GAME DEVELOPMENT ESSENTIALS:

GAME PROJECT MANAGEMENT

John Hight
Jeannie Novak

DELMAR
CENGAGE Learning

Australia • Brazil • Japan • Korea • Mexico • Singapore • Spain • United Kingdom • United States

DELMAR
CENGAGE Learning™

Game Development Essentials: Game Project Management
John Hight, Jeannie Novak

Vice President, Technology and Trades ABU: David Garza

Director of Learning Solutions: Sandy Clark

Managing Editor: Larry Main

Acquisitions Editor: James Gish

Product Manager: Sharon Chambliss

Marketing Director: Deborah Yarnell

Marketing Specialist: Victoria Ortiz

Director of Production: Patty Stephan

Production Manager: Stacy Masucci

Content Project Manager: Nicole Stagg

Technology Project Manager: Kevin Smith

Editorial Assistant: Sarah Timm

Cover: The Movies® image provided courtesy of Lionhead Studios

For product information and technology assistance, contact us at **Cengage Learning Customer & Sales Support, 1-800-354-9706**

For permission to use material from this text or product, submit all requests online at **www.cengage.com/permissions**
Further permissions questions can be emailed to **permissionrequest@cengage.com**

Library of Congress Control Number: 2007004566

ISBN-13: 978-1-4180-1541-1

ISBN-10: 1-4180-1541-5

Delmar
Executive Woods
5 Maxwell Drive
Clifton Park, NY 12065
USA

Cengage Learning is a leading provider of customized learning solutions with office locations around the globe, including Singapore, the United Kingdom, Australia, Mexico, Brazil, and Japan. Locate your local office at **www.cengage.com/global**

Cengage Learning products are represented in Canada by Nelson Education, Ltd.

To learn more about Delmar, visit **www.cengage.com/delmar**

Purchase any of our products at your local bookstore or at our preferred online store **www.cengagebrain.com**

Notice to the Reader
Publisher does not warrant or guarantee any of the products described herein or perform any independent analysis in connection with any of the product information contained herein. Publisher does not assume, and expressly disclaims, any obligation to obtain and include information other than that provided to it by the manufacturer. The reader is expressly warned to consider and adopt all safety precautions that might be indicated by the activities described herein and to avoid all potential hazards. By following the instructions contained herein, the reader willingly assumes all risks in connection with such instructions. The publisher makes no representations or warranties of any kind, including but not limited to, the warranties of fitness for particular purpose or merchantability, nor are any such representations implied with respect to the material set forth herein, and the publisher takes no responsibility with respect to such material. The publisher shall not be liable for any special, consequential, or exemplary damages resulting, in whole or in part, from the readers' use of, or reliance upon, this material.

Printed in China
3 4 5 6 7 15 14 13 12 11

CONTENTS

Chapter 2   Concept Development
describing the big idea 25

Part II: Documentation
& Pre-Production 65

Chapter 3   Game Design
defining the vision 67

Chapter 4   Technical Design
creating the blueprint for production 105

Chapter 5 Art & Sound Design

Chapter 6 Production Plan
bringing order to chaos 161

Part III: Management & Production 195

Chapter 7   Team Management
communication, objectivity, and leadership 197

Chapter 8   External Relationships
managing beyond the development team 223

Chapter 9   Putting It All Together
from idea to reality 247

Introduction
Game Project Management
making it happen

The key talent of any producer is the ability to *make things happen*. In the game industry—one of the most dynamic and fast-growing areas of entertainment—this talent is in high demand. However, very few books on the market focus on creating effective game project management skills.

Leadership is a much-needed resource in the game industry—where many talented artists, designers and programmers have found themselves being promoted into lead or producer positions without having the necessary management training. At the same time, some highly skilled producers from other industries (such as film, animation, and high-technology) are migrating to the game industry—and, although they have the leadership training and management skills, they often know very little about how to produce a game. This book fills in the gaps for both of these markets—covering basic concepts relating to game-specific projects, while also providing tips and techniques for effective leadership and management.

Game documentation is covered at length in this book. Although some large developers and publishers have admitted to doing away with formal documentation, an understanding of the elements associated with various forms of game documentation will help you clarify the roles and responsibilities of all team members and distinguish the game-specific project management process from traditional entertainment.

In this book, you will learn: the role of project management in developing great games; tips for creating ideas and implementing them through well-crafted documentation and project plans; the relationship between effective leadership and high quality games; and techniques for making your game projects run as smoothly as possible. As one of the few books of its kind on the market, *Game Project Management* is a much-needed, invaluable resource for students and game developers alike.

As the game industry continues to mature, game project management will become increasingly important. We hope that this book drives you to explore new and innovative ways of managing game projects.

John Hight
La Cañada, CA

Jeannie Novak
Santa Monica, CA

About the *Game Development Essentials Series*

The *Game Development Essentials* series was created to fulfill a need: to provide students and creative professionals alike with a complete education in all aspects of the game industry. As more schools continue to launch game programs, the books in this series will become even more essential to game education and careers. Not limited to the education market, this series is also appropriate for the trade market and for those who have a general interest in the game industry. Books in the series contain several unique features. All are in full-color and contain hundreds of images—including original illustrations, diagrams, game screenshots, and photos of industry professionals. They also contain a great deal of profiles, tips and case studies from professionals in the industry who are actively developing games. Starting with an overview of all aspects of the industry—*Game Development Essentials: An Introduction* —this series focuses on topics as varied as story & character development, interface design, artificial intelligence, gameplay mechanics, level design, online game development, simulation development, and audio.

Jeannie Novak
Lead Author & Series Editor

About *Game Project Management*

Game Project Management provides an overview of game project management techniques and procedures—including the history of game project management, concept development, game design documentation, technical design documentation, art style guide, sound design documentation, leadership, external management issues, and case study examples.

This book contains the following unique features:

- Key chapter questions that are clearly stated at the beginning of each chapter
- Coverage that surveys special topics in game project management—including documentation, tools, techniques, and team roles and responsibilities
- Thought-provoking review and study questions appearing at the end of each chapter that are suitable for students and professionals alike to help promote critical thinking and problem-solving skills
- A wealth of case studies, profiles, tips, and quotations from game industry officials
- An abundance of full-color images throughout that help illustrate the concepts and techniques discussed in the book
- A companion DVD that contains documentation, research, and both game and software demos

There are several general themes associated with this book that are emphasized throughout, including:

- Differences between games and other entertainment media (such as film)
- Leadership as a primary aspect of game project management
- Importance of documentation when managing game projects
- Significance of the connection between effective project management and hgh quality games

Who Should Read This Book?

This book is not limited to the education market. If you found this book on a shelf at the bookstore and picked it up out of curiosity, this book is also for you!

The audience for this book includes students, industry professionals, and the general interest consumer market. The style is informal and accessible, with a concentration on theory and practice—geared toward students, artists, producers, and game designers.

Readers that might benefit from this book include:

- Producers from other media (such as film) who are interested in migrating to the game industry
- Design, tech, art, sound, and test/QA leads who are interested in honing their project management skills
- College students in game development, project management, interactive design, communication, graphic design, and emerging technologies programs
- Art, design and programming students who are taking introductory game development courses
- Professional students in college-level programs who are taking game development overview courses
- First-year game development students at universities

How Is This Book Organized?

This book consists of three parts: history and concept development; documentation and pre-production; and management and production.

- Part I—History & Concept Development (Ch 1-2): This part focuses on the history and basic principles of project management—along with tools and techniques associated with the concept development process.
- Part II—Documentation & Pre-Production (Ch 3-6): This part focuses on the game design document, technical design document, art style guide, sound design document, and production plan—along with tools and techniques associated with the pre-production process.
- Part III—Management & Production (Ch 7-9): This part focuses on issues that might arise during production—along with a case study that guides the reader through the process of managing a hypothetical game project.

How to Use This Text

The sections that follow describe text elements found throughout the book and how they are intended to be used.

key chapter questions

Key chapter questions are learning objectives in the form of overview questions that start off each chapter. Readers should be able to answer the questions upon understanding the chapter material.

sidebars

Sidebars offer in-depth information from the authors on specific topics—accompanied by associated images.

quotes

Quotes contain short, insightful thoughts from players, students, and industry observers.

case studies

Case studies contain anecdotes from industry professionals (accompanied by game screenshots) on their experiences developing specific game titles.

tips

Tips provide advice and inspiration from industry professionals and educators, as well as practical techniques and tips of the trade.

notes

Notes contain thought-provoking ideas provided by the authors that are intended to help the readers think critically about the book's topics.

profiles

Profiles provide bios, photos and in-depth commentary from industry professionals and educators.

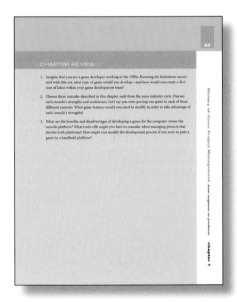

chapter review

A *chapter review* section at the end of each chapter contains a combination of questions and exercises, which allow readers to apply what they've learned. Annotations and answers are included in the instructor's guide, available separately (see next page).

About the Companion DVD

The companion DVD contains the following media:

- Game engines: *Torque* (Windows and Mac versions 1.4) and *Game Maker* (version 6.1)
- Game design documentation: GDD template (Chris Taylor/Gas Powered Games), *Sub Hunter* GDD (Michael Black/Torn Space), and *Uncivilized: The Goblin Game* [code name: Salmon] call for game design/submission (Wizards of the Coast)
- Game design articles: Harvey Smith/Witchboy's Cauldron and Barrie Ellis/One Switch Games
- Game project management spreadsheets: dialogue strings, translated text, game character animation list, budget spreadsheet, project schedule, status report, task assignment sheet, and change request form
- Game concept art: *Tabula Rasa, Viewtiful Joe 2, Resident Evil 4*

- Game demos/trial versions: 2K Games (*Prey*), Blizzard (*Diablo II*), Firaxis (*Sid Meier's Railroads!*), Stardock (*Galactic Civilizations II: Dread Lords*), THQ (*Company of Heroes*), Enemy Technology (*I of the Enemy: Ril'Cerat*), Star Mountain Studios (*Bergman, Weird Helmet, Frozen, Findella*), and GarageGames (*Dark Horizons: Lore Invasion, Gish, Marble Blast: Gold, Rocket Bowl Plus, Zap!, Tube Twist, Orbz, Think Tanks*)

About the Instructor's Guide

The instructor's guide (e-resource, available separately on DVD) was developed to assist instructors in planning and implementing their instructional programs. It includes sample syllabi, test questions, assignments, projects, PowerPoint files, and other valuable instructional resources.

Order Number: 1-4180-1542-3

About the Authors

In 1991, John built his first game, *Battleship*, for the Philips CDi player. Since that time he has worked on over 25 games and 9 edutainment products on various consoles and PCs. He's been fortunate to experience game development from many different roles: programmer, artist, writer, designer, and producer. Currently, John is Director of External Production at Sony Computer Entertainment of America in Santa Monica, CA. Prior to joining Sony, John held management and creative positions with Atari, Electronic Arts, Westwood Studios, and 3DO. In his role as Executive Producer and Director of Design for Electronic Arts, John contributed to the design and production of *Nox, Command & Conquer: Red Alert 2*, and *Yuri's Revenge*. He is currently working on games for the PlayStation 3 for both retail sale and direct-to-consumer digital distribution. John holds a B.S.E. in Computer Science from the University of New Mexico and an M.B.A. from the Marshall School of Business at the University of Southern California.

Photo credit: Luis Levy

Jeannie Novak is the founder of Indiespace—one of the first companies to promote and distribute interactive entertainment online—where she consults with creative professionals in the music, film, and television industries to help them migrate to the game industry. In addition to being lead author and series editor of the *Game Development Essentials* series, Jeannie is the co-author of three pioneering books on the interactive entertainment industry—including *Creating Internet Entertainment.* Jeannie is the Academic Program Director for the Game Art & Design and Media Arts & Animation programs at the Art Institute Online, where she is also producer and lead designer on a "course game" that is being built within the Second Life environment. She has also been a game instructor and course development expert at the Art Institute Online, UCLA Extension, Art Center College of Design, Academy of Entertainment and Technology at Santa Monica College, DeVry University, and Westwood College. Jeannie has developed or participated in game workshops and panels in association with the British Academy of Television Arts & Sciences (BAFTA), Macworld, Digital Hollywood, and iHollywood Forum. She is a member of the International Game Developers Association (IGDA) and has served on selection committees for the Academy of Interactive Arts & Sciences (AIAS). Jeannie was chosen as one of the 100 most influential people in high-technology by *MicroTimes* magazine—and she has been profiled by CNN, *Billboard Magazine,* Sundance Channel, *Daily Variety,* and the *Los Angeles Times.* She received an M.A. in Communication Management from the University of Southern California (USC), where she focused on games in online distance learning. She received a B.A. in Mass Communication from the University of California, Los Angeles (UCLA)—graduating summa cum laude and Phi Beta Kappa. When she isn't writing and teaching, Jeannie spends most of her time recording, performing, and composing music. More information on the author can be found at http://jeannie.com and http://indiespace.com.

Acknowledgements

We would like to thank the following people for their hard work and dedication to this project:

Jim Gish (Acquisitions Editor, Delmar, Cengage Learning), for making this series happen.

Sharon Chambliss (Product Manager, Delmar, Cengage Learning), for moving this project along and always maintaining a professional demeanor.

Nicole Stagg (Content Project Manager, Delmar, Cengage Learning), for her consistent responsiveness during production crunch time.

Ralph Lagnado (Image Research & Permissions Specialist), for his dedication and commitment to tracking and and clearing the many images in this book.

Jason Bramble, for his superhuman efforts in capturing and researching several screenshots for this book.

Niamh Matthews (Editorial Assistant, Delmar, Cengage learning), for her ongoing assistance throughout the series.

Gina Dishman (Project Manager, GEX
Publishing Services), for her diligent
work and prompt response during the
layout and compositing phase.

Per Olin, for his organized and visually-
pleasing diagrams.

Ian Robert Vasquez, for his clever and
inspired illustrations.

David Koontz (Publisher, Chilton), for
starting it all by introducing Jeannie
Novak to Jim Gish.

A big thanks also goes out to all the many people who contributed their thoughts
and ideas to this book:

Aaron Marks (On Your Mark Productions)
Barrie Ellis (OneSwitch Games)
Briar Lee Mitchell (Star Mountain Studios)
Chris Taylor (Gas Powered Games)
Christer Ericson (Sony Computer
Entertainment of America)
Christian Allen (Red Storm Entertainment)
Deborah Mars (Sony Computer
Entertainment of America)
Don Daglow (Stormfront Studios)
Drew Davidson (Carnegie Mellon University)
Ed Rotberg (Mine Shaft Entertainment)
Edward (Ned) Lerner (Sony Computer
Entertainment of America)
Frank T. Gilson (Wizards of the Coast)
Gordon Walton (BioWare)
Graeme Bayless (Crystal Dynamics/Eidos)
Harvey Smith (Midway)

Jeff Reese (Sony Computer Entertainment
of America)
Jeff Stewart (Petroglyph Games)
Jesper Sorensen (ncom.dk)
John Ahlquist (Ahlquist Software)
Mark Soderwall (LucasArts)
Mark Temple (Enemy Technology)
Michael Black (Torn Space)
Michael Booth (Turtle Rock Studios)
Michael John (Method Games)
Michelle Hinn (DonationCoder.com/IGDA)
Rich Adam (Mine Shaft Entertainment)
RJ Mical (Sony Computer Entertainment of
America)
Shannon Studstill (Sony Computer
Entertainment of America)
Starr Long (NCsoft)

Thanks to the following people for their tremendous help with referrals and in
securing permissions, images, and demos:

Andrew S. Cobleigh
Ai Hasegawa & Hideki Yoshimoto (Namco
Bandai Games America Inc.)
Alta Hartmann & Brian Jarrard (Bungie)
Benjamin Bradley & Joe Maruschak
(GarageGames)
Bob Sadowski (Seapine Software)
Brennan Reilly (Midway)
Brian Hupp (Electronic Arts)
Cathy Campos (Lionhead)
Chris Glover (Eidos)
Chris Hadley (Computer Laboratory,
University of Cambridge)
Christine Kalb (Autodesk Media &
Entertainment)
Courtney L. Walker Edelman (Microsoft)
Dave Timoney, Marlene Williams,
Todd Lubsen & Kim Aue (Gas
Powered Games)
David Fraser (Amstrad)
David Greenspan & Lin Leng (THQ)
David Swofford (NCsoft)
Emil Ayoubkhan (The Behemoth)
Erick Einsiedel & Teresa Cotesta (BioWare)

Frederic Chesnais & Cecelia Hernandez
(Atari)
Gabe Newell, Doug Lombardi & Jason
Holtman (Valve)
Grant Smith & Marc Franklin (Konami)
Greg Deutsch, Mike Mantarro, John Rafacz &
Aaron Grant (Activision)
Guillaume de Fondaumiere (Quantic Dream)
Janet Braulio (Nintendo)
Jessica Van Pernis & Sue Carrol (Apple)
JoAnn Bryden & Kathy Carpano (Hasbro)
Joe Keene & Daron Stinnett (Perpetual
Entertainment)
John Tam (Red Octane)
Jørgen Tharaldsen (Funcom)
Jun Shimizu (Q Entertainment)
Kate Ross (Wizards of the Coast)
Kristin Hatcher (Stardock Entertainment)
Lorne Lanning & Matt Lee (Oddworld
Inhabitants)
Marissa Gonzalez (GolinHarris)
Mark Beaumont, Estella Lemus & Michiko
Morita Wang (Capcom)
Mark Rein (Epic Games)

Michael Dornbrook (Harmonix Music Systems)
Mike Griffiths (Adit)
Mitch Soul (RAD Game Tools)
Paul Crockett (2K Games)
Paul W. Sams, Denise Lopez & Brie Messina (Blizzard)
Pete Hines (Bethesda)
Randy Buehler, Frank Gilson & Tim Mizrahi (Wizards of the Coast)
Reinel Adajar (Digidesign)
Rod Rigole (Vivendi UniversalGames)
Ruth Fankushen (BigStockPhotos.com)
Scott Rohde, Christian Phillips, Azucena Negrete, Kristi Olivas and Christina Cavallero (Sony Computer Entertainment America)

Simon Jeffery, Robert Leffler & Jana Rubenstein (Sega)
Sophie Jakubowicz & Jocelyn Portacio (Ubisoft)
Stephen Martin & Dennis Shirk (Firaxis)
Sue Carrol (Apple)
Suzi Schatz (Getty Images)
Todd Hollenshead (id Software)
Tony Fryman (Cyan)
Tony Liviabella (SN Systems)
Valerie Walls (lime, llc)
Vishal Gondal & Suhail Baghdadi (Indiagames)
Wendy Zaas (Rogers & Cowan)
Yoh Watanabe (Tecmo)

We would also like to thank the following reviewers for their valuable suggestions and technical expertise:

Graeme Bayless (Crystal Dynamics/Eidos)
Drew Davidson (Carnegie Mellon University)
Mahmoud Ghaffari (DeVry University)

Frank T. Gilson (Wizards of the Coast)
Steven Herrnstadt (Iowa State University)
Michael Matoush (Westwood College)

Questions & Feedback

We welcome your questions and feedback. If you have suggestions that you think others would benefit from, please let us know and we will try to include them in the next edition.

You may contact the publisher at:

Delmar, Cengage Learning
Executive Woods
5 Maxwell Drive
Clifton Park, NY 12065
800-998-7498

Or the series editor at:

Jeannie Novak
INDIESPACE
PO Box 5458
Santa Monica, CA 90409
jeannie@indiespace.com

DEDICATION

To my son William; to Lisa and Robert Abarta for their love and encouragement; to Helen Norkon for her support; and to my parents Bonnie and George for always believing in me.

—*John*

To Luis, who always helps us strive for balance. Thank you for making things happen.

—*Jeannie*

Part I: History & Concept Development

CHAPTER

1

History of Game Project Management

from engineer to producer

Key Chapter Questions

- Who were the first game developers and what were their associated games?

- How has game development changed from its early days to now?

- What did it take to develop a game in the 1980s?

- When did 3D graphics first appear and how did they impact projects?

- What are industry cycles and how have they affected development?

Back in 1988, it was easy, and necessary, for developers to get their hands dirty in all aspects of the game: code, art, music, design, and sometimes a little management. *Battleship* for Philips CDi was largely the work of John Hight and Greg Brooks. John scrounged video footage of World War II ships from the National Archives. As players selected the row and column of their shots, the battleship Midway fired its guns in a small window next to the playfield. The artwork was done using Studio 32 on a Macintosh, and the ocean waves were animated by cycling a portion of the 128-bit palette. The game was programmed in C, using the GNU compiler on Sun workstations. Greg set up AI programs to battle each other in his quest for the best opponent simulation. It took just two months to build. A story like this is rare these days. Most games take an average of 20 to 30 months to build and involve teams of 60 to 80 people. (Interestingly, the development process associated with mobile, casual, and web games is reminiscent of early game development—with groups of 5 to 10 people working from 6 to 9 months—yet these projects can benefit from many aspects of proper project management.) This chapter focuses on how the industry has changed and how project management has evolved in response.

One Lone Programmer: The Early Days

The first computer game was created by programmer A. S. Douglas in 1952 as part of his doctoral thesis on human–computer interaction at the University of Cambridge. It consisted of simple naughts and crosses (tic-tac-toe) programmed on a vacuum tube computer called EDSAC (Electronic Delay Storage Automatic Calculator).

© 2006 Computer Laboratory, University of Cambridge Information

Adit Limited

EDSAC, one of the first programmable computers, was built in 1949 at the University of Cambridge in the United Kingdom.

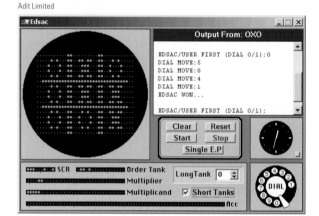

This is a Windows simulation of the original "naughts and crosses" computer game on the EDSAC.

EDSAC was one of the first computers, and it literally filled a room. The programs were crude by today's standards: a few lines versus millions of lines of code. Douglas adapted EDSAC's monitor tubes to fashion a 35 × 16 pixel screen. There was never a commercial application of his game. The first video game system was also developed by an engineer. Ralph Baer, engineering manager for a military electronics firm, built the first video game system in 1966. His *TV Game* used video signals to place game objects on the screen of an ordinary television set. Some historians credit Baer with having the idea for TV games as early as 1951. Although there are other instances of games on various technologies, Baer's was the first to use a standard television set as the display device, thus paving the way for video games in the home.

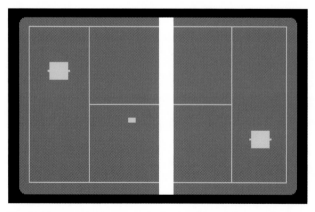

The first home video game was a simple table tennis game for the Odyssey created by Ralph Baer.

:::::Industry Cycles

Diagram by Per Olin

1972	1976	1976	1983	1984	1990	1990	1994	1994	1999	2000	2004	2005
First Introduction		Cartridge Games		8-Bit		16-Bit		32 & 64-Bit		128-Bit		HD

The video game industry tends to grow and shrink in cycles closely tied to the introduction of new home consoles. Coin-op arcade games were the trendsetters—and popular arcade games were eventually ported to home console systems. As the consoles became more powerful, the arcades moved to location-based entertainment—simulation rides and highly customized interfaces. The market usually slumps when new consoles are announced, as consumers forgo purchasing home machines and games for the existing platforms in anticipation of improved technology. PC games have enjoyed a slow but steady growth and have helped publishers even out the loss of revenue prior to a new console offering. To date, there have been seven distinct phases for video games, as shown in the accompanying diagram. Interspersed throughout this chapter are highlights that will help you put industry cycles into perspective.

In 1971, Nolan Bushnell's first game, *Computer Space,* was released by Nutting Associates. The cabinet featured a CRT display mounted in a "mod" freeform fiberglass console that looked a lot like a giant telephone receiver. The game design involved piloting a rocketship and firing on enemy flying saucers. A two-player version was also released.

A year later, Magnavox released the first consumer game console, the Odyssey, based on Baer's designs. That same year, Bushnell released his second arcade game, *Pong,* and founded Atari. There is much controversy surrounding *Pong,* since Bushnell previewed the Odyssey and its tennis game prior to releasing *Pong.* The first *Pong* game was built by engineer Al Alcorn and installed at Andy Capp's Tavern in Sunnyvale, CA. The game was so popular during its first two weeks that an overflow of quarters in the coin box caused it to malfunction.

Computer Space was the first arcade game.

::::: Industry Cycles: First Introduction (1972-1976)

The first home video
game console:
Magnavox Odyssey.

The first home game consoles were viewed as toys. Games were integrated into the game systems and couldn't be updated or changed. Projects involved one or two people defining a simple game and then implementing it via low-level machine code. The first systems were the Magnavox Odyssey, Atari Pong, and Coleco Telstar.

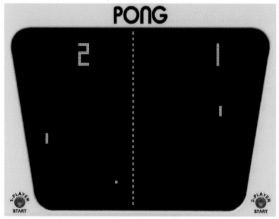

Pong was the first widely known video game.

Atari's Bushnell launched the video arcade industry by building more *Pong* arcade cabinets. By 1974, Atari designed a home version of *Pong*, and Sears wanted to buy 150,000 units of the console. Bushnell secured $10 million in venture capital to quickly expand Atari to meet growing demand. This was a turning point for project management in video games. They were no longer being created by engineers moonlighting in their garages. Video games were now serious business, and corporations were formed to bring them to market.

Atari expanded again with the introduction of the VCS (Video Computer System) in 1977, and it quickly became the best-selling home game system in the world. The games were still designed and developed by programmers, but now the company included marketing, manufacturing, and operations staff.

The Atari VCS (later known as the 2600) brought video games into millions of homes. Yet Atari's programmers received no credit, and they complained that their wages were low relative to their contributions. Many programmers left—including a group that founded Activision, the first third-party publisher.

The Commodore PET. PET (Personal Electronic Transactor) was introduced in 1977 with a 1 MHz processor and 4K of RAM.

Computers were either hobbyist kits or research projects. They included Xerox Alto and the MITS Altair 8800 (kit). Apple Computer co-founder Steve Wozniak wrote *Breakout* for his friend Steve Jobs, who worked at Atari. The MITS Altair was one of the first hobbyist computers. Microsoft co-founder Bill Gates wrote the BASIC language interpreter for this machine.

Coin-op arcade games became an attraction in nightclubs with games such as *Pong* (Atari), *Tank* (Kee Games), and *Star Trek* (For-Play). The coin-op mentality led to the creation of games that were easy to get into. After all, anyone with a quarter should be able to walk up and play. They were designed to be repetitive and addictive so that players would drop in another quarter to get just a little further. Playtesting involved placing an arcade machine in a bar and watching the coin drop for a few weeks. (Many mobile and casual games of today are designed for "everyone" and involve quick play. Interestingly, several titles *are* arcade games from the past!)

:::::: Industry Cycles: Cartridge Games (1976-1983)

As coin-op arcades became more popular, people wanted to bring the experience home. With the introduction of cartridges, home consoles became general purpose. This gave them longer life by allowing consumers to buy additional games. It also created a market for independent game developers who could now specialize in designing and programming games. Activision became the first third-party developer. New systems included: Fairchild Channel F, Atari

The Atari 2600 (also known as the VCS [Video Computer System]) was one of the first home console systems.

2600, Odyssey 2, Intellivision, Vectrex, and Colecovision. After rapid growth for a decade, the home video game market crashed in 1983. Many investors got burned, and both hardware manufacturers and software developers were forced to work more efficiently.

Coin-op became a staple form of entertainment. Releases included: *Asteroids* (Atari), *Space Invaders* (Taito), *Pac-Man* (Namco), *Defender* (Williams), *Spy Hunter* (Midway), *Mario Bros.* (Nintendo), *Dragon's Lair* (Cinematronics), *Q*bert* (Gottlieb), and *Zaxxon* (Sega).

The home PC market was also born during this era. This removed the barrier to entry for developers, who no longer had to build their own development systems. Programmers now had access to relatively low cost and reliable development platforms. PC systems introduced during this era included Apple II, Commodore PET, Tandy TRS-80, Atari 800, Sinclair ZX80, IBM PC, Timex Sinclair 1000, Commodore 64, Compaq Portable PC, and Coleco Adam. PC releases included *Impossible Mission* (Epyx), *Ultima* (Origin Systems), *Zork* (Infocom), and *Microsoft Flight Simulator* (Microsoft/subLOGIC).

The Apple II was one of the first computers designed with games in mind.

Renaissance Men: The 1980s

By the early 1980s, dozens of companies jumped into the growing home console market. Games were still relatively cheap to build, so new games were released every month. There was little or no market research conducted and no planning or forecasting. Individual games were still being designed by a single engineer with no experience in creating consumer products. There was little innovation in hardware or game design, and consumers began to tire of this newfound toy. By 1983, the video game market suffered a crash and most U.S. companies went out of the business. Atari was sold off and became a computer manufacturer.

Everyone thought the video game industry was dead, but two years later, Nintendo introduced the Nintendo Entertainment System (NES) and brought life back into the industry. The cycle would repeat itself—but now hardware manufacturers had learned to innovate before their products became stale. The market was ripe for the resurgence of small developers.

The pioneers of game development were engineers and programmers. Some were professionally trained as software engineers and many were self-taught. Degrees in computer science weren't that prevalent, and games were frowned upon by academia.

The first text adventure, *Colossal Cave*, required players to enter text directions to navigate, obtain objects, and interact with the game world.

In the early 1980s, games were developed in a few weeks by a single engineer. Graphics were simple block shapes with between 16 and 128 colors, and the memory (RAM) required to hold a game was limited to 16K. Sound was a luxury and was often rudimentary at best. Some games were simple text adventures, requiring the player to enter directions to move and explore. Hardware companies like Atari and later Nintendo developed most of the games for their respective platforms.

By the end of the 1980s, project timelines had increased to a few months. Games were developed by two or more people. Memory had increased to 64K graphics improved, and sound was much better. These early developers had to learn a variety of skills: programming, writing, computer graphics (pixel-pushing), and sound design. It was common to see these Renaissance men huddled together in a room full of electronics: a workstation or PC to write code, a Macintosh for digital art or sound design, and a synthesizer to create music and sound effects. A stack of empty Jolt cola bottles would serve as bookends for Knuth's *Art of Programming* series or a well-worn copy of Kernighan and Ritchie's *The C Programming Language*.

This was a golden era for independent developers. The growth of personal computers made it easy for developers to create games for machines like the Radio Shack TRS-80, Apple II, Atari 800, IBM PC, Commodore Amiga, and the Apple Macintosh.

The Internet was a long way from its current state, but it fostered an active community of programmers who used it to send e-mail and communicate ideas via news forums. Code snippets were shared and algorithms were discussed. There was no concern for protecting intellectual property. Some programmers held the belief that code should never be subject to copyright or patent.

The Commodore Amiga was a favorite system for hobbyists and early game developers in the United States and Europe.

> On the Amiga and the Lynx, one person could develop a whole game. It's still possible for one person to do a whole title on the PS3; it's just that it would take you, like, 60 years! Seriously, to create a popular "A" title on the Amiga, you could create a game with 2 to 3 people, on the Lynx with 1 to 4, on the 3DO with 4 to 15, and on the PS3 with 20 to 60. However, bear in mind that not all the outrageously successful titles over the years were "A" or even "B" titles; always, always remember *Tetris*. I wish I could play *Tetris* right now! The success of that title is a parable for these modern times.
>
> — *R.J. Mical (Senior Software Manager, SD Tools Group, Sony Computer Entertainment of America; Co-Creator of the Amiga, Atari Lynx, and 3DO)*

There was no standard user interface library; everything on screen had to be custom programmed. Programmers wrote their games in BASIC, Assembler, or C using simple text editors to format their code. It could take a long time to compile their programs, so they would type in their changes, start a build, and go to lunch. Upon returning, they faced an output file full of syntax errors that had to be corrected before the game would run.

In the early 1980s, game budgets were a modest $1,000 to $10,000. Teams were composed of a few relatively unknown individuals. Project management was informal in the early 1980s. There was usually a single milestone: the final game. By the end of the decade, that would all change.

In 1982, Trip Hawkins used his earnings and experience as a director of marketing for Apple, plus some Silicon Valley venture capital, to found Electronic Arts (EA). It was unique among publishers at that time by actively promoting its game developers. EA put game designers' names

The Sega Master System was released in 1985 in Japan. It was released in 1986 in the United States but remained a distant second to the NES in sales.

on their flashy packages and included their photos in promotional materials. Less highly visible but more important was what EA did for project management. In the early years, EA dealt only with external developers. As part of its review process, EA introduced formal technical design reviews (TDRs),which required developers to create detailed task lists and conduct risk analysis on their game designs. This disciplined approach is the core of the TDD that we use today (discussed in detail in Chapter 4).

::::: Industry Cycles: 8-bit (1984–1990)

Image courtesy of Nintendo

The Nintendo Entertainment System revived the home video game market in the mid-1980s.

During the 8-bit era, the notion of a technical design was conceived and best practices were adapted from both the software development and manufacturing industries. New consoles introduced during this era included the Nintendo Entertainment System (NES), Sega Master System (SMS), and Atari 7800. New console game releases included *Final Fantasy* (Square), *Metal Gear* (Konami), *Metroid* (Intelligent Systems), and *Super Mario Bros.* (Nintendo). This was the so-called golden era. Tools were easy to use, projects were easy to manage, the market was growing, and small developers could thrive.

The Good, the Bad, and the Funny: Tales from the Front

*T*he good: Being trained by a producer from A&M Records in the early days of EA, when we were the first game managers ever to be called "producers." Having people walk up to me and say, "I played your game for an entire summer when I was X years old, and it just made that whole year great for me!" or "I could never really talk with my grandfather, but when we played your game together we always had a great time."

The bad: Being part of a team where everyone pours their hearts and souls into developing a game, and then missing whatever special chemistry it needed to make it right and having the end result just be okay.

The funny: In 1985, we had a great argument inside Electronic Arts. *Adventure Construction Set* had been a big hit, and I wanted to create an *Adventure Construction Set 2*. An EA manager told me, "This isn't an industry about sequels. It's about coming up with great new games, not trying to coax more money out of old ones." What is EA famous for today? Successfully sequeling the best roster of franchises in the industry! (Of course, you'll notice I tell a story where it turned out my side of the argument was right, and I never mention all the times when I argued something where my point of view turned out to be wrong!)

Don L. Daglow (President & CEO, Stormfront Studios)

Coin-op games were pushing graphics technology with the ability to support multiple simultaneous players. Examples included *Gauntlet* (Atari), *Arkanoid* (Taito), *Streetfighter* (Capcom), *Out Run* (Sega), *Castlevania* (Konami), and *Punch-Out!* (Nintendo).

Advances in processors and lower-cost memory made it possible for sophisticated handhelds such as Nintendo Game Boy and Sega Game Gear. *Tetris* first appeared on the PC and was soon ported to the Game Boy and nearly every other platform.

PC systems dropped their text-based interfaces and sported graphical user interfaces (GUI), WYSIWYG ("what you see is what you get"), and mice. PC introductions included Amstrad CPC 464, Apple Macintosh, Atari ST, PC with Windows, and Commodore Amiga 1000.

Games were among the first to capitalize on these so-called ergonomic interfaces. PC games released included *Madden NFL* (Electronic Arts), *Elite* (Acornsoft), *Secret of Monkey Island* (LucasArts), *SimCity* (Maxis), *Pirates!* (Microprose), and *Leisure Suit Larry in the Land of the Lounge Lizards* (Sierra).

The original *Castlevania* was a side-scroller dungeon-crawl.

The Amstrad CPC (Colour Personal Computer) 464 was popular in Europe.

Battle for the Living Room: The 1990s

The popularity of home computers and the difficulty of operating them caught the attention of consumer electronics companies, which were eager to bring interactivity to the living room through the television set. Philips Electronics and Sony, buoyed by the success of its compact disc (CD) standard, collaborated on an interactive CD (CDi) standard. This "greenbook" standard was a first—containing the specifications for a home console that any electronics manufacturer could license and build. By 1990, Philips established a publishing entity to foster a development community and set standards for content creation.

Although the CDi player was never a commercial success, Philips pioneered many of the principles of project management used today. Philips not only hired producers from Hollywood to establish production processes and standards, but it incorporated EA's TDR process—refining it to include requirements for source control and asset archiving. Its

Myst was one of the best-selling games of all time and one of the first to be released on CD.

producers maintained detailed game specifications, and its quality assurance teams prepared detailed test plans. Philips even published a guide to production that described the various roles of the development team, the green-light process, and formal definitions for alpha, beta, and gold master phases.

The programmers had their fun in the 1980s; now it was time for the artists. Memory (RAM) kept getting cheaper and processors kept getting faster. The use of 16 bits meant that artists weren't limited to a fixed 128- or 256-color palette. Artists could now incorporate thousands of colors. Drawing tablets were also widely available on PCs. The barriers were removed so that producers could enlist traditional artists to create imagery.

::::: Industry Cycles: 16-Bit (1990–1994)

Image courtesy of Nintendo

Super Nintendo
Entertainment System

New consoles released during the 16-bit era included Sega Genesis, NEC TurboGrafx 16, Nintendo SNES, and SNK Neo-Geo. New console game releases included *Sonic the Hedgehog* (Sega), *Donkey Kong Country* (Nintendo), *Earthworm Jim* (Virgin), and *Need for Speed* (Electronic Arts).

Diagram by Per Olin

Sega Genesis	1989, 16-bit, 64 colors, $189
IBM PC	1990, compatible with Windows 3.0, $2,000
Nintendo SNES	1991, 16-bit, 256 colors, Super Mario World included, $199
Philips CDi	1992, 16-bit, CD, IR controller, $599
3DO	1993, 32-bit, MPEG-1 movies, $699
Atari Jaguar	1993, multiple processors, 64-bit bus and registers, $149
Sega Saturn	1994, 32-bit, $399
Sony PlayStation	1994, 32-bit, 16.7 million colors, RISC processor, 3D graphics, revolutionary controller, $299
IBM PC	1995, compatible with Windows 95 and Pentium processor, $1,700
Nintendo 64	1996, 64-bit, 32 thousand colors, $199
Sega Dreamcast	1998, 128-bit, 16.7 million colors, 7 million polygons per second, modem and internet support, $199
IBM PC	1999, compatible with Windows 98 and Pentium III processor, $1,500

PC games (using Windows 3.0 and Pentium processor) included: *Creatures* (Apex), *Doom* (id Software), *Civilization* (Microprose), *Lemmings* (Psygnosis), and *Myst* (Brøderbund). New coin-op releases included *Mortal Kombat* (Midway), *Bomber Man* (Irem), *Ridge Racer* (Namco), *Virtua Racing* (Sega), *Dance Dance Revolution* (Konami), and *Golden Tee Golf* (Strata). Coin-op games had traditionally been leading edge but were now struggling to stay ahead of the console and PC markets. The arcade emphasis began to shift toward specialized location-based entertainment.

Some of the most memorable console games were released during this time. Top-sellers included *Sonic the Hedgehog* for the Genesis, *Super Mario World* for the SNES, *Road Rash* for the 3DO, *Crash Bandicoot* for the PlayStation, *Doom* for the PC, *Super Mario 64* for the Nintendo 64, and *Soul Calibur* for the Dreamcast.

Sega Genesis

PC AT

By the 1990s, a whole generation of game developers had arrived on the scene. They had grown up playing games at home or in the arcades. Artists and musicians began to get involved, too. The quality of games improved dramatically as this new crop of talent dreamed up new ways to entertain people.

Diagram by Per Olin

Nintendo GameBoy	1989, black & white, $99
Atari Lynx	1989, color, $189
Sega GameGear	1990, color, $149
Sega Nomad	1995, color, $180
Nintendo GameBoy Color	1998, color, $79

Game budgets in the '90s ranged from $50,000 to $1,000,000. These big budgets allowed developers to bring in specialists from various disciplines to form development teams of 6–20 people. The notion of a dedicated project manager, or producer, arose out of a need to manage these teams. Prior to this time, a producer wore other hats—including designer and programmer. Scheduling and project management borrowed principles from packaged goods software development and film/video production. Formal definitions for alpha, beta, and master milestones were introduced by game publishers.

The PC and Macintosh became standard tools for game development. Symbolic debuggers allowed programmers to step through their code and fix errors quickly. For the first time, engineers could view their code on their PC (or in a window) as it ran on a game development system (or in another window). This allowed engineers to develop larger and more complex games.

Artists had programs to create 2D and even 3D images. They could manipulate palettes to maximize the appearance of graphics on the screen. Tablets allowed artists to draw with a stylus instead of a mouse.

Musicians used low-cost samplers, sequencers, and waveform editors to create music and sound effects. Actors lent their voices so that games could talk. For the first time, gamers could enjoy quality sound via MIDI and 16-bit stereo on the consoles and PCs.

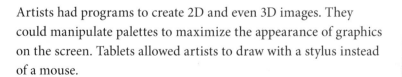

Nintendo Game Boy

Sega Game Gear

History of Game Project Management: from engineer to producer   chapter 1

Nintendo Game
Boy Color

The decade opened with Nintendo controlling the home console market and it ended with many manufacturers rising and falling. By the end of the decade, Sony and its PlayStation had the dominant market share.

Sony learned from its rivals. It instituted publishing standards as stringent as those of Philips and 3DO. It organized attractive third-party publishing programs to attract top developers away from Nintendo and Sega. Most importantly, Sony applied its long experience in consumer electronics to make game consoles attractive for everyone—not just computer enthusiasts. This mass-market awareness brought new elements to manage: marketing assets (demos, screenshots, previews), Hollywood screen talent, and soundtracks by renowned recording artists.

Nintendo

Super Mario 64 is often heralded as the best 3D platform game ever made.

The PlayStation also brought 3D graphics to consoles and, with that, a whole new art pipeline. Up to this point, graphics had been created by traditional artists who were self-taught in the skill of pixel-pushing. Now art was being created by character modelers, object modelers, environment modelers, texture artists, lighting and effects artists, and animators. Specialized technical artists were required to write scripts to convert the graphics and animation from standard packages to a form usable by the game engine. For the first time in development history, the artists outnumbered the programmers on the team. Developers embarked on a quest for visual realism.

::::: Industry Cycles: 32- and 64-Bit (1994–1999)

     Nintendo

Sega Saturn   Sony PlayStation   Nintendo 64

During this era, 3D graphics processors were introduced in game consoles. People stopped talking about pixel resolution when comparing new consoles. Instead they tracked the number of polygons displayed per second. New consoles included 3DO, Atari Jaguar, Sega Saturn, Sony PlayStation, and Nintendo 64. Console games embraced 3D technology with a vengeance. New releases included *Super Mario 64* (Nintendo), *Resident Evil* (Capcom), *Tomb Raider* (Eidos), *Crash Bandicoot* (SCEA), *Metal Slug* (SNK), *Rayman* (Ubisoft), *Gran Turismo* (SCEA), *Tony Hawk's Pro Skater* (Activision), *Dead or Alive* (Tecmo), *Medal of Honor* (Electronic Arts), and *Golden Eye 007* (Rare).

::::: *MissionForce: CyberStorm:* Always Stand Your Ground

Sierra Entertainment

I was producer/director on the original *MissionForce: CyberStorm*, back at Dynamix. (May that great studio rest in peace.) We had just finished the first game, and we had a plan to sequel the original with some great content additions, but using the same core game engine, within a year. We started down that path and were well on our way when I was called in by the new GM [general manager], who wanted to tell me how *Lords of the Realm II* was doing well, and that he felt *CyberStorm 2* needed to be real-time now. (The original had been turn-based.) I was asked to investigate what it would take to retool the game as real-time... so, after expressing my concerns, I did so. We threw out much of the old turn-based, hex-based engine to adopt a real-time, square-tiled system, and started building. Six months in, we demonstrated our progress to the press... and the editor from *CGW [Computer Gaming World]* looked at what we had, and responded "You know... of all the games last year, I felt *CyberStorm* was the one that really needed to be turn-based..." Well, our fears had been realized. I spoke with the GM, and he responded with, "So... how can we turn it back into a turn-based game?" We responded with introducing a turn-based system into our new real-time engine, and ended up with a hybrid that was much of the worst of both worlds. The lesson here? Stand your ground. If you have something that works... and works well... and you're told to do something patently foolish... say NO. Had I stood my ground, worst case I would have been fired... but at least then I wouldn't have been directly responsible for delivering a game that could have been so much more.

— *Graeme Bayless (Director of Production, Crystal Dynamics)*

::::: *Spyro the Dragon 2: Ripto's Rage!:*
From Geek Points to Skill Points

Sony Computer Entertainment America

When working on the second *Spyro the Dragon* game, a number of the staff were pulling a late night playing *StarCraft*. (This is a great deal of what happens during those all-nighters, by the way.) Mark Cerny came into the office after dinner and was appalled at our audacity; he took Post-Its, wrote "Geek Point" on each of them, and affixed them to the back of all the players. The next day, we added "geek points" as a special set of secrets to the game; the later-renamed "skill points" have become a staple of every Insomniac title since.

— *Michael John (Lead Designer, Method Games)*

Half-Life was one of the first FPS games with an intricate storyline.

New coin-op releases also went 3D, such as *Tekken* (Namco), *Crazy Taxi* (Sega), and *Time Crisis* (Namco). PC systems included PC with Windows 98 and Pentium III, and the Apple iMac. The PC market was slower to adopt 3D. There were a number of 3D graphics cards with competing standards. Microsoft was pushing Direct X, while developers were more inclined toward OpenGL. PC games released included *X-COM: UFO Defense* (Microprose), *Command and Conquer* (Westwood Studios), *Starcraft* (Blizzard), *Baldur's Gate* (Interplay/BioWare), *Quake* (id Software), *Ultima Online* (Electronic Arts), *Unreal* (GT Interactive/Epic), *Everquest* (SOE), *Half-Life* (Valve), and *Roller Coaster Tycoon* (Hasbro Interactive).

With the introduction of 3D, production teams increased dramatically in size—which, in turn, made the role of producer necessary in even the smallest projects. It also added a level of complexity to testing. Testers now had to catch object collisions and "holes in the geometry" where player characters could literally fall outside the game world. Producers and team members had to get up to speed on 3D geometry just to understand what the programmers and artists were talking about.

Console is King: The 21ˢᵗ Century

By the turn of the century, all games began to incorporate 3D graphics. Innovations in hardware technology supported realistic-looking characters and environments. Each increase in hardware performance and storage yielded a leap in realism. The goal for many developers was now to create an experience identical to reality: rippling water, flowing hair, shifting wind, dynamic moving lights, reflections on moving objects, facial lip-synching, varied character animation and emotions, and real physics and collisions.

This emphasis on realism has caused team sizes to soar. Core teams for full-scale, major project development now number 30 to 80 people with 50 to 100 subcontractors being hired at various stages. The producer's job is more important than ever. Producers often oversee budgets ranging from $5 million to $30 million. Project management is handled by specialized managers in each field: software, art, animation, music, and design. Even in mobile, casual, and web game development (where titles can still be created with 5 to 10 people working 6 to 9 months for under $1 million), there has been an influx of licensed products, sequels, and overblown team/budget sizes.

::::: The Highs and Lows of *Nox*

Electronic Arts

One low point in my game development career was being flatly told in 1999 that we were not going to be allowed to release a map editor with our fantasy game, *Nox*. It would "confuse customers," "degrade the quality" of the game, and be a "QA nightmare." I knew this was utter crap and would damage our online community, but was powerless at the time to override this out-of-touch decision. During that same period, games such as *Quake, Unreal*, and *Half-Life* were actively encouraging their communities with editors, source code, and "mod" SDKs. In some cases, this led to entirely new games such as *Half-Life: Counter-Strike*. The icing on the cake was the built-in support for community-created content in *The Sims*, released the same month, by the same company. At the same time, a high point I recall very fondly was when *Nox* was released. I joined many Internet servers and watched people from all over the world play the game. There's nothing quite like knowing you have built something that entertains millions of people all over the planet. Many of my best experiences have been those of intense collaboration with groups of amazingly talented people who are working together on a game we are all excited about. I have been lucky enough to have this experience several times during my professional career, and it is a daily occurrence at Turtle Rock Studios. It is, in fact, the primary reason I founded the studio.

— *Mike Booth (Chief Executive Officer, Turtle Rock Studios)*

Outsourcing Labor

The rising cost of development has led many developers to outsource work to foreign markets where labor rates are lower. The difference in culture, language, and time zones requires detailed upfront planning, complex (multilevel) project schedules, and frequent team communication.

Tekken has seen six sequels with versions released for the arcade, console (PlayStation), and portable (PSP) platforms.

Hollywood production values have increased consumer expectations faster, but domestic markets haven't grown fast enough to support these big-budget games. Publishers are instituting plans to develop games for a global community and release versions of their games in multiple territories. Some publishers attempt to create games that have universal appeal. Others look toward customizing the experience for local territories. Project managers specializing in localization of games are a critical part of a team. They often need to manage dozens of versions and still ensure simultaneous worldwide release.

Sega Dreamcast, Sony PS2, Nintendo GameCube, and Microsoft Xbox.

:::::Industry Cycles: 128-Bit Consoles (2000-2004)

Image courtesy of Nintendo

The 128-bit console era marked the beginning of big budget games. Megahits could expect to sell five million units or more. Publishers began to focus on fewer games with larger budgets. Producers were now expected to work alongside marketing to define target audience, forecast market potential, and estimate return on investment (ROI). Round two of the console wars saw Sega Dreamcast,

Animal Crossing, a 128-bit game released for the GameCube, involves interaction with animal villagers and domestic goals such as home improvement.

Sony PlayStation 2, Nintendo GameCube, and newcomer Microsoft Xbox all vying for the top. In the end, Sony would emerge with almost half the market. New console games released included *Kingdom Hearts* (Square), *Jak and Daxter* (SCEA), *Halo* (Microsoft), *Animal Crossing* (Nintendo), *SSX* (Electronic Arts), *Star Wars: Rogue Squadron 2* (LucasArts), and *Grand Theft Auto: San Andreas* (Take-Two Interactive). This period saw record profits for some publishers and devastation for others. It was winner-take-all. Producers were forced to relocate as publishers went out of business or merged with rivals. It became increasingly difficult for start-ups to compete if they lacked a foundation of in-house 3D expertise or technology.

New coin-op releases included *San Francisco Rush* (Atari Games), *Gauntlet Dark Legacy* (Midway), *Blade of Honor* (Konami), *Tekken 5* (Namco), and *Wave Runner GP* (Sega). The PC finally had reliable 3D technology. Microsoft updated the OS to Windows XP and Intel rolled out the Pentium 4 at 3.0 GHz. While there were some widely successful releases, the overall market began to decline. Notable PC games included *Max Payne* (Gathering of Developers), *The Sims* (Electronic Arts), *Half-Life 2* (Valve), and *Zoo Tycoon* (Microsoft). New handhelds included Nintendo Game Boy SP and DS.

Electronic Arts

The Sims (*Open for Business* shown) is arguably the most successful game franchise to date.

Diagram by Per Olin

Nintendo Game Boy Advance	2001, cartridge, $100
Nintendo Game Boy Advance SP	2003, cartridge, backlit, $79
Nintendo DS	2004, dual-screen, touchpad, WiFi, $130
Sony PlayStation Portable (PSP)	2004, UMD games and movies, WiFi, $249
Nintendo Game Boy Micro	2005, cartridge, backlit, $89
Nintendo DS Lite	2006, dual-screen, touchpad, WiFi, $130

Diagram by Per Olin

Sony PlayStation 2	2000, 128-bit, 75 million polygons per second, DVD, backwards compatible with PlayStation, $299
Microsoft Xbox	2001, 115 million vertices/second (theoretical), hard drive, internet support, $299
Nintendo GameCube	2001, 64-bit, 12 million polygons per second (real-world), connectivity to GameBoy, $199
PC	2003, with Windows XP and Pentium 4 processor (3.0GHz), $1,000
Microsoft Xbox 360	2005, hard drive add-on (core) or included (premium), 500 million triangles per second, 720p/1080i resolution, $299-$399
Nintendo Wii	2006, no hard drive – but ships with 512mb of flash memory, 480p resolution, $250
Sony PlayStation 3	2006, 20-60GB hard drive, 1080p resolution, $499-$599

Image courtesy of Nintendo

Sony Computer Entertainment America

Image courtesy of Nintendo

Game Boy Advance (left), PlayStation Portable [PSP] (center), and DS Lite (right).

Through all the innovations, console manufacturers have kept the cost of their systems low relative to PCs. Despite the higher cost of games, consoles currently command the lion's share of the market. PCs have become largely commoditized, while consoles are getting more and more expensive. This has caused price differentials to shrink greatly with respect to the PC's lower end, although compatibility problems (such as onboard video) are an issue.

Microsoft Corporation

Sony Computer Entertainment Americca

Image courtesy of Nintendo

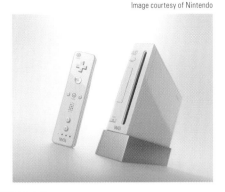

Xbox 360 (left), PlayStation 3 (middle), and Wii (right).

Microsoft Xbox 360	2005, downloadable games, $299
Sony PlayStation 3	2006, 1080p resolution and BluRay, $499
Nintendo Wii	2006, motion controller (Wii remote & Nunchuk), $249

:::::Industry Cycles: HD Consoles (2005- ?)

Activision

The high-definition (HD) era has once again raised the bar for visual realism. HD consoles are being released in conjunction with affordable HD TVs and the introduction of competing HD disc standards. The new consoles also support Internet connectivity as a standard feature. For round three in the console wars, we have Microsoft Xbox 360, Nintendo Wii, and Sony PlayStation 3. New console games released include *Call of Duty 2* (Activision), *NBA Live 06* (Electronic Arts), and *Dead or Alive 4* (Tecmo). Internet and wireless connectivity of modern consoles have been factors in fueling the rapid growth of the console market. Services such as Xbox Live have changed the way console gamers play, bringing them into the vast world of online multiplayer games that only PC gamers had access to five years ago.

Call of Duty 2, which was the first top-selling Xbox 360 game, raised the bar in its realistic portrayal of World War II combat.

World of Warcraft has over 7 million subscribers worldwide.

The PC market, which traditionally offered publishers a buffer during the transition to new consoles, is currently in decline. Gone are the multimillion-unit sellers, with the notable exception of *World of Warcraft* (Blizzard). Other top-sellers include *Guild Wars* (NCsoft), *Sims 2* (Electronic Arts), and *Age of Empires III* (Microsoft). Microsoft intends to help reverse the PC game software sales slide with its new Vista operating system and retailer point-of-service (POS) displays for showcase titles.

The producers who started out as lone engineers in the early days have traded in their code and tech journals. In the 21st century, most producers have a background in business—or at least a knack for it. An understanding of technology is still required, since each game pushes the envelope a little further, and milestones are usually governed by progress in software development. Project management requires accurate forecasting, attention to detail, and effective communication now that games are released simultaneously in multiple languages and on multiple platforms. Weekly progress reports and tracking are mandatory. Release dates are critical, since publishers now stand to gain or lose millions and their stock reflects this variance. Hundreds of jobs are added or lost as projects are green-lighted or cancelled. Some may say this is why we have lots of licenses and sequels, since publishers are risk-averse. Experimentation can and does still occur at a lower level—with casual, web, and mobile games in which team sizes and budgets permit original work and fast turnaround time.

The history of games is tightly intertwined with the development of computers. Consumer desire to play games at home fueled the development of low-cost and high-performance graphics processors. Early games could literally be designed in a few hours and developed in a few days; currently, games require months of design prior to production. The process of getting a game into production takes a great deal of work and planning. This first step in project management, concept development, is the subject of the next chapter.

chapter 1

:::CHAPTER REVIEW:::

1. Imagine that you are a game developer working in the 1980s. Knowing the limitations associated with this era, what type of game would you develop—and how would you create a division of labor within your game development team?

2. Choose three consoles described in this chapter, each from the same industry cycle. Discuss each console's strengths and weaknesses. Let's say you were porting one game to each of these different consoles. What game features would you need to modify in order to take advantage of each console's strengths?

3. What are the benefits and disadvantages of developing a game for the computer versus the console platform? What trade-offs might you have to consider when managing projects that involve both platforms? How might you modify the development process if you were to port a game to a handheld platform?

2

CHAPTER

Concept
Development
describing the big idea

Key Chapter Questions

■ What are the major components of a concept?

■ Why is platform choice important to concept development?

■ How do you come up with ideas for games?

■ What does a publisher do?

■ What is the green light process?

You're singing in the shower, talking to an old friend over the phone, or lying awake at night. Suddenly it hits you — that perfect idea for a game. Your thoughts take shape and you can begin to see the game in your head. That little spark can ignite the firestorm that is concept development. One great idea can lead you to the first step in creating a game. This chapter takes you through the process of turning these ideas into proposals that get funded for development.

What Is a Concept?

Concepts are the short story version of a game idea. They include everything some-one needs to know about a game and nothing more. They should be in a format that can be digested in five minutes or less.

Concepts, short for concept proposals, are mainly used to propose products to publishers, in the hopes of getting funding for more detailed preproduction and, ultimately, the creation of a game. These proposal documents are also used to cre-ate unified vision and purpose for a development studio or the development team (referred to as "developer" throughout this book).

The concept addresses four key questions:

1. What is the game?
2. Who will buy the game?
3. Why will they buy the game?
4. Why should this game be published?

The answer to this last question lists the developer's competitive advantages with regard to the game and describes how the game fits into your overall business strategy.

The concept has the following sections:

- high concept
- premise and story synopsis
- unique selling points
- game features
- genre of game
- target platform
- target customer
- competitive analysis
- financial analysis
- team
- proof of concept (optional)

Concept Document Guidelines

In my opinion, a good concept document must incorporate a clear and concise presentation of a game's main elements. There needs to be some indication of what makes the game unique and why it will be successful. . . . Another thing to consider is that this is not intended to be a game design document (GDD), and as such it should almost never be longer than two pages. That said, the single most important feature of a good high concept document is that it will lead to a contract from a publisher. Experience tells us that this will usually require a good selection of pretty pictures as well as the basic information indicated above.

— *Ed Rotberg (Chief Technology Officer, Mine Shaft Entertainment)*

Who Writes the Concept?

The concept is created by a small team, usually six or fewer people, including the producer, creative director, lead designer, concept artist, and technical director. The creative director contributes the overall vision for the game. The concept is usually written by the creative director and edited by the producer of a project.

The producer is responsible for overseeing the conceptual process and documenting the decisions made. The creative director is responsible for presenting game ideas and leading discussions with the team. The lead designer will ultimately have responsibility for executing the design of the game, so it's a good idea to have that person involved from the very beginning. Artists are helpful to create concept drawings and storyboards to help illustrate ideas. They also provide input on design choices that affect the look of the game such as the setting, time period, characters, and style. The technical director (TD) contributes to the concept process by describing ways to show off the capabilities of the technology. This may be special software that the team has the ability to create or exploit, or features of a new hardware platform. The TD can also provide input on what is realistic to achieve in the game. A good TD balances healthy skepticism with a desire to push the technology to keep the team from setting goals too low. The game has to be leading edge two to three years from now, so goals should be sufficiently high to keep it from looking dated by the time it is released. Some companies, such as Blizzard, have avoided this "leading edge" focus and instead create high-quality titles in terms of gameplay and story, even if they utilize older graphics engines.

High Concept

The *high concept* is a short sentence or two that provides the vision or "big idea" for the game. This is usually the first thing in the concept, right after the title. High concepts should be simple and easily understood. If you can't get your idea across in a few sentences, then it is likely too complicated or too vague to be a commercial success.

Painting a Clear Picture

The best high concepts are those that paint a clear picture in the mind of the audience and team about what experience the game will deliver. While there is inspiration involved in great high concepts, most of them come from a lot of hard work and refinement.

— *Gordon Walton (Studio Co-Director, BioWare Austin)*

THQ

Just like in *Crazy Taxi*, players drive pedestrians to dropoff points for money in *Simpson's: Road Rage*.

Some high concepts try to describe a game by referring to other games. "*Crazy Taxi* meets *The Simpsons*" is arguably a good description of the game *The Simpsons: Road Rage*. However, it means nothing to someone who hasn't played *Crazy Taxi,* and it also relegates the design to being a "me-too" product.

The high concept for the *Gran Turismo* series is to be "The Real Driving Simulator." All *Gran Turismo* games hold this as their core vision, and all aspects of the design support this high concept:

- accurate reproductions of cars from well-known manufacturers
- realistic handling and performance
- real world tracks and racing conditions

A good high concept for a game is one that's very easy to understand for the average consumer. It's trite and stereotypical but that's why the Hollywood style pitch statement works so well: "It's like *Jurassic Park,* but the dinosaurs have rocket launchers strapped to them."

— *Starr Long (Producer, NCsoft)*

The developer, Polyphony Digital, extended this high concept into motorcycle racing with their newest game, *Tourist Trophy*. The high concept for this game plays off of their heritage: "The Real Riding Simulator."

High concepts do not always reveal much about the story that unfolds in the game. That is covered in the premise and story synopsis.

Tourist Trophy simulates racing production motorcycles on real world tracks.

The X

Electronic Arts uses the term "the X" to identify the main feature or major message of the game. Throughout the concept phase and well into preproduction, a team of programmers, artists, and testers reviews the design and any playable prototypes. The team provides feedback to the designers to ensure that the game supports "the X."

Don Daglow on the Creative High Concept:::::

Don L. Daglow has served as president and CEO of Stormfront Studios since founding the company in 1988. Stormfront's major titles include the upcoming action-adventure *Eragon* (Xbox 360, PS2, Xbox, PC; to be published by Vivendi Universal Games, based on the 20th Century Fox film) and *The Lord of the Rings: The Two Towers* (PS2/Xbox, published by EA, based on the film by Peter Jackson). Electronic Games has called Don "one of the best-known and respected producers in the history of the field," and in 2003 he received the CGE Award for "groundbreaking achievements that shaped the Video Game Industry." Prior to founding Stormfront, Don served as director of Intellivision game development for Mattel, as a producer at Electronic Arts, and as head of the Entertainment and Education division at Broderbund. He designed and programmed the first-ever computer baseball game in 1971 (now recorded in the Baseball Hall of Fame in Cooperstown), the first mainframe computer role-playing game (*Dungeon* for PDP-10 mainframes, 1975), the first sim game (Intellivision *Utopia*, 1981), and the first game to use multiple camera angles (Intellivision *World Series Major League Baseball*, 1983). Don co-designed Computer Game Hall of Fame title *Earl Weaver Baseball* (1987) and the first massively multiplayer online graphic adventure, the original *Neverwinter Nights* for AOL (1991–1997). In 2003 he was elected to the board of directors of the Academy of Interactive Arts and Sciences. He also is a past winner of the National Endowment

Don L. Daglow
(President & CEO, Stormfront Studios)

for the Humanities New Voices playwriting competition. Don holds a BA in Writing from Pomona College and an EdM from Claremont Graduate University.

Picture you're at a party. The music and the voices are loud. You're introduced to an incredibly attractive person who asks what you do. Casually, you reply, "I produce video games."

"You do?!!! That's fascinating! What kind of game are you working on now?"

You're about to answer, but a friend across the room calls out to this unbelievably attractive person. They wave back and respond "Be there in a sec!"

They turn back to you, eager to hear about the exciting game you're working on. This is your moment. You're in a noisy room and the most attractive person you've ever met is about to walk away. In this brief instant, what single sentence do you say about your game that will make this heavenly person want to come back over to you later and hear more?

It can't take too long, because they're about to go. It can't be too complicated, because the music drowns out every fourth word you say. And it must be utterly fascinating.

Now, isn't that a lot more interesting than "A high concept is the single short sentence that clearly states the features or premise that will compel the maximum number of players to buy your game"?

Premise and Story Synopsis

The *premise* tells more about the main character, primary goal, or philosophical theme of the game. The premise is usually a few sentences written in second- or third-person voice. The premise (third-person) for *Half-Life* is:

> Gordon Freeman, a doctor of theoretical physics, conducted experiments in teleportation in the ultra secret Black Mesa Research Facility. One of his experiments causes a resonance cascade that opens a dimensional rift to Xen—a world inhabited by terrifying, bloodthirsty monsters.

This same premise could also appear in second-person voice, which can be even more dramatic and speak directly to the player:

> You are Gordon Freeman, a doctor of theoretical physics, who has conducted experiments in teleportation in the ultra secret Black Mesa Research Facility. One of your experiments causes a

resonance cascade that opens a dimensional rift to Xen—a world inhabited by terrifying, bloodthirsty monsters.

By contrast, the third-person high concept for *Half-Life* is:

> Scientists gun down face-hugging aliens in this engrossing sci-fi first-person shooter that delivers both a compelling solo game and solid online play.

A second-person version might read:

Valve

In *Half-Life 2*, players gun down creepy aliens with high-tech weapons.

> You are a scientist who guns down face-hugging aliens in this engrossing sci-fi first-person shooter that delivers both a compelling solo game and solid online play.

This may not sound special, but back in 1998 when the game was released, first-person shooter (FPS) games were notorious for thin solo games. Most people bought FPS games to compete online or at LAN parties.

The *story synopsis* provides more detail about the protagonist, setting, and backstory. It also gives a hint of the antagonist and how the story will unfold.

Unique Selling Points

A good concept grabs the prospective players and leaves them shaking their heads thinking, "That's a great idea!" These "winners" have one or more *unique selling points* (USPs) that set them apart from the competition.

A rule of thumb is that any new game concept should have at least three unique selling points, or USPs. These are elements that customers would see on the back of the box to entice them to buy the game. A great game can have only one USP, but it should be truly unique, something that has never been seen before.

USPs aren't merely marketing fluff; they are the core pillars of your game and should guide the decision-making process throughout production.

A common USP is to base a game on a well-known brand or license. Games derived from the *Lord of the Rings* trilogy have characters and settings that are unique and cannot be duplicated in other games without violation of copyright.

Sony Computer Entertainment America

Players fly among hundreds of ships in *Warhawk*.

USPs may also center on the use of new technology. *Warhawk* is one of the first games to use the motion sensors in the new PlayStation 3 console.

The most lasting of USPs are those that provide an innovative game mechanic. *Dune II* brought real-time action to strategy games which, up until then, had traditionally been turn-based. *The Sims* provided complex and often unpredictable AI with its simulation of human behaviors.

USPs tend to sound like the slogans for the game. Examples of USPs include:

- Switch on the fly between 3 player characters
- Fly, drive, run, and swim—all in one world
- First game to be set in the mythical underwater realm of Atlantis
- Epic military battles above ground, squad-based exploration below it

What is "Fun"?

Inspiration comes from a wide array of sources, ranging from personal experience to good fiction... from dreams and imagination to other existing content. At the end of the day, however, the concept is 1% of what makes a great game... the other 99% is how you execute on it. Like most studios with talented individuals, I'm confident I could have 100 great ideas generated with one week's work. Turning those great ideas into great games is the hard part. A good high concept really needs to answer a few key things. First, what is "fun"? When building a game, one of the most important aspects is to fully understand what is fun about the game, and constantly remind yourself of it. If you lose the "fun", you end up with a product that may be an accurate simulation... or a great story... but that isn't terribly fun to play. Second, a concept needs to understand the market it is targeting, and should discuss those in the proposal... why will this game work with the target audience? Finally, every concept should be able to clearly define their "differentiation." What makes this product different? Without your "USPs," you're unlikely to get the product off the ground.

— *Graeme Bayless (Director of Production, Crystal Dynamics)*

Original vs. Licensed IP

Working on either original or licensed IP [intellectual property] is great, but the benefits and disadvantages are almost completely opposite. A good license gives you a look, feel, and back story—and it lets you get right to task of making the game. An original IP provides you with complete creative freedom—but you have to develop your own look, feel, and back story before you can start making the game. An original IP is free to start and can be sold later. However, you have to market and establish it all on your own. A license brings exposure and brand recognition, but you have to pay for that up front.

— *John Ahlquist (Founder, Ahlquist Software)*

Licensed properties are already in the mind of the consumer. You have to make almost no effort to explain it to them. The downside is that you are limited to only do things that fit within the universe of that IP. In addition you sometimes have to create gameplay that is great at fitting within the licensed IP but isn't necessarily fun. Original IP lets you do just about anything with the game but it usually requires a fair bit of explaining to the consumer.

— *Starr Long (Producer, NCsoft)*

I love the freedom an original IP gives, but it also means you have to build your entire audience for the game. Also, the freedom to innovate in any and all ways is overwhelming at times. What a licensed property gives you is a built in audience—but, more importantly, it gives you boundaries. The inherent boundaries of an established IP basically force you to focus your innovations.

— *Gordon Walton (Studio Co-Director, BioWare Austin)*

The benefits of licensed intellectual property (IP) are obvious; brand recognition and established fan base. But after working on the "big two" game licenses (*Lord of the Rings* and *Star Wars*), I have to say that original IP is much more fun and less taxing on the development team. Licensed IP can tie you down from the get-go with story and character continuity, and the bulk of your design decisions have to be approved by licensing. Depending on how your contract was negotiated, you may have marketing executives designing your game for you! Original IP lets you focus on the things that matter. Creative people want to create.

— *Jeff Stewart (Game Designer, Petroglyph Games)*

Clearly, there are advantages and disadvantages to developing a game with original IP vs. one using a licensed property. *The potential upside is enormous if you establish a successful original IP.* This includes sequels and the potential for licensing the IP even further. (Remember Pac-Man cereal?) This is probably the biggest plus. While there may be more assurance of success with a licensed property, the potential for ongoing and overall success is much, much higher with original IP. *There is far greater freedom of creativity.* With a licensed property, each aspect of the title must meet the licensor's approval. This can often be a major stumbling block. Sometimes the creative freedom of an original IP can make the actual technical development easier because of this. *The team typically feels a greater sense of ownership with the product, making motivation easier.* With a licensed property, though, *there is far less risk for the publisher, and more insurance of a profitable title.* In addition *there is less need for development of characters and story,* since the player can be assumed to have a certain level of familiarity with either or both. This often makes a game more accessible to the player at the outset. And finally, *there are often many high quality assets available to the team for including into the product.*

— *Ed Rotberg (Chief Technology Officer, Mine Shaft Entertainment)*

This industry is rife with bad licenses… all because someone decided that grabbing a license somehow made it all better than building an original IP. While this certainly CAN be true, it is not automatically so. The basic idea behind licensing is that you have an audience already there for your product. If ten million people are fans of <insert property here>, and you sell your game to even 10% of them, you've done a million units. Simple math… but also flawed, as a single calculation being off can throw your numbers way out of whack. For myself, I prefer to stay away from any license unless I consider it to be an appropriate and gameable license (by "gameable" I mean a license that naturally could be turned into a game). For example, while Titanic represents one of the most successful films of all time, it isn't terribly appropriate as a gaming license. On the flipside, licenses like Spiderman and John Madden have been staples in gaming that carry such power as to be well worth the millions they cost. In the simplest form, the argument between the two camps comes down to this… it is easier to market a licensed title, and in theory you have a built-in market with predispositions towards purchase of your game. On the other hand, if you can build your own franchise, you can reap the rewards of being a franchisee, and potentially create a revenue stream that transcends the game. The risks for creating your own IP are higher, as you can't depend on the power of the license to save you if your game isn't great… but if you make a truly great game without a license, you can realize rewards far greater than that of a licensed title.

— *Graeme Bayless (Director of Production, Crystal Dynamics)*

You can't own a licensed property, of course, unless you buy it. Entering into a licensing agreement means that you are giving up a certain amount of creative control. Also, the licensor gets a significant cut of revenue and may demand significant up front fees. If you have original IP, you get to be in the driver's seat. That said, a good licensed property may suggest a game from within its core concepts. This saves a lot of design time. Also, the main reason we enter into licenses is to take advantage of the powerful awareness already present for the property in the marketplace. If you do license, make sure the game you are creating will matter to the demographic and psychographic of the licensed property's market base. A sophisticated real time strategy game based on a girl's toy won't sell.

— *Frank T. Gilson (Senior Developer of Digital Games, Wizards of the Coast)*

Features

Game *features* describe the player's interaction with the game. These are the things consumers see in the advertising or on the back of the box. Features may not be unique but they are important for gameplay and the overall game experience. Examples include:

- point-of-view (first-person, third-person)
- online/multiplayer
- number of levels or missions (outline each)
- weapons, gadgets, inventions, vehicles
- voice recognition
- high definition/1080p resolution
- seamless world with continuous streaming

Each feature should be evaluated to determine whether it supports the USPs. If not, then question whether the feature is really necessary. Games that have a strong cohesion between features and USPs fulfill customer expectations. They also tend to be more polished and immersive.

> A really awesome looking and sounding game can still be a hollow waste of $60 if it doesn't incorporate great gameplay.
>
> — *Frank T. Gilson (Senior Developer of Digital Games, Wizards of the Coast),*

Features should drive task prioritization. Since features typically involve new technology or game mechanics, they may require considerable research and development (R&D) or trial and error. A seasoned producer will try to get these done early to allow time for rework and polish. The other reason to get major features done early is to ensure that they won't fall prey to the inevitable trimming that occurs when projects begin to run late or over budget. However, don't forget that excellent gameplay should be stressed above graphics and sound that do not directly impact fun and replayability.

Genre

Games are categorized by *genres* or styles of game design. Some of the commonly recognized genres include those that follow.

© 2005 Tecmo, LTD

Dead or Alive 4 demonstrates detailed character models and animation.

Sony Computer Entertainment America

Ratchet and Clank: Size Matters brings the popular PS2 series to the handheld PSP.

Action

The *action* genre is one of the most popular game genres in the United States. All action games involve fast-paced movement and quick reflexes, allowing for a great deal of eye-hand coordination and little time for reflective thought. Subgenres include fighting, platformer, racing/driving, and shooter.

Fighting

Design in *fighting* games involves two combatants striking each other with fists, kicks, and handheld weapons. Some fighting games allow up to four players, with two on each side. Players memorize combinations of button presses to activate elaborate moves. Each fighting character has one or more signature attacks or finishing moves.

Platformer

In a *platformer* (or platform game), the player controls a character that leaps or climbs from one platform to another while fighting enemies and collecting power-ups. Platform games are especially popular among younger audiences.

:::::Retro Arcade: A New Twist on Classic Design

Microsoft Corporation

Geometry Wars is a popular downloadable retro-arcade game.

Retro-arcade games mimic the style and pacing of coin-op video arcade games from the 1980s. Some, like *Battlezone II*, are actual sequels of these games. There can be hundreds of levels by making slight modifications to graphics and attributes of enemies and playfields. This style of game is popular for downloadable games due to the low memory requirements.

Racing/Driving

Design in *racing/driving* games centers around driving a vehicle on a track or through city streets. Racing games in the action genre focus less on advanced physics and more on having fun and capturing the feeling of speed. (Racing simulations, discussed later in this chapter, focus more on emulating how vehicles behave in a real-world scenario.)

Burnout Revenge focuses on speed and special effects.

::::: Vehicle Combat

A specialized form of driving games, known as *vehicle combat* games, involves players driving and shooting at, or simply crashing into, each other to gain points and upgrades.

Sony Computer Entertainment America

Twisted Metal: Head-On pits drivers against other cars in a destructive arena.

Shooter

Design in *shooters* centers around the player controlling a single character wielding various projectile weapons and firing at enemies. This includes both first-person shooters (FPSs) such as *F.E.A.R.* and third-person shooters such as *Max Payne*. Military shooters such as the *Call of Duty* series combine FPS with military combat simulation.

Vivendi Universal Games

Activision

First-person shooters show the game world through the eyes of the player. *F.E.A.R.* (left) has a fantasy horror look, while *Call of Duty 2* (right) goes for historic realism.

Quantic Dream

Games such as *Indigo Prophecy* bring more complex, non-linear storylines to the adventure genre.

Sony Computer Entertainment America

God of War 2 continues the saga of Kratos.

Courtesy of Blizzard Entertainment, Inc

World of Warcraft immerses players into persistent state worlds.

Adventure

The goal of most *adventure* games is to solve a problem, often shrouded in mystery. In classic adventure games, the player is put in the role of "detective," uncovering clues to puzzles and riddles by exploring environments. The storyline in classic adventure games was often more important than the player's character. The best-selling graphic adventure game of all time, *Myst*, did not provide the player character with a specific identity. Pure adventure games were thought of as a dying breed until the release of daring games such as *Indigo Prophecy*, which challenge the linear storyline and unintuitive puzzle solving that has marked classic adventure games.

Action-Adventure

The *action-adventure* hybrid has become a genre in its own right. Like adventure games, the emphasis is on exploration and problem solving. But unlike classic adventure games such as *Myst*, action-adventure games often involve quick reflexes, fast-paced movement, and some combat. Like classic adventure games, story progression in an action-adventure game is often linear with scripted events.

Massively Multiplayer Online Games

Massively multiplayer online games (MMOGs) allow thousands of simultaneous players in the same game world. Some games allow combat between players, player vs. player (PVP). Players pay a regular subscription fee to maintain their accounts. *World of Warcraft*, currently the largest MMOG, boasts over seven million subscribers.

:::::Party: Bring Your Friends!

In party games, players compete in various mini-games to earn points and ultimately win a match. Party games are light-hearted, designed for ease of play among two to eight players in the same room.

Mario Party 7 supports up to eight players with shared controllers.

Puzzle/Maze

Players must solve visual or mental puzzles to proceed in a *puzzle* game. The game design is often derivative of arcade games but level advancement is more difficult. Some games such as *Lumines* require faster response from the player as levels progress.

Role-Playing Games

Role-playing games (RPGs) are derived from classic pen-and-paper *Dungeons & Dragons*® games. Players customize their characters by selecting race, class, and skills. Design involves adventuring and killing monsters to gain loot and experience points that can be traded for better weapons and enhanced abilities, respectively. Most RPGs are set in medieval fantasy worlds, and some have modern or futuristic settings.

Strategy

In *strategy* games, players focus on managing resources such as units (people, vehicles, weapons), food, money, and materials. Strategy games can be either turn-based or real-time.

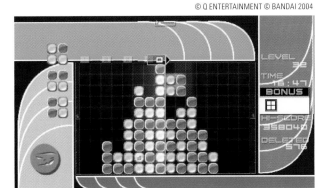

Lumines is a fast-paced puzzle game featuring falling blocks and discs, along with a hypnotic soundtrack.

The Elder Scrolls IV: Oblivion is an RPG containing rich environments such as lush forests and complex cities in which characters interact through combat and conversation.

Gas Powered Games

The RTS *Supreme Commander* promises land, air, and sea battles with hundreds of units.

Most *real-time strategy (RTS)* games allow players to command entire armies rather than single characters. Activities might include base building and resource gathering to add depth and complexity. Like FPSs, RTS games are quite popular among competitive online players.

Simulation

Simulation games are always based on real-world rules, whether related to vehicles, processes, or participation in competitive activities such as sports.

Vehicle

One of the longest-running *vehicle simulation* series is *Microsoft Flight Simulator,* a flight sim in which would-be pilots fly private and commercial aircraft to and from real-world airports. The first game in the franchise was released in 1982. There are hundreds of combat flight sims based on aircraft from World War I to futuristic enivironments. As mentioned earlier in this chapter, many driving/racing games (such as the *Gran Turismo* and *Forza* series) are also considered to be vehicle simulations.

Microsoft Corporation

Sony Computer Entertainment America

Microsoft Flight Simulator X (left) and *Gran Turismo HD* (right) are flight and racing simulations, respectively.

Process

Process simulations involve goals such as creating cities (*SimCity* and *Tycoon* series) or evolving social networks—and even life itself (*Spore*). Whereas urban planning process sims such as *SimCity* and *Rollercoaster Tycoon* have set goals that allow the player to successfully build and maintain venues and urban communities, most process simulations have no real ending. Often, the goal is to build or maintain balance in a process, whether it's a community or life itself.

Sports

Sports games reproduce the rules and look of classic sports. They are sometimes put in the *simulation* category because they emulate real-world rules, but sports is often considered a genre all its own. Popular sports include American football, basketball, baseball, golf, and soccer, but there are sports of all kinds covered in electronic games, including table tennis, volleyball, badminton, cricket, rugby, and archery.

Survival-Horror

Design in *survival-horror* games mixes adventure and survival. The camera is usually third-person, but some games, such as *Resident Evil 4*, include first-person shooter (FPS) controls. Although survival-horror can be thought of as a subgenre of action-adventure, it is being recognized as a genre in its own right. One of the only genres that describes the story behind the game rather than style of play, the survival-horror moniker could represent the film industry's growing influence on the game industry.

Spore is the latest life simulator from Will Wright, designer of *The Sims*.

Sports games, like *Tiger Woods*, attempt to accurately simulate the experience of playing professional sports.

Players can take in the surroundings with an over-the-shoulder point of view in *Resident Evil 4*.

Open world games are also known as *sandbox* games. They give the player the freedom to travel throughout the world without restrictions. Missions or quests are used to create a sense of progression. Not all games fit into strict genres. Many sandbox games blend aspects of one or more genres together. For example, *Grand Theft Auto: San Andreas* combines third-person shooting, driving, and role playing with an open-world "sandbox" game. *The Elder Scrolls IV: Oblivion*, officially an RPG, contains a huge open game world with emergent AI for its NPCs (non-player characters). Players may spend weeks discovering new areas and encountering different monsters and NPCs.

Platform

Choosing your primary delivery platform is a critical decision. Making the wrong decision will limit the potential of your game and result in poor results at retail. So-called killer-apps are so desirable and so deftly tuned to their particular delivery platform that customers will buy hardware just to play the game.

Console

Consoles are the most popular devices for consumers. They're easy to use and they sport a simple handheld controller. Sony PlayStation 3, Microsoft Xbox 360, and Nintendo Wii are all examples of next-generation video consoles. The PlayStation in its various forms has reached over 100 million consumers worldwide.

Microsoft Corporation

Sony Computer Entertainment America

Nintendo

Next-generation consoles: Microsoft Xbox 360, Sony PlayStation 3, and Nintendo Wii.

Hardware manufacturers sell their consoles at a discounted price, sometimes below their actual cost of production and distribution. So how do they make money? They charge a license fee for every disc or cartridge produced. Roughly 14% of the retail price paid by consumers for a game goes to license fees.

Console manufacturers typically review all game concepts and give their approval for new games. They also review games in production, and developers are required to follow guidelines for the interface. In this way, manufacturers control quality and consistency of games released on their platforms.

Development hardware consists of a high-end PC connected to a proprietary development kit or "dev kit" provided by the console manufacturer. During the early stages of a new console's release, these dev kits are allocated to those developers with the greatest chance of delivering hit products at the launch of the console. Priority is also given to games that are exclusive to a given platform.

Computer (PC)

Many developers start out by creating their games for the computer (PC) platform. There are no restrictions or approvals required to create games for the PC. The hardware is relatively inexpensive, and there are thousands of resources to drawn upon. The margins can be better as there are no license fees, and manufacturing costs are generally lower than consoles. So what are the downsides? Unlike consoles, there is no single configuration for the PC. Developers spend a great deal of time trying to determine the minimum specification or

Courtesy of Dell Inc

The PC (Dell Precision 690 and 490 shown) has come a long way since its first release in 1981.

"min spec" for their games. Interface choices involve keyboards, mice, and a host of potential peripherals. Operating systems change frequently, and new hardware additions may create compatibility issues for games after their release. Keep in mind that a game can work well on one platform but not necessarily translate to others. RTSs have traditionally been hits on the PC platform but weak performers on consoles.

Market Considerations

The market considerations that influence platform choice are the following:

1. popularity and suitability of your genre on a given platform
2. potential installed base for a given platform
3. target customer
4. release windows

Popularity and Suitability

RTS games are almost exclusively developed for PCs. They use onscreen cursors or selection boxes to grab and move armies, or units. Players battle each other competitively in multiplayer matches over the Internet. Fighting games and action/character games are typically designed for the console. They use simple controls and require nimble reflexes to play.

Until recently, FPSs were just for the PC. The commercial success of games such as *Halo* on Xbox, *Gears of War* on Xbox 360, and *Resistance: Fall of Man* on PlayStation 3 indicate that FPSs have made the leap from computer to console.

Role-playing games (RPGs) can be found on all platforms. *Final Fantasy*, *Knights of the Old Republic*, and *Fable* are all examples of successful console RPGs. However, massively multiplayer RPGs (MMORPGs) are more successful on the PC. This will likely change, since the next generation of consoles all include broadband connectivity as a standard feature.

Sports games can be found on all platforms, and they are the most successful game genre. The market is dominated by a few big publishers vying for costly, exclusive licenses to leagues, players, and stadiums. Publishers such as Electronic Arts (EA) rely on their sports franchises to produce income every year as player rosters change.

Potential Installed Base

Console developers need to decide which platform has the greatest chance for success. Which will catch on and which will falter? While it's generally true that superior technology is a good indicator, it is by no means a guarantee of success. People buy games, not hardware. If the games available for a new platform aren't enticing, then consumers won't make the leap.

Some publishers hedge their bets by offering games simultaneously on multiple platforms. This strategy allows publishers to spread costly development across multiple SKUs (stock keeping unit, a common term for a unique numeric identifier, used most commonly in business to refer to a specific product in inventory or in a catalog). This may not be the best strategy for all games. Developing for multiple platforms usually means designing for the lowest common denominator and not taking full advantage of the capabilities of a given platform. It can also mean that a publisher has to shoulder the full burden of marketing. Popular games that are exclusive to a single platform often receive additional marketing support from hardware manufacturers. They also get first access to scarce development hardware.

So how do developers decide which console will prevail? Research services such as NPD offer predictions for installed base of all announced platforms months and years ahead of their release. These predictions rely on the past performance of current platforms and they assume full support of the development community. They also assume that production can stay ahead of demand.

Customer

Every game should have a target *customer* or core audience in mind. The most basic demographics include age, gender, geographical location, educational level, household income, and other interests (TV shows, music, clothing, hobbies). While it is true that a game designed for teenagers will often appeal to their younger siblings, the opposite rarely happens.

Few games appeal across all territories. Games made for American tastes may find little appeal in Europe or Asia. Some genres are also territory specific. A review of sales data and top-ten lists over the last five years would lead us to believe that adventure and puzzle games do well in France but have lackluster results elsewhere; both Germans and Americans enjoy strategy games; party games are big in Japan.

Boys still consume more games than girls, but the market for girls is beginning to show promise. EA's top-seller, *The Sims*, boasts a female audience that outnumbers the men. Publishers are more willing to invest in new themes in the hopes of gaining share in the rapidly growing female market.

Disposable income plays a role too. Few adolescents can afford to shell out $50 every month for a new game. They rely heavily on marketing and word of mouth to influence their purchases.

Finding Your Target

Finding the target customer is key... you likely have limited funds that must be applied against reaching the right people. This requires doing lots of market research, focus testing, and playtest analysis. More importantly, it requires that both the marketing and development groups be willing to both spend the time validating the concepts, and react to the feedback given. While I'm not advocating design-by-reaction, I do believe you can learn a great deal about your target audience by market research and focus testing... and you absolutely should use that to target your marketing.

– Graeme Bayless (Director of Production, Crystal Dynamics)

Players with Disabilities

Game developers have not been looking for instances where their game is "accidentally" accessible for a certain group of people with disabilities. For example, maybe their game works really well with an alternative controller that [a quadriplegic] might use. Of course, we don't find this out until a gamer with that particular disability is determined to play your game and discovers that it does work with a controller that they use to navigate a regular PC screen with. So even if you have not thought about gamers with disabilities— ... if there are features that work well with "controller b" (and usually these are posted on sites targeted for gamers with disabilities), then you should put out a press release and/or put this information on your game packaging. Right now, there is not a rating system for games with accessible features but we're working on it! All this being said...if you are going to announce that your game has a feature that is accessible, you should investigate that thoroughly through asking groups like the IGDA Game Accessibility SIG for an evaluation or to put you in touch with a user group that could evaluate that claim. A lot of games claim to have closed captioning—and, in reality, they have ... an important ambient cue; missing that [cue] means that the gamer is going to die 100 times before someone tells them "Oh, you have to listen for three clicks then turn around and launch a grenade in order to get through level one." That's embarrassing ... and unethical because you may have just sold a lot of copies of your game—only to [be faced with] a lot of really angry gamers who may not trust your publisher again.

— Michelle Hinn (Vice President, Game Division, DonationCoder.com)

ESRB Ratings and Player Markets

I've found that the ESRB rating system provides convenient shorthand for discussing the target audience for games. While it certainly influences the content in terms of violence/ language etc. in a game, it also is a good way of identifying the target look and feel for a game. A game rated 'E' will probably be built with lighter, more saturated colors, and a twitchy control scheme. As games tend toward T and M, the color palette changes to less saturation and contrast, and the controls will tend to get looser in favor of more realistic movement. Also the content of stories changes a great deal. I find it ironic that the current political climate is to kick up a fuss about the ESRB ratings system's accuracy, when in fact we tend to use the ratings as a touchstone of stylistic choices throughout the development process.

— Michael John (Lead Designer, Method Games)

The Importance of Market Research

Make market research a part of your pre-production. Doing game design in a vacuum will make a game that the designers like, and that could be sold to similar people, but perhaps no one else. However, game designers and creative personnel need to have buy in to the market research process. They should be developing test cases and questions, helping to set up and administer the research, and analyzing the results. Part of that process should identify the customer. This initial work and research can be done by far fewer people, and is much cheaper than full game production. Just make sure what you end up with is something you really want to create. The actual marketing of a game product needs to start early with marketers playing prototypes and understanding the ongoing focus testing. It should fully leverage fan sites, forums, and beta tests. Magazine print ads and TV spots often don't have as much impact as online interactive marketing.

— Frank T. Gilson (Senior Developer of Digital Games, Wizards of the Coast)

Concept Testing

Some publishers will extract elements from the concept and test it on groups of potential consumers. This testing typically happens via online surveys with a minimum of 300–400 respondents. The results of the survey help publishers determine the ideal target market for a concept. It may also convince developers to alter or emphasize certain features. *Concept testing* occurs throughout the development of the game to help refine the market positioning. Once the game is playable, focus testing in small groups is conducted to give publishers live feedback about the game and its positioning.

Competitive Analysis

The *competitive analysis* section describes the games that will likely attract the same target customers as the proposed game. It should include a listing of relative strengths and weaknesses for each competitor and a side-by-side feature comparison across all competitors and the proposed game.

Financial Analysis

The *financial analysis* section is where the producer needs to make the argument for doing the game. Many great ideas have been shot down because they failed to convince anyone that they could provide a profit. The components of the analysis are budget, projected sales, and return on investment (ROI).

The budget is an estimate based on the scope and resources the developer plans to put into the project. This is a target number that will be refined as the design becomes more solid. Projected sales can be derived by looking at sales data from past games that targeted the same customer.

Sequels can usually claim a hefty percentage of the original game's sales unless a better game is due to release at the same time. For games based on original IP, try to identify trends in the customer's interests and connect those back to the proposed game.

Once the budget is set and sales estimates can be made, a simple return on investment (ROI) can be calculated; it will be discussed further in this book. Expected ROI varies from publisher to publisher. Most publishers require at least a 15% return.

NPD Data

NPD Funworld® tracks retail sales data and consumer interest for console and PC games. Sales data are made available to subscribers on a monthly basis. Be aware that Wal-Mart, a major game retailer, does not report into these databases, so figures in the United States may be as low as 60% of actual sales.

Team

This section describes the development *team*. Make sure you include their names, education, biographies, and notable games they worked on. It's important to have all the bases covered: producer, creative director, technical director, art director, lead designer, lead engineer, lead artist, and animator. List the proposed team size and composition. Significant development partners or licensed technology should be noted, especially if the engineering or graphics team is thin.

Proof of Concept

The *proof of concept* is a presentation that demonstrates the core aspects of the game. It may be as simple as a series of storyboard panels that are edited together into a linear sequence. It could be as complex as a complete interactive prototype that looks and plays like a portion of a finished game.

Playable code is optional and not required for a concept proposal. However, it can make the difference between approval or rejection for new game ideas that are difficult to describe or visualize.

Market Conditions

A great game will succeed no matter when it is launched, assuming that enough people know about it. If you have a great game and good awareness, you can increase your chance of success by picking the right release window.

New Console Introduction

The most significant release window is when a new game console is introduced. Games released simultaneously with a new console are called "launch titles." They help drive the sale of new hardware by showcasing the capabilities of the latest technology. These pioneers are betting that the hardware sales will take off and they will have first-mover advantage over their competitors. The danger here is that the new hardware will have a small installed base for too long and that ROI will need to stretch over an uncomfortably longer time period.

Developers of launched titles must create their games alongside the hardware they are meant to run on. This means working with few or no tools and not modifying the underlying specifications. The R&D costs are higher than working on an established platform. Specifications are subject to change and there is tremendous pressure to deliver in conjunction with the hardware launch.

Holiday Season

The next most important window is the *holiday buying season*. In the United States, the period between Thanksgiving and Christmas is the most active period for the retail sales of game hardware and software. Over half of the annual revenue derived from game sales in North America occurs during this period. The Christmas season is also significant in Europe, where up to half of worldwide game sales take place. There are often too many products released in this time period, and good games have lost money as a result of oversaturation in the market.

Competition

Newcomers are well advised to stay clear of the 900-pound gorillas. Know your *competition* and try to avoid releasing your game in the same quarter (three-month period). It is usually better to come out ahead of the competition than after it. The "big" games in any given genre are notorious for coming in late; they are more concerned about maintaining reputation and market share than about hitting a deadline.

Selecting Your Concept Team

During concept development it is inefficient to maintain a staff of more than 10 people. Small groups of talented people can communicate directly, meet frequently, and divide tasks with minimal project management. The ideal concept team is composed of experienced leads from design, technology, and art, all formulating plans for the game. In cases where new technology R&D is needed, as with the introduction of next-generation consoles, you may need skilled engineers early on to build production tools and to determine technical constraints.

Illustration by Ian Robert Vasquez

While it's important to recognize the creativity of individuals, it's critical to have multiple people lend their wisdom and experience to new proposals. Egos need to be kept in check. The goal is to make a great game, and this is a shared endeavor.

The best teams learn to trust and respect each other. Individual team members are comfortable discussing the issues, and no one is out to make anyone else look stupid. Team members take their responsibilities seriously, and their professionalism fosters genuine interest in making the best game possible with the resources available.

Coming Up with New Ideas

The best way to spark new ideas and encourage team participation in a project is to brainstorm. There are many ways to conduct a brainstorming session; here's just one technique:

Illustration by Ian Robert Vasquez

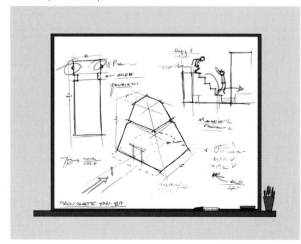

Try to include participants from various disciplines: design, technology, art, marketing, quality assurance, and so on. Include the quiet types; they are often good listeners and offer excellent ideas that everyone else overlooks. It's also a good idea to bring in fresh members during multiday sessions.

The best environment for a session is a conference room with a large whiteboard. Keep water and light snacks on hand so that everyone maintains energy. As with all meetings, establish why everyone is there and how long you expect the meeting to run. If the discussion is still strong when the meeting time is up, everyone can decide whether to continue. Don't force creativity to fit within a given timeframe. If the meeting is no longer productive, then bring it to an end and reschedule.

> We get our inspiration for game concepts from playing tons and tons of games but we also get inspiration from film, television, books, philosophy, and science.
>
> — *Starr Long (Producer, NCsoft)*

Experiential Concept Development

Play a lot of games. Read many books, magazines, and newspapers. Have a real, full life outside of work so that you can encounter new media and how everything is connected. Even just sitting in a coffee shop reading a weekly can give rise to a game concept. A good high concept needs to connect 'fun' with 'replayability' as well as encompass an idea you would be passionate about working on.

— *Frank T. Gilson (Senior Developer for Digital Games, Wizards of the Coast)*

Creative Inspiration

Inspiration for a game concept can come from almost anywhere. Sometimes it's from a good book. Sometimes it's from conversations with friends. On occasion, it has been from a particularly vivid dream. Historically, raw, rough ideas have been polished and purified in the fires of an organized brainstorming session.

— *Ed Rotberg (Chief Technology Officer, Mine Shaft Entertainment)*

Real World Ideas

I have used favorite scenes from movies, favorite architectural structures and spaces, lots of things from the 'real world' in coming up with inspiration for puzzles and challenges. The game industry has traditionally assumed that the best designer is the hardcore gamer, and I don't believe this is necessarily so. Hardcore gamers tend to be self-referential in their designs. This is not to say that a designer doesn't need to know games—it's crucial to understand the language and tradition of games thoroughly. But I think that the best inspirations come from outside the game world.

— *Michael John (Lead Designer, Method Games)*

Illustration by Ian Robert Vasquez

Nominate one person in the group to write down ideas on a whiteboard. It's a good idea to rotate this task through the group so that everyone has a chance to play moderator. As the suggestions are shouted out, the moderator captures the essence in a simple phrase on the board. By the end of a 15-minute session, you should have a wall full of ideas. You also might want to use Post-It notes *on* a whiteboard. Once all the ideas are written each on a note, categories for the ideas can be written on the whiteboard. The Post-It notes can then be organized properly underneath various category headers.

Let's take a look at the five phases of group idea generation:

1. Brainstorm
2. Prune & Discuss
3. Assign
4. Follow Up
5. Decide

Phase 1: Brainstorm

First, identify the issue you want to address. This may be as broad as coming up with a list of game features or as narrow as giving your game a name. The moderator should write this in large letters at the top of the board. Next, the moderator should ask the group to provide ideas. The first rule of brainstorming is to eliminate negativity. Creative energy needs to be encouraged. The free flow of ideas will come to a crashing halt if you take time out to criticize every idea. The craziest suggestions can often lead to innovative ideas. Don't hinder your group by making them choose each word carefully. No idea is too bold or too mundane to be considered during this phase.

Phase 2: Prune and Discuss

Nominate someone else to be the scribe. That person's job is to copy down the list of ideas and discussion points. Sort through all the ideas and discuss them one by one. Eliminate ideas that fail to win support. If an idea is good but doesn't address the main issue, put it aside; the scribe should note this for later discussions.

Rank the remaining ideas. Which ones best address the issue? Which ones are the most novel? Recopy the ideas, leaving space in between for notes. Discuss each one and try to interconnect ideas to form larger concepts.

Phase 3: Assign

Finish the session by assigning ideas or groups of ideas to be researched and detailed out. Set a time for the next meeting to review the results. Delegate this activity so that multiple ideas can be explored in parallel.

Phase 4: Follow up

Meet with the group(s) again to go over the results of the brainstorming session and the assigned tasks. In addition to verbal or written reports, participants can bring images to tape on the board, sound clips, or even movie snippets to follow-up sessions. This can help establish a mood or style more efficiently than words alone.

Phase 5: Decide

The best games have a clear vision that is shared by all team members. Don't wait until production to decide what features your game will have. Make firm decisions and be clear about which ideas are "in" and which ones are shelved. Get group buyoff on this.

Now, be flexible. It's true that most games change their core features from concept to final release. If you establish a process for debate and a track record for making decisions, the team and your publisher will appreciate this.

The next step is to pick the team you need to assemble a strong proposal.

Will Your Game Be Revolutionary . . .

In crafting your USPs, you need to understand whether your game is evolving an existing genre or is truly revolutionary.

Revolutionary games are those groundbreaking games that bring a truly new and highly desirable experience to interactive entertainment. They join the classics that everyone refers to when discussing their list of favorite games. If they are successful, they launch a new genre of games, as *Castle Wolfenstein* did for FPS games.

It is extremely difficult to create a revolutionary game. Most good designers have dozens of ideas that could be considered revolutionary. Few of these ideas acquire the momentum to become a game. Some

KATAMARI DAMACI® ©2003 NAMCO BANDAI Games Inc.
Courtesy of NAMCO BANDAI Games America Inc.

Katamari Damacy is a Japanese game that involves rolling over objects (and people!) in the world to create a giant ball.

Gran Turismo revolutionized racing games by adding RPG elements that allowed players to "advance" (upgrade) their cars.

lack commercial viability or require technology that is too advanced or costly. Some aren't deep enough to sustain an entire gameplaying experience. Some are too complex to be appreciated, let alone understood, by a majority of people. Many good concepts are offered at the wrong time. Consumer tastes change over time. A decade ago, adventure games were quite popular. Now they are nonexistent.

Most games are in some way derived from previous work. Games, like ideas, are rarely unique. Revolutionary games don't need to completely shy away from known genres. In fact, some games can blend the principles of other games to form something "new." *Gran Turismo* revolutionized racing games by combining RPG elements. Winning races gives you cash which, in turn, you use to upgrade your car. Players select cars that are very familiar to them, perhaps the same models they drive in real life. Through the course of play, they can modify their cars and develop a strong attachment to them.

. . . or Evolutionary?

Quake IV (left) and *Madden 06* (right) both evolved out of existing franchises.

It is easier to evolve an existing genre. For one thing, you have a ready market. It's much easier to explain your game to customers if you can refer to similar games or, better yet, the previous game in a successful series. You should spend time to research what features are considered core to a given genre. If you remove one or all of these features, the game may be difficult to market. Successful games fulfill customer expectations.

Care should be taken to select USPs that push the genre in a direction that makes the game more accessible to a larger audience than previous games in the genre. The *Tomb Raider* series saw gradually declining revenue largely because it failed to introduce new USPs. Customers saw each sequel as the same game design with a new story and improved graphics. This wasn't sufficient to hang on to the existing customer base, let alone grow it.

Beware of following the fan base too closely. Hardcore, loyal fans are typically more aggressive players than the average customer. They will shout for features that enhance the experience for them but may alienate the majority of less experienced players. This is especially true in online games such as FPSs, RTSs, and MMORPGs. If you follow the sequels of popular games in this genre you will see that a considerable number of features are refinements to the interface that make it easier for the player to win. So-called power user features like hotkeys, statistics, and pop-up controls shouldn't be required for novice players to successfully play the game. Otherwise you will eventually be selling to a decreasing fan base.

Is There Room for New Ideas?

Vivendi Universal Games

In recent times, most of the best-selling games (such as *Grand Theft Auto: San Andreas*, *Halo 2*, *Half-Life 2*) are sequels of top-selling products. This isn't because designers have run out of good ideas for new games. Consumer expectations have been elevated by increasingly more powerful hardware and games racing to keep up with the technology. Hundreds of new games are released every quarter but very few are successful. It's a "winner take all" industry. Publishers have learned that it's safer to put big money into something that consumers are familiar with.

Half-Life 2 is a good old-fashioned shoot-em-up with a great story and slick graphics.

So how do you give them something new and succeed commercially? There are several ways:

- *Evolve an existing property*. The best place to innovate is within the framework of an existing game or intellectual property (IP). Use the fictional setting and characters that consumers are familiar with. Decide which game components to leave as-is, select components to refine or improve on, and develop new game elements. Don't be afraid to cut a feature if it simply doesn't fit or wasn't perceived as being at the core of the design.

- *Revolutionize an existing property.* Take that well-known "brand" and extend it into new territory. *The Sims* used the popularity of *SimCity* to pull consumers from a city planning game to an interactive dollhouse/life simulation. If Maxis hadn't drawn from its *SimCity* constituency initially it might not have gained the momentum to make it one the best-selling games of all time.

- *Plan for sequels.* If your IP is truly unique and you want to set about creating a totally new IP, consider planning a progression of games. Start out small and build a core following with the first game. Focus on quality and innovation. As awareness builds, use the goodwill established with the first game to create a second game with all the bells and whistles. Often this first game may be self-published or developed on a modest budget. Examples of wildly successful games that followed this route (either intentionally or serendipitously) are: *Grand Theft Auto* and *Doom.*

Electronic Arts   Electronic Arts

SimCity, first released in 1989, gave rise to dozens of *Sim*-branded games, including *SimCity 4* (left). The *Sims* franchise (*The Sims 2: Open for Business*, right) brought gamers from the city view down to the people.

There is always room for new ideas. Consumers want new experiences. Good designers know how to minimize the risk of introducing new ideas by limiting their innovations to one or two core features. Producers limit risk by keeping the budget and schedule in line with conservative sales projections. If the idea is truly fun it won't matter that the game didn't have a blockbuster budget. Save that for the sequel.

Publishers

New game concepts are usually funded by publishers. They take the upfront risk and, in return, you get paid for your efforts. If you're lucky, your title is a big success and you earn royalties over and above the initial advances from your publisher. The terms of a development agreement vary widely, but they all have a common theme:

- The publisher pays the developer on a monthly basis for milestones reached.
- The publisher provides editorial feedback on the milestones and expects the developer to make changes based on the feedback.
- The publisher handles marketing, testing, localization, and distribution of the game. In addition, they may cover third-party costs like sound or movie production.

Choosing a Publisher

Investigate the various publishers before sending out your game concept. Talk to other developers. Find out which have published games in the same genre as your game. Look up games on the Internet. There are many websites with detailed game reviews and online databases of published games.

Gamasutra

You can find an extensive list of publishers and developers on Gamasutra at www. gamasutra.com.

If they don't have a product scheduled in the same window as yours, they may be more interested in your ideas. If they have a competitive product in the same window, you don't want to tip your hand by showing them your concept. Here are some of the things you want to look for in a publisher:

- Financial stability and good track record for timely payments.
- Global distribution; ideally they have their own distribution channels with no middlemen.
- Experienced producers and marketing brand managers, both in terms of years in the business and familiarity with your game's genre.
- Shared vision. Do they understand your game . . . and you?
- Willingness to collaborate. Do creative discussions flow easily or are they forced and one-sided?
- Good relationship with hardware vendors (consoles). This is important for access to proprietary development technology during the prelaunch phase of a new console.
- Responsiveness. Do they return your phone calls and e-mails promptly? Do they seek answers to your questions or merely shrug?

Choosing a publisher is as important as choosing your team. Most game projects last for two years or more, so it's critical to work with someone you trust and respect.

Non-Disclosure Agreements (NDAs)

Before you present your game concept to a publisher, you will be asked to sign either a submission agreement or a mutual nondisclosure agreement (NDA), a legal document that protects the publisher from later claims that may arise on their as yet unannounced products. A mutual NDA specifies that the publisher will do their best to safeguard your ideas and not exploit them, and it requires that you not disclose any ideas that the publisher shares with you. Publishers will not sign a "one-way" NDA that protects your ideas but not theirs. Publishers receive hundreds of new game concepts every year, and it is very likely that the concept you're presenting is similar to a concept they've already seen or have in development. Publishers need to protect themselves against frivolous claims that their latest game was based on someone else's idea.

> Ideas are cheap; it's the execution that is valuable.
>
> — Wise words from seasoned developers

How do you protect yourself? Sometimes publishers will furnish a mutual NDA. This may protect you from outright theft of your entire concept, but it does not prohibit a publisher from signing up a game similar to yours. The best way to protect yourself is to prepare a winning concept and demonstrate the passion and ability to execute it.

Most publishers use standard "boilerplate" language in their NDAs. It is unlikely that they will agree to alter this language. You may want to have an attorney review the agreement before you sign to make sure you aren't giving up any ownership or rights. Don't let your attorney talk you into having her draft a new NDA. Unless you have a long track record of success, no publisher will waste their legal resources to change these standard agreements before meeting you.

Meeting a Publisher

There are several ways to get your product in front of a publisher. It's their business to find the next big thing, and a lot of people facilitate this process. There are thousands of people trying to break into the business, so you need to rise above the crowd. You can go directly to a publisher or work through an intermediary.

Business Development

Most publishers have an in-house business development person who actively seeks out new properties or licenses to build games around. They also meet with developers and solicit proposals for games based on their licenses or, occasionally, original ideas. These are the people you will likely send your proposal documents to. Some publishers split duties so that business affairs deals with license and contracts while product development, usually an executive producer, handles new proposals.

Agents

If you're new to the game business or inexperienced at negotiations, agents can be useful. Most charge 5% of the overall cost of the deal. Some agents may be willing to take an ownership stake in lieu of fees in your company. In this case, make sure they can bring value beyond your first publishing contract. Some agents are experienced at running a business and can help you avoid costly mistakes in a new venture.

A good agent will review your game proposal and help you polish it. The agent should be able to get you an introduction or, better yet, a pitch meeting with multiple publishers. Before signing up, talk to past and current clients. Find out what the agent can do for you. The games business is small and it doesn't take much investigation to find out "who's who."

Trade Shows

There are several tradeshows that you can attend to meet publishers and network with people in the industry.

E^3

Electronic Entertainment Expo (E^3) has been the premier event in the game industry. Every major publisher, hardware manufacturer, and services provider has attended this trade show, which has filled the spacious Los Angeles convention center with throngs of attendees scuttling between the three major halls. The focus of this conference has been on presenting new products and software for entertainment and education. E^3 has been more of an event for retailers and the press and not necessarily the best place to land a publishing deal. However, it has also been a great place to network and gain insight about short-term trends. E for All Expo, the consumer video and computer game expo that replaces E^3, launches in October 2007 in Los Angeles, CA — while the E^3 Business & Media Summit makes its debut in July 2007 in Santa Monica, California.

Tokyo Game Show (TGS)

Tokyo Game Show (TGS) is held every fall in Japan. New hardware from console manufacturers is sometimes unveiled along with the latest games. Sony and Microsoft both have a large presence, although Nintendo is absent, preferring its own event. The show is similar to the original E3; large halls are filled with dazzling booths and hundreds of games. Unlike E³, TGS is open to the general public after the first day.

GDC

The Game Developer's Conference (GDC) is geared toward developers and publishers. It offers a wide variety of educational panels and talks categorized by professional tracks. The main conference lasts for three days but it is usually preceded by one- to two-day special topic mini-conferences. GDC takes place alternatively in San Jose and San Francisco, California in March. Regional GDCs also occur in Europe, Australia, and Asia.

D.I.C.E. Summit

D.I.C.E. stands for Design, Innovate, Communicate, Entertain. This two-day summit is sponsored by the Academy of Interactive Arts and Sciences or AIAS. According to the Academy's website, D.I.C.E. "was created to explore approaches to the creative process and artistic expression as they uniquely apply to the development of interactive entertainment." Unlike E3 or GDC, this gathering is low-key; no flashy expo areas, just meeting rooms and informal gatherings. The attendees are evenly mixed between publishers and developers. The publishing reps tend to be more product focused than marketing oriented. D.I.C.E. usually takes place in Las Vegas, Nevada, during the first part of the year.

SIGGRAPH

For over 30 years, ACM SIGGRAPH has hosted an annual conference for computer graphics. The latest techniques and creative imagery for 3D and interactive graphics are on display. The conference is more oriented toward programmers and artists than game developers. However, a symposium run by Dr. Drew Davidson of Carnegie Mellon University—*sandbox: An ACM SIGGRAPH Video Game Symposium*—was launched at SIGGRAPH in Summer 2006 and promises to be an exciting ongoing addition to the conference. SIGGRAPH is held at various locations across the United States—most recently in Los Angeles, Boston, and San Diego.

Industry Associations

There are a few professional organizations for game developers, such as IGDA, AIAS, and ESA.

IGDA

The *International Game Developers Association* (IGDA) has thousands of members from all fields of discipline in the game industry. They publish a monthly magazine, *Game Developer*, and a monthly newsletter. They also sponsor the Game Developer's Choice Awards at GDC. IGDA has chapters in North America, Europe, and Asia.

AIAS

The *Academy of Interactive Arts and Sciences* (AIAS) hosts the annual D.I.C.E. conference in Las Vegas and the Into the Pixel art show. Members come from both publishing and development professions. AIAS recognizes the achievements of its members each year by presenting Interactive Achievement Awards.

ESA

The *Entertainment Software Association* (ESA) is a trade organization for publishers. It sponsored the annual E^3 conference and currently provides information about legislation of interest to the industry.

Presenting Your Concept

Most concepts are in the form of written proposals or pitch documents that can be easily transmitted and read on a plane. Interactive proposals on DVD are gaining popularity. These include music, sound effects (SFX), and animation. More and more publishers are requesting that interactive proof of concept or demonstration of technology accompany each proposal.

If you're lucky you'll get the opportunity to present your concept in person to a development executive. If your idea has merit, be prepared to present it multiple times as more people in the company are invited to see it.

Use your best speaker. The person with the most passion and charisma may not always be the author of the concept. Now is not the time for big egos. Make sure your presentation is focused and highlights both the high concept and USPs of your game. Who is your customer? Why does it make sense for this publisher to pick up your game?

If your proposal catches on, you will get a product "champion" within the publishing organization. This may be a producer, an executive producer, or a business development executive. Keep your advocate armed with everything needed to convince the rest of the company that your concept should be published. If you have time constraints due to operating costs or another offer, let your advocate know. Stick with your champion once you have one! Don't try to work multiple contacts within a single company, or you'll lose your support quickly.

Be prepared to customize your proposal to suit a publisher's needs. This should include minor changes only; big changes are an indication that there isn't a shared vision. Once your champion feels confident about you and the proposal, the next step will be to green-light it for preproduction.

The *green light process* is the vehicle by which new product concepts are proposed. The outcome is decisive: (1) proceed into preproduction, (2) modify the proposal and resubmit, or (3) pass on the proposal. The green light signifies that a concept has commitment and support from the highest level of the organization.

The actual green light meeting is a formality. Ideally, representatives from all parts of the organization "do their homework" and come to the meeting prepared to render an opinion. Proponents of a new product need to supply green light reviewers with complete information following a consistent template.

Proposals include the concept as outlined earlier, project plan, contract terms, and a working prototype or mock-up. The proposal addresses four key questions: (1) what is the game? (2) who will buy the game? (3) why will they buy the game? (4) why should we make this game? This answer to this last question lists the competitive advantages a publisher and/or developer has vis-à-vis this game and describes how this game fits their overall company strategy and corporate brand.

Green light authors include the producer and the creative director or lead designer. The development staff prepares the description of the product. The marketing brand manager from the publisher provides sales forecasts and market analysis. The proposal materials need to be distributed well in advance of a green light meeting so that all attendees have adequate time for research and review.

Typical green light reviewers include:

- President and/or head of publishing, to weigh the input of all parties and render the final decision
- Heads of Marketing & Sales from North America, Europe, and Asia, to review market analysis, sales forecasts
- Finance, to review budget and cash flow needs
- Legal, to review rights, contract terms, and license issues

- Operations, to review schedule, quality assurance, localization, and distribution plan
- Technical reviewer, typically a technical director, to review technology issues and engineering talent
- Creative reviewer, typically a game designer, to review the game concept
- Artistic reviewer, typically an art director, to review the conceptual art and talent
- Production reviewer, typically a fellow EP, to review the project plan and developer
- Authors of the proposal

While it is best to have everyone meet face to face, it also works to conduct this via videoconference. The meeting should not conclude until a decision is made.

Not every proposal makes it to a green light meeting. The president or head of publishing typically selects which products are scheduled. Proposals that lack fundamental support or are incomplete are sent back to their proponents.

Projects undergo the green light process at two points: (1) before moving from concept into preproduction and (2) before moving from preproduction into production. Products that fall into this latter category are automatically scheduled for green light review, as they often have development staffs "on hold" and money has already been spent on preproduction.

Projects moving from preproduction into production require more items to review. These review materials include game design, technical design, art style guide, sound design, task schedule, staffing plan, detail budget (including third-party costs), production plan, prototype or interactive demo, risk analysis, marketing plan, market research, sales forecasts (by territory), and R.O.I. analysis. Since some members of the green light committee are also contributors, it is important to include some objective members who are not direct contributors to the game.

The green light meeting (and any communication leading up to it) are often lively. Discussion needs to challenge the authors and uncover any problems facing the project. To assure candid responses, the developer, licensor, and key talent are usually not invited to attend unless they are needed to provide information or to answer questions.

Very few projects make it into production. This should not be seen as a failure on the part of the authors if a game isn't approved. Rather it should be seen as a success in the system. By the same token, a good green light committee doesn't always take the safe road by not approving anything. The reviewers all have a responsibility to uncover elements that could sway the decision from a "no" to a "yes" so that the authors can go back and improve on their plans.

:::CHAPTER REVIEW:::

1. Using one of the techniques discussed in this chapter, come up with an original game concept. Make sure the concept addresses the four key questions discussed in this chapter.

2. What market, genre, and platform have you chosen for your game? How do you feel your choices will affect the game development process?

3. Put together a concept document for your original game idea containing all the features (such as USPs and competitive analysis) discussed in this chapter. Run a mock pitch session and show how you might pitch this concept to a publisher or other funding source.

Part II:
Documentation
& Pre-Production

Game Design

defining the vision

Key Chapter Questions

- What are the major components of a game design document (GDD)?
- What is a branching script, and what types of games use it?
- What is a non-interactive sequence?
- What types of rewards does the designer create for the player?
- What should be included in a level description?

Some argue that design needs to be organic and games should not rigidly adhere to documents. It is true that designers should live in their own designs and be prepared to modify the design once they get a chance to play their games. But if no formal GDD exists, then there is no plan and no direction for the development team. This leads to chaotic workflow and dysfunctional teams that rely on daily verbal direction. This may have been a fun way to develop small games in the 1980s, but it is a ridiculous way to build big budget games today.

In this chapter, we'll go over the basic components of the *game design document (GDD)*. This document describes all the creative aspects of the game. It serves a wide audience: designers, software engineers, artists, sound designers, producers, and publishers. The GDD is the definitive guide for developing a game. Many developers affectionately refer to this document as the "bible."

Games lacking a well-defined design are fated to waste time and money. You don't have to look far to hear tales of brilliant and talented people embarking on multiyear, multimillion-dollar projects with little more than a high concept and an abundance of optimism. Times are changing. As the stakes go up, both publishers and developers are rethinking their processes and devoting more time to game design itself.

Design Team

The core design team for the GDD usually consists of a half dozen people. The team may also be supported by contributions from others, including specialized contractors.

The design team is led by the creative director or game director, who has principal responsibility for authoring or editing the GDD. The game director is responsible for the design philosophy, contributing the "big idea" by describing elements such as the design premise, player character, major non-player characters (NPCs), features, and game mechanics.

The lead designer and the game designers delve into the details by defining items such as individual levels/missions, events, skill/ability progression, and the user interface. The lead designer establishes templates used by the design team to specify these details and establishes procedures for communicating design to the rest of the development team.

The technical director and the programming team review the design and provide guidance on feasibility and complexity of design choices. They also influence the design by recommending new technical features.

The art director and artists contribute to the design with concept sketches and ideas for the visual aspects of the game. Character and environment choices are influenced by their visual possibilities.

The audio director and sound designers help define the mood and tone of the game design by providing sample music and sounds. They research sounds and artists that best support the vision of the design.

The producer keeps the various contributors moving forward, following the vision of the game director and lead designer. During the design phase, ideas are often discarded or modified. The producer communicates changes among the team members and—when key decisions are made—upward and outward to publishers and company management. If the vision is muddy or things begin to go off track, the producer needs to encourage clarity and focus.

Face the Design

The core value of documentation is to make the design team face the design of the product in its entirety. That means both the trivial, easy aspects and the complex, difficult aspects. A good design document will confront the entire scope of the product—laying out a clear plan for what should be attempted and how the attempt should be made. It should be written clearly enough to be comprehensible to an outsider as well. What happens when reality meets design, though, is another story.

— *Rich Adam (CEO, Mine Shaft Entertainment, Inc.)*

Always Strive for Comprehensiveness

All of those documents have one key requirement in common: comprehensiveness. It's always so tempting to not write down the obvious, to skip over those two items you haven't figured out yet, or just to gloss over elements that everyone already understands. The problem is that assumptions aren't always shared, the things we think we'll figure out next week sometimes take until next year, and what's obvious to you may be way over my head. In any document that is a plan, you always want to specifically call out each item or asset, identify what it will be, and state when it will be done, how its completion is defined (e.g. "approved by producer", "attains frame rate of 30 fps", etc.), and who will do it (by name or function).

— *Don L. Daglow (President & CEO, Stormfront Studios)*

Story

All games tell a *story*. Even early arcade games had a premise, a hero, and a villain. Arguably not as much thought and effort went into the story as the technology, but times have changed. Production values in games now rival feature films. Good storytelling is now expected, not merely appreciated.

Outline

Stories for games unfold over days, not just hours, of play. With new technology, stories are destined to get even longer and more complex. The GDD needs to block out the story in an

MS. PAC-MAN® © 1982 NAMCO BANDAI Games Inc.
Courtesy of NAMCO BANDAI Games America Inc.

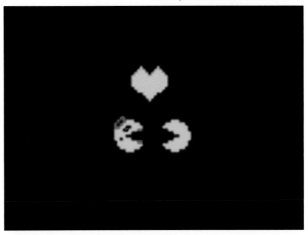

After completing a few levels, *Ms. Pac-Man* players were rewarded with this romantic interlude.

outline to help organize it and to provide a framework for categorizing components of the game.

The *outline* is the high-level overview of the game. The main (highest-level) entries for the entire game should not extend beyond two pages. If you have considerably more than this, you will need to create another level of hierarchy.

Sony Computer Entertainment America

Kratos contemplates suicide at the beginning of *God of War*.

Plot Points

The *plot points* are the special moments that create interest or suspense in the story. They usually reveal some portion of a mystery or help us understand the motivation of an NPC. These are the important elements designers hope the player doesn't miss. Plot points should be emphasized by special activities or a change in the pace or mood. Often these become the central theme for a mission or quest in the game.

The following is an excerpt from the *God of War* plot:

> *Kratos is remorseful after mistakenly murdering his own wife and child in a temple massacre. He stands at the highest cliff in Greece and states that "the Gods of Olympus have abandoned me." He then casts himself into the clouds below.*

This powerful opening sets the stage for the player character's vengeful battle with the gods and their minions.

Sony Computer Entertainment America

Kratos battles enemies as he slides across a rope. The multi-tiered architecture of Athens provides a stunning backdrop.

Environments

Each *environment* should be described in sufficient detail in the GDD for an artist or level designer to create. Avoid specifying where each tree and shrub should go; artists can assemble compelling worlds once they have a sense of what needs to go in them.

You should describe the time period and any special props required for each scene. Designers will need to know which environments are interconnected and what sort of action needs to take place in an environment. Combat may require arena-style spaces, whereas exploration may need more confined channels and corners to hide things behind.

It's also important to note which characters, NPCs, special objects, and effects will appear in an environment. For example, if a dragon is going to crash through the roof of a tavern, then the tavern needs to be big enough to accommodate it. If the dragon needs to set the tavern ablaze, then the tavern should probably be composed of wood.

Many game design documents contain both traditional set drawings and overhead maps to complement environmental descriptions. These are useful tools for helping a production team make sense of the world they are building.

Script

The *script* contains all dialogue and text in the game. This is the document in the GDD that defines the story and action. It is used by members of the development team to create characters, to play recorded lines, and to display text.

Standard Formats

Games adapt the same standard script format used in films, plays, and television programs. This format was designed for linear stories where each actor's lines appear in a specific scene and in a predetermined order.

This script excerpt from *God of War* is in standard form and uses color to distinguish revisions. The scene is from the opening to the game, discussed previously.

Sony Computer Entertainment America

```
RED = REWRITE/RE-RECORD, GREEN = RECAST
PURPLE = NEW FOR 10/19


SCENE 01

Kratos stands on a bluff overlooking the Aegean Sea. He is
resigned to his fate, his decision made.

                    KRA01-01
                    KRATOS
                (moody, like a ton of
                 bricks)
            The gods of Olympus have abandoned
            me... Now there is no hope.

Kratos steps off the cliff, beginning his fall to the
ocean.

                    NAR01-02
                    NARRATOR
                (tragic)
            And Kratos cast himself from the
            highest mountain in all of Greece.

Kratos continues to plummet downward.

                    NAR01-03
                    NARRATOR
            After ten years of suffering, ten
            years of endless nightmares... it
            would finally come to an end.

The ocean is rushing up towards Kratos.

                    NAR01-04
                    NARRATOR
            Death would be his escape from
            madness.

As Kratos races toward the sea and the rocks and foam loom
even larger, we...

                                    FADE TO BLACK.
```

Script excerpt from the introduction to *God of War*

Branching

The standard script format works for some games, but most games involve nonlinear storytelling where player choices determine which scene or line occurs next.

Most games have nonlinear stories where scenes may appear in a different order depending on player actions. Non-player characters (NPCs) usually have multiple possible lines in response to player choices. Each response line can branch into a separate story thread.

Branching scripts are a collection of modules, where each module contains the following components:

1. Name of the NPC that is speaking.
2. Dialogue line of the NPC for the given scene or interaction.
3. List of possible responses (dialogue or actions) for each player character (PC); these could be lines or actions.
4. Branch identifier for each response: scene number, character, line number.

Each player response branches into a module containing responses from the NPC, which, in turn, may branch into more choices for the player. Ultimately, some or all of these branches may converge or split off into wholly separate storylines or threads.

© (P) 2004 Lionhead Studios Limited.

In *Fable: The Lost Chapters*, villagers react to the player's actions. This one seems to be happy with the player's choice!

Adaptive Branching

Some games employ sophisticated *artificial intelligence (AI)* to modify branch options on the fly. The AI remembers the player's past choices and behavior and scripts the NPC responses accordingly. For example, if the player has been good and helpful, then a villager NPC may offer him food or shelter but a thief may shun him. If the player has been evil or selfish, then the villager may run the other way while the thief offers to join forces. This sort of adaptive branching is common in *role-playing games (RPGs)*.

Dialogue

The main purpose of the script is to describe the entire dialogue in the game. Dialogue often changes from printed word to final performance. This is necessary because actors deliver more convincing performances when they are allowed to improvise. Some words are mandatory, since they are connected to clues in the game. This may be reinforced to the player by highlighting the word on screen.

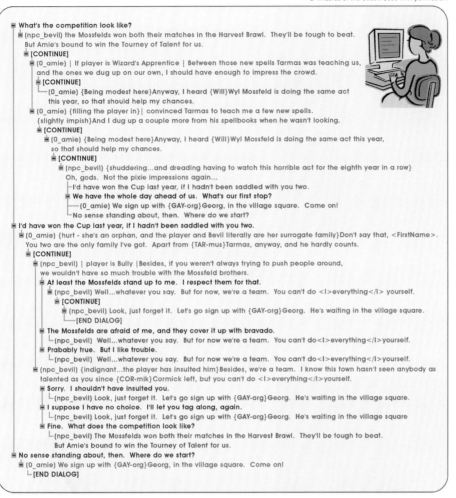

- What's the competition look like?
  - (npc_bevil) the Mossfelds won both their matches in the Harvest Brawl. They'll be tough to beat. But Amie's bound to win the Tourney of Talent for us.
    - [CONTINUE]
      - (0_amie) | If player is Wizard's Apprentice | Between those new spells Tarmas was teaching us, and the ones we dug up on our own, I should have enough to impress the crowd.
        - [CONTINUE]
          - (0_amie) {Being modest here}Anyway, I heard {Will}Wyl Mossfeld is doing the same act this year, so that should help my chances.
      - (0_amie) {filling the player in}| convinced Tarmas to teach me a few new spells. {slightly impish}And I dug up a couple more from his spellbooks when he wasn't looking.
        - [CONTINUE]
          - (0_amie) {Being modest here}Anyway, I heard {Will}Wyl Mossfeld is doing the same act this year, so that should help my chances.
            - [CONTINUE]
              - (npc_bevil) {shuddering...and dreading having to watch this horrible act for the eighth year in a row} Oh, gods. Not the pixie impressions again...
                - I'd have won the Cup last year, if I hadn't been saddled with you two.
                - We have the whole day ahead of us. What's our first stop?
                  - (0_amie) We sign up with {GAY-org}Georg, in the village square. Come on!
                - No sense standing about, then. Where do we start?
- I'd have won the Cup last year, if I hadn't been saddled with you two.
  - (0_amie) {hurt - she's an orphan, and the player and Bevil literally are her surrogate family}Don't say that, <FirstName>. You two are the only family I've got. Apart from {TAR-mus}Tarmas, anyway, and he hardly counts.
    - [CONTINUE]
      - (npc_bevil) | player is Bully | Besides, if you weren't always trying to push people around, we wouldn't have so much trouble with the Mossfeld brothers.
        - At least the Mossfelds stand up to me. I respect them for that.
          - (npc_bevil) Well...whatever you say. But for now, we're a team. You can't do <I>everything</I> yourself.
            - [CONTINUE]
              - (npc_bevil) Look, just forget it. Let's go sign up with {GAY-org}Georg. He's waiting in the village square.
                - [END DIALOG]
        - The Mossfelds are afraid of me, and they cover it up with bravado.
          - (npc_bevil) Well...whatever you say. But for now we're a team. You can't do<I>everything</I>yourself.
        - Prabably true. But I like trouble.
          - (npc_bevil) Well...whatever you say. But for now we're a team. You can't do<I>everything</I>yourself.
      - (npc_bevil) {indignant...the player has insulted him}Besides, we're a team. I know this town hasn't seen anybody as talented as you since {COR-mik}Cormick left, but you can't do <I>everything</I>yourself.
        - Sorry. I shouldn't have insulted you.
          - (npc_bevil) Look, just forget it. Let's go sign up with {GAY-org}Georg. He's waiting in the village square.
        - I suppose I have no choice. I'll let you tag along, again.
          - (npc_bevil) Look, just forget it. Let's go sign up with {GAY-org}Georg. He's waiting in the village square
        - Fine. What does the competition look like?
          - (npc_bevil) The Mossfelds won both their matches in the Harvest Brawl. They'll be tough to beat. But Amie's bound to win the Tourney of Talent for us.
- No sense standing about, then. Where do we start?
  - (0_amie) We sign up with {GAY-org}Georg, in the village square. Come on!
    - [END DIALOG]

Besides, if you weren't always trying to push people around, we wouldn't have so much trouble with the Mossfeld brothers.

1. At least the Mossfelds stand up to me. I respect them for that.
2. The Mossfelds are afraid of me, and they cover it up with bravado.
3. Probably true. But I like trouble.

In *Neverwinter Nights 2,* branching dialogue (top) is entered using a proprietary script editor. During gameplay (bottom), possible player responses appear as numbered choices.

Dialogue windows, such as those shown in *Neverwinter Nights*, may be used when the camera is zoomed out or when there are multiple responses.

In branching scripts, these highlighted words may be hyperlinks that the player selects to branch to other script modules. The script should clearly indicate words or phrases that are mandatory so that the audio director and actor know that they need to follow the script as written.

Many scripts contain descriptions of environments, camera and lighting directions, and background information in addition to the dialogue. This can be useful in the early stages of planning out a game, but it often has little value in game design. Similar to a movie, the dialogue of the script needs to convey the story, not the descriptive text that no one hears.

Updating the Script

The voice or live action recording usually takes place during the last quarter of production. At this point, very little should change, so it's deemed safe to record the lines. There are usually multiple takes for each line and many lines get improvised. Once the final lines have been chosen for use in the game, the script should be updated. The script will be used by designers to determine what line is in each audio and FMV asset. It's important that the script reflect the actual words.

Voice actor Mike Yurchak in action.

Some scripts contain alternate lines to allow for multiple responses from NPCs. The alternates should be included in the script and clearly labeled so that designers know that they are available for use.

Linking to Audio Assets

Full-scale games typically have tens of thousands of recorded lines, so a systematic approach to tracking text and audio is needed. Each line in a game script has a unique asset identifier (ID) to help keep track of the associated data for each line of dialogue. Audio producers typically use Excel spreadsheets to contain the script information:

Asset ID	File	Character	Scene #	Line #	Alternate	Text
1000	GPM_JN_100_1_0	Jeannie	100	1	0	You want to see the Queen?
1001	GPM_JN_100_1_1	Jeannie	100	1	1	You're kidding about the Queen, right?
1002	GPM_JN_100_1_2	Jeannie	100	1	2	Nobody wants to see the Queen.
1003	GPM_JN_100_2_0	Jeannie	100	2	0	I have a favor to ask.
1004	GPM_JN_100_3_0	Jeannie	100	3	0	Take this envelope to the Queen.
1005	GPM_JN_101_1_0	Jeannie	101	1	0	She must have been in a bad mood.
1006	GPM_JN_101_1_1	Jeannie	101	1	1	Look on the bright side, you've still got nine other fingers.
1007	GPM_JH_098_1_0	John	98	1	0	You'll need to see the Queen.
1008	GPM_JH_099_1_0	John	99	1	0	Careful, she's nervous today. Awaiting some important news.
1009	GPM_JH_102_1_0	John	102	1	0	Didn't anyone tell you? She always punishes the messenger.
1010	GPM_JH_102_1_1	John	102	1	1	Ask Stumpy what happened to him.

This table shows how dialogue strings are tracked for recording.

The take number is used for tracking multiple takes or variations. During initial recording, the audio director may request a few performances. The general rule of thumb is to get three takes on everything, even if the first performance is perfect.

Localization Considerations

The script is also used for *localization* and translation into other languages. The meaning needs to be preserved through the translation process. Translators will also attempt to choose words that synchronize with the mouth motions of English-speaking actors.

Asset identifiers (IDs) are critical, since there is no other way, short of hiring bilingual producers, to ensure that the correct translation is associated with each line of dialogue and text.

Nintendo

This image from *Fire Emblem: Path of Radiance* shows how the interface leaves plenty of room for other translated text.

Diagram by Per Olin

Asset ID	File	Character	Scene #	Line #	Alternate	Text	Translation
3000	GPM_NR_500_1_0	Narrator	500	1	0	Players	Spieler
3001	GPM_NR_500_2_0	Narrator	500	2	0	Team	Team
3002	GPM_NR_500_3_0	Narrator	500	3	0	Game Type	Spielart
3003	GPM_NR_500_4_0	Narrator	500	4	0	Map	Karte
3004	GPM_NR_500_5_0	Narrator	500	5	0	Join Game	Spiel beitreten
3005	GPM_NR_500_6_0	Narrator	500	6	0	Options	Optionen
3006	GPM_NR_500_7_0	Narrator	500	7	0	Resume Game	Spiel fortsetz

This table shows how translated text is tracked by asset ID.

The Challenge of Localization

Localization creates many challenges ranging from dealing with the increased size of text in many languages over English to the varying ratings-boards in each country. If you do not have someone on staff with extensive current localization experience, I would recommend outsourcing the localization to a group with that experience. Without question, localization has a lot of "gotchas" that can trip up the inexperienced.

— Graeme Bayless (Director of Production, Crystal Dynamics)

Two issues that always seem to come up in localization are (1) some text is buried somewhere in the code and forgotten, and (2) last minute changes are inevitable, and cause a tracking nightmare for the localization team. The team I worked with most recently, Ready At Dawn Studios, created a special in-house tool they call "Linguist" which attacked both of these problems: text strings were strictly forbidden within the code, and text was entered by reference only. The Linguist tool used an internal xml-based database of all the text strings in all the languages, and was distributed in its entirety to the various localization specialists. Linguist was not only a repository of all game text, but also contained a color coding system which showed the translator whenever any string in the master (English) version had been added or modified. This tool was overwhelmingly the best solution I've seen for localization.

— Michael John (Lead Designer, Method Games)

Localization has two key elements: language and culture. Most major publishers now localize games with translations (and, if included, recorded voices) that are written and produced in the target country for the game's language version. The Spanish spoken in Mexico is different from that of Spain, which is different from that of Argentina. Americans, Australians, Canadians and UK gamers all speak English but all have alternate words, spellings and pronunciations. Which versions to separate and which to lump together (and how) are decisions best made by native speakers. There are many examples of cultural differences, but an easy one to discuss is the presence of blood on screen. This is formally or informally taboo in Germany and other countries, while in some cultures its presence is expected. As the game ratings system has evolved the standard in the US has changed. Again, native speakers and residents of the countries involved need to be part of these decisions to ensure they are culturally appropriate.

— Don L. Daglow (President & CEO, Stormfront Studios)

I have several important concerns with localization. One is the fact that Asian language character sets are taller than western languages. Thus, you'll need to provide for double byte character display in your software. Also, your UI elements will need to have enough vertical room. Another concern is the length of strings in a language like German. Almost anything you say in German is going to be longer than English. Gender of terms is an additional issue. English doesn't care about that...but many languages do. A big problem can be concatenation of strings. If your game does a fair amount of that, it will make localization much harder, especially when compounded across all the other issues. Don't forget to consider the problems you'll run into localizing voice over!

— *Frank T. Gilson (Senior Developer of Digital Games, Wizards of the Coast)*

Michelle Hinn on Localization for Accessibility :::::

Michelle Hinn is an instructor in the department of Library and Information Sciences at the University of Illinois—where she teaches game design courses and is the program coordinator and academic advisor for the Women in Math, Science, and Engineering living/learning community at the university. She was recently named one of *Next Generation Magazine's* "100 Most Influential Women in Gaming" based on her work as chair of the IGDA Game Accessibility Special Interest Group. Michelle is also the head of the game division of a shareware/donationware company, DonationCoder. com. She has a B.A. in Music Performance, a B.S. in Psychology, an M.A. in Multimedia Design from Virginia Tech—and she is currently completing her PhD in Human-Computer Interaction at the University of Illinois. Michelle has worked at Microsoft Game Studios where she focused on piloting usability tests for Xbox multiplayer games. Additionally, she has worked for Computer Sciences Corporation, the National Center for Supercomputing Applications (NCSA), and the University of Nevada at Reno. She is the co-editor of *Visions of Quality: How Evaluators Define, Understand, and Represent Program Quality* and is working with the Game Accessibility SIG on a book on game accessibility. She is on the editorial board of ACM's *Computers in Entertainment* magazine. Michelle has also authored several award-winning papers on the topic of universal accessibility from organizations such as the American Evaluators Association and the International Visual Literacy Association—and she was one of the three 2006 recipients of the IGDA's Most Valuable Player Award.

Michelle Hinn
(Vice President,
Game Division,
DonationCoder.com;
Chair, IGDA Game
Accessibility Special
Interest Group)

Issues related to localizing to other languages also arise when it comes to closed captioning features. There's the verbal . . . and also ambient audio to be considered. For some games, an explosion will sound the same if it's a true-to-life sound. However, when we have games in which an audio cue may be more culture-specific (such as a sound that everyone understands to represent "uh oh" in a more cartoon-like fashion in one culture but is not universally understood that way), then you either have to worry about coming up with a culturally equivalent sound . . . or somehow captioning it in a way that conveys its meaning. This is mainly important when it comes to ambient sounds that are important to navigating through a game but it's also important if you want to convey a particular mood that is dependent on audio cues and/or music.

When we think about closed captioning, we usually think of the hearing impaired. But if you think more deeply about it, then you [might recall] how much you use closed captioning in noisy places (like a bar or a gym) or in quiet places (such as playing a game at work and putting on headphones, [which] might be a little too obvious that you are not working on that weekly report)! . . . We all know the famous bad translations in games, and we are all in danger of [making this mistake. The] gaming community has a lot to learn from the deaf community with regard to alternative ways to convey meaning. They have been dealing with issues for quite some time related to cultural barriers when trying to sign to someone who is from a country that speaks another verbal language. So we can get to the point where we [provide] closed captioning and think more deeply about more universal meanings . . . that will result in easier localization in different languages. . . . It will also result in having games that take closed captioning beyond just the verbal language expressed in a game but also the ambient sounds . . . that are increasingly being relied upon as game cues.

:::::*Ghost Recon 2:* Global Politics

Ghost Recon 2 was set in North Korea, and we had taken pains to craft the story so not to cause too much of a stir. However, somehow the North Korean government picked up on the game, and they issued a press release saying that our game was proof of American aggression, and that we would die "gruesome deaths." The Stars and Stripes newspaper called us for the story, and I explained to them that our game was not about current events, and was fiction, etc., etc. Then, one of the major game sites picked up on the story. Quoting me from the S&S article, they said something like "Christian Allen is undeterred by North Korean threats..." I was like, wait a minute, that's not what I said!

— *Christian Allen (Creative Director, Red Storm Entertainment)*

Non-Interactive Sequences

Non-interactive sequences are the cinematic sequences of the game. The action and camera movements are pre-scripted. Player control may be taken away or restricted during these sequences to ensure that the player doesn't miss an important plot point or clue. You wouldn't want the player to be running off down the hall just as the dying king whispered the location of the ancient treasure!

Pre-Rendered Cinematics

In the past, most games used pre-rendered cinematics for their non-interactive sequences. Some of these rivaled the best special effects sequences of Hollywood films. Blizzard is famous for their beautifully rendered movies. Other games combine live action video to bring realism to their characters.

Courtesy of Blizzard Entertainment, Inc

Electronic Arts

World of Warcraft (left) features detailed introduction cinematics to establish the backstory for character races, while actors in *Command & Conquer: Red Alert 2* (right) speak directly to the player, sometimes goading them into action.

For most games, the cinematic sequences look much better than the game. The transition to these cinematics often takes the player out of the world, since it involves ending the action, fading the screen to black, and then fading up on a movie. Some critics feel that this detracts from the experience.

Oddworld Inhabitants

Clever developers such as OddWorld Inhabitants (*Abe's Oddysee* shown) design their cinematics to seamlessly transition back into the game

In-Game Cinematics

With the advent of next-generation video consoles and 3D video processors, the graphics in games are approaching photo-realism. New consoles, such as the PlayStation 3 and Xbox-360, make it difficult to discern the difference between real-time and pre-rendered graphics.

More designers are taking advantage of this technology and rely-ing on the in-game engine to tell the story. The control is still taken away from the player, but it stays in the world, switching the view between characters as they interact. Sometimes higher-resolution models are swapped in and the camera zooms in for close-ups as the actors speak.

Attention to detail—wrinkles, mottled skin, and glistening eyes—help reinforce the realism of *Half Life 2*.

Storyboards

Storyboards are used to describe what the camera should see during non-interactive sequences. Storyboards may also be used to describe special scripted moments such as a complicated battle sequence or an environmental puzzle.

Sony Computer Entertainment America

Title Screen

DOMINUS: The gods of Olympus have abandoned me...

Shot 01A

DOMINUS: ...my last hope was with them. Now my life is in their hands.

Shot 01B

Shot 01C

NARRATOR: And Dominus cast himself from the highest mountain in all of Greece.

Shot 01D

Dominus buffeted by wind.

Shot 01E

Camera tracks behind Dominus falling.

Shot 01F

NARRATOR: After three years of suffering, three years of endless nightmares...

Storyboard sequence from the introduction to *God of War*

Some designers use storyboards to lay out a typical pathway through a mission or level. This helps everyone on the development team to visualize what the player will see and experience as they play the game. It is a great tool for assessing the tempo or pacing of the game before the level is actually built.

Non-linear Storytelling

The player is the central character in the unfolding story. Unlike movies, games can incorporate the player's choices to determine which pathway to follow. Interactive fiction requires that the writer weave multiple plot threads and characters into a network of decisions.

The Elder Scrolls IV: Oblivion provides players with a nonlinear storytelling experience.

In a linear story, the experiences are pre-scripted and player actions cannot change the outcome of the story. The approach to developing story for these games is similar to that of a movie.

The key to good nonlinear storytelling is to make player choices meaningful and interesting. Too many games have throw-away lines to give the appearance of choices. In poor scripts, only one or two choices really matter and the rest either lead to a dead end or connect back to the same thread.

Choices should also be tempered by the personality of the character. If characters are allowed to vacillate from angel to devil on a line-by-line basis, they will appear to be chaotic, lacking purpose or direction. *Fable* attempts to offer the player a range of behavior, but very quickly players lock into being either good or evil. The neutral route tends to be bland when compared to the extremes!

Player Character (PC)

The *player character (PC)* is the avatar or personification of the player in the game world. There may be one PC, a group of PCs, or even an army.

 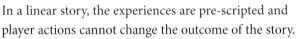 

In any given game, there may be one PC (Snake from *Metal Gear Solid 4: Guns of the Patriots,* left), a group of PCs (trio from *Demon Stone,* middle), or even an army (order army from *Dragonshard,* right).

Eidos Interactive Ltd

Lara Croft from *Tomb Raider* was one of the first video game vixens.

Some games are centered on a single, hopefully memorable, character. We are asking the player to pretend to walk in the character's shoes. A player's decision to accept or reject a game is influenced by sympathy or interest in the character. When *Tomb Raider* was first released, for example, there was much debate whether teenage boys (the dominant market at the time) would be willing to play as a girl.

Regardless of a character's origin, it needs to be described so that artists can create models, animators can define moves, writers can craft words, and level designers can build domains for each character in the game.

Types

There are many different types of PCs, which can sometimes be distinguished by the type of attack or activity each is designed to perform: melee, projectile, siege, stealth, jumping/climbing, driving/flying, and communication. These can be combined or special types can be created to suit the needs of the game design. The GDD needs to outline the major types so that designers can create scenarios to emphasize them.

Midway

Two players can team up to battle enemy fighters in *Mortal Kombat: Shaolin Monks*.

Melee

Melee characters are designed to fight toe-to-toe with their enemies. In fantasy games, they are the warriors; in strategy games, they are the soldiers. These characters take a lot of damage, and they can deal a lot of damage to other characters. Don't make the mistake of creating these characters to be "boring" when compared to other types. These characters are the simplest to use and, as a result, they are the most accessible to a wide range of players.

Projectile

Projectile characters are designed to lurk behind the front lines firing their weapons from a safe distance. In fantasy games, they are the wizards; in strategy games, they are the snipers. These characters are more complicated to use. They are typically fragile and vulnerable to direct attack.

Siege

Siege characters are designed to break down enemy defenses or sustain a lot of damage. In fantasy games, they are the giants; in strategy games, they are the catapults. These characters are slow moving but deal a tremendous amount of damage. They are vulnerable when faced with many attackers at once, so they are often accompanied by melee escorts.

Stealth

Stealth characters are designed to sneak behind enemy lines and steal or disrupt activities. In fantasy games, they are the thieves; in strategy games, they are the engineers. These characters have special abilities and rarely face their attackers in melee combat.

Soldiers typically fire on each other using rifles in *SOCOM*.

This trebuchet from *Civilization III* is used to break down walls and buildings.

Players need to sneak up on enemies in *Metal Gear Solid IV: Guns of the Patriots*.

Game Design: defining the vision

chapter 3

Nintendo

Mario is probably the most famous platform game character.

Climbing / Jumping

Climbing characters are designed to crawl up ladders or leap from one platform to the next. They explore levels and jump over hazards while grabbing power-ups along the way. These are often the stars of character platform games.

Flying / Driving

Flying / driving characters are designed to operate vehicles or ride beasts. They navigate obstacles or follow tracks in time-sensitive races. The character may be the actual vehicle or beast itself.

Sony Computer Entertainment America

Sony Computer Entertainment America

Dragons battle in the skies of *Lair*, and capital ships rule the skies in *Warhawk*.

Courtesy of Sega Corporation

In *Caution: Seaman*, a fish talks to the player.

Communication

Some characters are simply built to interact with the player. They may use voice chat to interact. These characters usually have a variety of facial expressions or mannerisms to convey emotions. Some games use a real-time image of the player projected into a fantasy world.

Customization

Many games allow the player to select from a group of character choices or even create *customized* characters. Role-playing games (RPGs) usually offer a wide variety of variables so that players can tune their characters to suit their tastes or fantasies. Many games offer advanced editing features so that players can manipulate fine details of the PC. Some games provide players with the ability to import their own facial imagery so they can approximate their own likeness in the game. Customization creates a greater sense of ownership and connection to the player's character. It also helps players in multiplayer games like MMOs distinguish one another.

Courtesy of Blizzard Entertainment, Inc

Sony Computer Entertainment America

In *World of Warcraft*, players can choose from eight different races and customize their characters' appearances. *MLB 2006* allows gamers to capture their facial image using the EyeToy and map it to a ballplayer character.

Abilities

Character abilities need to be distinct and meaningful. Animation should support the use of an ability to make it feel special to the player. When a player acquires a new ability they should immediately be given the opportunity to use it to defeat an enemy or solve a puzzle. This positive reinforcement encourages players to earn more abilities.

Moves

All of the PC's movements, attacks, and special moves need to be specified. The basic movements include the mundane such as walk, run, jump, fall, and die. There should be multiple variations of these moves, since they are played frequently. An animation list details each movement and indicates how many frames of animation should be allocated. These individual animations must be smoothly blended so that the character responds naturally to player controls. This animation blending may be handled by transition animation and specialized software routines. Attacks must be blended into the basic moves as well as defensive moves such as block, crouch, or sneak. All of these moves need to transition into moves where the PC absorbs damage: hit, fallback, fall down, and death. Real-time physics systems, like the ragdoll physics in the Havok engine, eliminate the need to have canned animation when characters die or react to blows.

© Valve Corporation. Used with permission.

Half Life 2 uses ragdoll physics to create exaggerated reactions to force.

Diagram by Per Olin

Asset ID	Filename	Description	Frames	Loop
1000	HNTWLK	Hunter walk cycle	240	Y
1000	HNTWWK	Hunter wounded walk cycle	240	Y
1001	HNTRUN	Hunter run cycle	240	Y
1001	HNTWWR	Hunter wounded run cycle	240	Y
1002	HNTDCK	Hunter duck	120	N
1002	HNTRLF	Hunter roll forward	150	N
1003	HNTCRC	Hunter crouching	120	N
1003	HNTCRL	Hunter crawling cycle	240	Y
1003	HNTDGR	Hunter dodge right	120	N
1003	HNTJMP	Hunter jumping	150	N
1003	HNTKNL	Hunter kneeling	120	N
1003	HNTRSR	Hunter roll sideways right	150	N
1004	HNTCLM	Hunter climbing cycle	180	Y
1004	HNTDGL	Hunter dodge left	120	N
1004	HNTRSF	Hunter roll sideways left	150	N
1005	HNTLVR	Hunter flipping lever	120	N
1006	HNTBTN	Hunter pressing button	120	N
1007	HNTODR	Hunter pushing open door	150	N
1008	HNTKDR	Hunter kicking open door	150	N
1009	HNTCDR	Hunter closing door	150	N
1010	HNTOBX	Hunter opening box	150	N
1011	HNTSWB	Hunter swinging blunt object	60	N
1012	HNTMRH	Hunter melee right hook	45	N
1013	HNTMRP	Hunter melee right punch	30	N
1014	HNTMLJ	Hunter melee left jab	30	N
1015	HNTMLP	Hunter melee left punch	30	N
1016	HNTMRK	Hunter melee right kick	30	N
1017	HNTMLK	Hunter melee left kick	30	N
1018	HNTMRD	Hunter melee roundhouse kick	60	N
1019	HNTFGN	Hunter firing gun	30	N
1020	HNTLGN	Hunter loading gun	90	N
1021	HNTEGN	Hunter equipping gun	90	N
1022	HNTSGN	Hunter storing gun	90	N
1023	HNTDGN	Hunter dropping gun	60	N
1024	HNTPU2	Hunter picking up object (2 hand)	90	N
1025	HNTPU1	Hunter picking up object (1 hand)	60	N
1026	HNTITT	Hunter idle (toe tap) cycle	240	Y
1027	HNTIHH	Hunter idle (hands on hips) cycle	240	Y
1028	HNTITK	Hunter idle (thinking) cycle	240	Y
1029	HNTISN	Hunter idle (scanning) cycle	240	Y
1030	HNTHTP	Hunter hit (punched)	30	N
1031	HNTHTK	Hunter hit (kicked)	30	N
1032	HNTHTS	Hunter hit (stabbed)	30	N
1033	HNTHTT	Hunter hit (shot)	30	N
1034	HNTNBK	Hunter knocked back	60	N
1035	HNTNBR	Hunter knocked right	60	N
1036	HNTNBL	Hunter knocked left	60	N
1037	HNTNDN	Hunter knocked down	60	N
1038	HNTKBK	Hunter killed back	90	N
1039	HNTKFW	Hunter killed forward	90	N
1040	HNTKRT	Hunter killed right	90	N
1041	HNTKLT	Hunter killed left	90	N

Table showing a sample animation list for a game character.

Special Powers

Game worlds are fantastic, so PCs often have special powers like telekinesis, mind control, and invisibility. Don't assume that people know how these powers should work or what they look like; describe them!

Progression

The GDD must outline the expected *progression* of each PC. As players progress through the game, they expect their characters to improve. RPGs use an experience point system to assign values to upgrades. In this system, experience points are earned by slaying enemies, discovering hidden items, or completing quests. These points are then exchanged for new abilities or to enhance existing abilities.

Some games have *technology trees*—graphical representations that establish predetermined pathways, or trees, for upgrades. Players look at the end of the tree for the ultimate ability they want, and then they invest experience points in the root abilities of the tree so that they eventually get what they want. This mechanic leads to clear delineation of character types while still giving players the ability to fine-tune their characters.

This same principle can be applied to armies. Real-time strategy (RTS) games use tech trees to determine which units each player can build.

Driving games, such as *Gran Turismo 4*, allow players to make permanent upgrades to their cars.

These progression systems give players more ownership by allowing them to customize their character, army, or vehicle. Since players earn this right by playing, they have a sense of accomplishment each time they acquire a new ability. This also contributes to replayability, thus extending the life of the game and value to the consumer.

Spiderman uses his web to swing between buildings in *Ultimate Spiderman*.

© 2006 Wizards of the Coast, Inc. Used with permission.

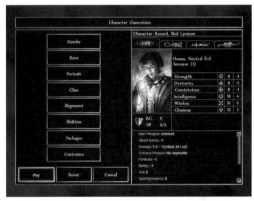

Character upgrade screens (such as this one from *Neverwinter Nights*) shows the progression of a player character (PC).

Courtesy of Blizzard Entertainment, Inc

World of Warcraft allows players to trade earned skill points for upgraded character abilities.

Electronic Arts

Sony Computer Entertainment America

In *Red Alert 2*, superweapons can be accessed only after prerequisite buildings are erected.

In *Gran Turismo*, players race for money so they can make performance improvements to their vehicles.

Rewards

The most common *reward* system includes money or coins, which can be used to purchase new inventory items or simply kept for bragging rights. Players of the popular *Mario Bros.* series would compare their experiences: Who got the most coins? Who got through a level the fastest? Who uncovered all the secrets?

As mentioned previously, some games use an experience system to award points which can then be traded for upgrades. Power-ups are special one-shot items that are automatically given to the players when they find them.

Toy Factor

Blizzard's *Diablo* rewarded players with a seemingly endless supply of unique weapons and armor. Gamers would replay levels many times in the hopes of finding something new for their character. Some players hosted "trading post" games to exchange unique items. Characters became toys to outfit and display.

Sony Computer Entertainment America

Discovering treasure in *Neopets: The Darkest Faerie.*

Rare rewards are usually found at the ends of levels or in secret areas. When designing these, put some effort into the presentation. A treasure chest shouldn't just creak open; it should be a spectacular event filled with glowing light and heroic music.

Playing can be its own reward. Revealing plot points through non-interactive sequences is one way to reward players for their hard work. A more common reward is to include secret areas filled with a special bonus: a rare weapon, a powerful power-up, or something notable that the player will tell others about.

Vulnerabilities

Every good hero has his Achilles' heel. Spiderman must protect his identity. Superman stays away from kryptonite. If the PC is all powerful there is no real threat, no tension, and gameplay becomes boring.

The PC may have several *vulnerabilities*. This forces players to develop new tactics to counter attempts by enemies to exploit their weaknesses.

Inventory

Most PCs develop by acquiring items in the world. These *inventory* items may be used immediately or saved for later use.

Some games have advanced inventory management, while others simply replace the currently equipped item when a better version is found.

Courtesy of Blizzard Entertainment, Inc

The GDD needs to identify all the possible inventory items and what they do for the player. A sample description should include:

1. Name of item
2. Look of item (including an image of the item)
3. Usage (examples of how the item is used)
4. Special abilities to player when equipped (e.g., protection from magic or poison)
5. Degradation (for items that wear out) and capacity (e.g., rounds of ammunition)
6. Special effects for graphics and sound effects (e.g., fire circles, bouncing shots, and lightning bolts)
7. Rarity (how rare the item is relative to others; usually expressed as common, uncommon, rare, and unique [for one-of-a-kind items])

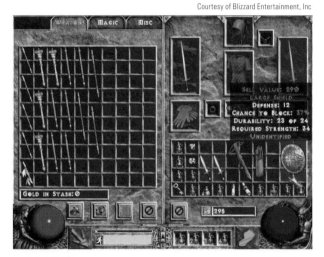

Diablo II contains a grid-based inventory system that limits how much can be carried and forces players to frequently arrange items.

The most common inventory items are weapons, armor, one-shot items, and special-use items. Even games that don't contain any degree of violence may have one-shot and special-use items to help define PC capabilities.

World of Warcraft uses color to distinguish how rare the weapons are; in this case (purple), the weapon is very rare.

Weapons

Weapons include anything the PC can wield to inflict damage on enemies or the environment. The weapon description should indicate the type of damage dealt (e.g., projectile, explosive, piercing, cutting, bashing, burning, or magic) and the amount of damage dealt.

More is not always better. Players appreciate having fewer weapons that have very distinct looks and noticeably different effects or power. The exception is MMORPGs; they tend to have hundreds of weapons with very slight variations and much reuse of imagery. MMORPGs probably have this increased number of weapons due to character advancement (characters exist at a wide variety of levels) and enemies (e.g., it might be necessary to have both fire *and* ice weapons to fight different bosses and monsters).

The armor displayed in the *Diablo II* inventory screen looks powerful and distinctive.

Armor

Armor includes articles of clothing and gear that equips the PC. Some may have a strictly aesthetic purpose and offer no intrinsic protection. Armor descriptions should include how the armor protects the PC and any special resistance or vulnerability (e.g., steel shields can be damaged by acid or can conduct electricity).

Armor is often the most noticeable item for a character. It is important to make powerful or rare armor items look distinctive and desirable. Players appreciate the ability to color or tint their armor or clothing to further customize characters.

One-shot Items

One-shot items are carried by the player but extinguished after a single or limited number of uses. These include items such as food, potions, magic scrolls, bandages, keys, and power-ups.

One-shot items are sprinkled throughout a mission or level to provide repetitive rewards to the player. They are also used to balance the difficulty or warn of upcoming danger. Platform games often leave a trail of food or health power-ups right before the big boss encounter.

Items such as food in *World of Warcraft* provide repetitive rewards to the player.

Special Use Items

Special use items are unique to a specific game. They may be carried by the player or used throughout the game or for a particular sequence. Examples include binoculars, flashlights, sensors, communicators, and grappling hooks.

These special-use items give a game personality and distinctiveness. If they are fun and interesting to use they be a USP for the game.

Doom 3 creates tension by forcing the player to use a flashlight in dark areas.

Non-Player Characters (NPCs)

Non-player characters (NPCs) are all the persons that the PC encounters or interacts with in the game. They may be allies or enemies. Their behavior is controlled by the AI of the game code.

Examples of NPCs include the following:

1. Enemies the PC may encounter
2. Supporting actors for story purposes
3. Vendors for purchasing inventory items
4. Innocent victims to be rescued (or tormented)
5. Henchman to assist the PC
6. Beasts of burden to transport the PC or carry excess inventory

NPC types, abilities, and vulnerabilities are the same as with the PC, although NPCs are generally more specialized and often serve a single

In *Jak & Daxter*, Jak has a sidekick (Daxter), who provides him with clues and story points.

purpose. With the exception of henchmen and beasts of burden, they may have no inventory beyond what is visible on them. NPCs are numerous in the game world. Game designers usually try to reuse their 3D models and animation by substituting different heads and clothing to create the appearance of a much larger cast.

Sony Computer Entertainment America

Boss Characters

Most games feature at least one boss character. These are really tough villains that have multiple tactics which usually follow a pattern and distinct vulnerabilities that the player must discover. *Shadow of the Colossus* features nothing but bosses, and each of the 16 missions is designed around defeating a single, unique boss character.

Shadow of the Colossus is unique in that it has bosses and no other enemies.

Features

The features are the significant aspects of the game that define the player's experiences. In an RPG, the features are centered on the development of the player's character and the epic story that unfolds. In an action-adventure game, features usually involve the player's control of the character and the unique abilities and weapons they learn to master. In an RTS, features center on new units for the player's army and regions to conquer.

The GDD needs to take the high concept and USPs and expand on them. The vision must be clear and the scope of the game must be limited so that the features are easily understood by the development team. Features are typically the bullet point list used to market the game and ultimately appear on the back of the box. It's the game designer's job to fulfill the promise of each feature by incorporating it into the design in a logical and entertaining way.

As an example, let's look at the material that appears on the back of the box for *Gran Turismo 4*. The tag line reads: "the drive of your life." Features include:

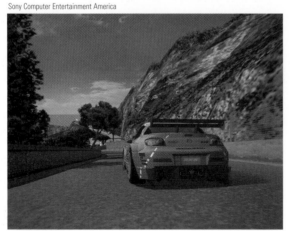

Sony Computer Entertainment America

- 650 cars spanning a century of automotive history
- 100 tracks from across the world
- Spectators who react to your every move
- New game modes: Photo Mode and B-Spec Mode

Photo mode in *Gran Turismo 4*

For sequels, features are the improvements or "reasons to buy" a game over its predecessor. The same holds true for games that evolve a given genre of game. If you want to introduce a new FPS game, it had better offer some significant improvements over the latest installment from the contenders (*Doom, Quake, Half-Life, Unreal, Halo*).

The features listed on the back of the box for *Quake 4* include:

- Extremely detailed graphics (on high-end PCs with top 3D cards)
- Detailed facial expressions
- Varied character animations (motion capture)
- Dynamic lighting and shadows
- High polygon count characters and scenes
- Tactical team-based attack formations for NPC AI
- High-caliber voice acting

Quake 4 (right) has obvious graphical improvements over the original *Quake,* and even *Quake 3* (left): full 3D environments with dynamic lights and normal mapping.

Be sure that features are fully realized in a game. If you can't be better than the competition on a given feature, then at least match them. Otherwise, you should consider dropping the feature and spending resources on something that will garner praise and provide enjoyment for the player.

Michael John (Lead
Designer, Method
Games)

Michael John is an independent lead game designer, with over 10 years of experience making console video games. His credits include the notable character-action games *Spyro the Dragon (series)* for PlayStation, and *Daxter* for the Sony PSP. Michael also co-authored the "Cerny Method" along with Mark Cerny, which is often cited for popularizing the importance of pre-production in video game projects.

Game design documentation should be split into two categories, which are the *macro design* and the *micro design*. These two documents are fundamentally different in focus and content.

Macro design documentation must be as brief and concise as possible for your game. Any details not absolutely necessary to a basic understanding of the game should be eliminated. If the detail would be obvious to someone playing the prototype, it should be eliminated. (For instance, including a detailed description of how the character reacts to the controller would be useless if you have a prototype of it.) Story should be included only in rough outline form. The macro design document should be written so that it can be read and fully understood in under an hour by any member of the team. In my experience, this puts its total length at between 5 and 10 pages. Because of its brevity, organization and clarity are crucial (I am a big fan of bullet lists) in a macro design document.

A completed macro design should also include a game layout matrix. This is usually a spreadsheet, with the game's various levels or areas in the rows, and the elements to be included in each level in the columns. The game matrix should fit on a single sheet of paper (I admit to cheating and using ledger paper), because its purpose is to give the designer a quick overview of the game's structure, balance and pacing. Liberal use of color in the game matrix is also helpful—you use color to identify genres of gameplay (e.g., minigame, puzzle, boss...) and you can then take a step back and blur your eyes a bit (or remove your glasses if you're blind like me) and see whether or not your game is properly balanced.

The other half of the picture is micro design. Micro design is generally done on the fly during production, and is where level design falls in the process. In my practice, micro design is actually a collection of documents, and includes the level maps (in 2D format), and the Level Design Documents (LDDs).

Micro design is the opposite of macro design in terms of level of detail. The LDD in particular should be done in painstaking detail. I insist of designers working with me that it include a blow-by-blow verbal walkthrough of all expected events in the level. The expectation is that only those team members intimately involved with the level at hand will actually read through it in its entirety; however for those people, the LDD and map should provide all the information necessary to implement the level.

Part of the reason that micro design is so thorough is that it functions as an additional test for the designer of the level's flow and accuracy. A remarkable number of errors, missed opportunities, or just plain dumb ideas are exposed when writing out a narrative description of the action in a level. (Note: this micro design system applies only to narrative-style games (linear or non-linear), and would not apply very well to generative-style games such as *The Sims*.)

Gameplay Mechanics

The *gameplay mechanics* are the meat of the design. This section in the GDD describes the core of what makes a game fun and unique. For games based on existing genres, this is a description of how the game is evolving the genre. For truly revolutionary designs that defy categorization, the gameplay mechanics must sufficiently describe the players' activities so that the desired experience is well understood.

Pillars

The *pillars* of the game literally define the game. These are usually the top two or three reasons that consumers would buy and play the game. The pillars come from gameplay features, unique story or license aspects, or design principles that set the game apart from the rest. The three main pillars of gameplay in *Titan Quest,* for example, are exploration, combat, and rewards. In *Dragonshard*, the pillars include epic battles above ground and D&D-style adventures below ground.

All features and gameplay mechanics are weighed against the pillars. Anything that detracts is culled from the game. Things that reinforce are given higher priority. This results in clearer vision for the design and greater consistency for the player.

In *Dragonshard*, one pillar of gameplay was to have D&D-style adventuring in caverns under the earth.

RTS games such as *Dragonshard* are designed for replayability.

Repetition

Linear, story-driven games may have little or no repetition. Each mission or level involves a great deal of special case encounters. Other games provide a basic set of rules and an open sandbox in which to try out different tactics. Too much *repetition* becomes boring. Not enough repetition cheats the player of achieving mastery.

Games with inherent replayability, such as FPS and RTS games, rely on repetition and sophisticated artificial intelligence (AI) behaviors. These games easily substitute online human opponents for AI to make competitive matches interesting.

When players fight one another or AI in RTS games such as *Dragonshard*, they often play using the same map. Yet each game feels different to them because choices in army size, unit composition, and tactics result in widely different experiences and outcomes.

Game designers often need to repeat aspects of the game to get the most out of costly programming or graphics. Clever designers learn how to introduce variations so that the repetition seems natural to the player.

In some games, such *as God of War*, save points are sprinkled throughout the environment.

Save/Load Scheme

Game designers need to consider how and when players will be able to save their progress in a game. If too much time elapses between save points, players will be frustrated at having to repeat long sections of the game when their characters die. If the player can save at any time, there is little or no consequence for dying. This encourages trial and error gameplay, where players constantly reload from a save point to maximize results.

Reward Them for Not Saving!

Consider giving rewards to players for not saving. You can still provide the option of "save-anywhere-anytime" for those who want it, yet reward those who do not—*and* provide replayability for those looking for that "no-save-perfect-victory"!

— *Frank T. Gilson (Senior Developer of Digital Games, Wizards of the Coast)*

Pacing

Missions or scenes should introduce new features and build on them. Cohesive gameplay teaches players their roles and reinforces what they've learned. Many good games fail to achieve blockbuster status because they fail to introduce features in a logical and entertaining progression.

Players cannot sustain a constantly increasing pace. Eventually they simply become worn out. Arcade games of the 1980s repeated the same game mechanic for each level, gradually increasing the speed and frequency of enemies until the player could no longer keep up.

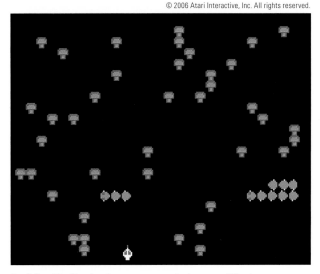

Each level in *Centipede* gets progressively more difficult.

Players currently spend an average of $50 or more for a game; they are entitled to finish it. Good game designers create quiet moments between crescendos of action. These quiet moments are usually good spots for non-interactive sequences, or peaceful travel from one locale to another, or possibly a move that plays while the next level is being loaded into memory. These quieter sequences shouldn't be boring. They can be filled with rich eye candy, provocative music, or poignant story points. Entertain the players as they rest up for the next big battle.

Care should be taken to systematically introduce new concepts or abilities. Treat these as special gems. Don't be stingy by withholding the best for last and don't squander them by flooding the player with everything all at once. It's helpful to graph out the first time each item is introduced to the player to get a sense of how frequently new things are introduced across all missions.

Level or Scene Descriptions

In films, scenes are self-contained areas where one or more cameras will record the interaction of characters. In games, scenes may be much larger, since cameras are free to follow the actors as they move freely about the environment. As such, *level* or *scene descriptions* are typically overhead maps of an area. These may represent all or part of a mission or level in a game.

Firaxis Games Inc.

This map from *Civilization III: Conquests* is similar to the drawings used by designers to describe the layout of a level.

Important aspects of scene descriptions are the following:

1. Overhead view or map
2. Location of NPCs
3. Pathways or patrol loops followed by NPCs
4. Location and type of rewards
5. Puzzles, traps, and locked areas
6. Secret or bonus areas
7. Trigger points for non-interactive sequences
8. Environment (e.g., drizzling rain, shimmering light)
9. Sound emitters (e.g., croaking frogs, humming electronics)
10. Non-interactive sequences

Levels should be as pleasing to look at as they are to play. Good designers consider visual aesthetics when creating a scene. Some studios, such as Blizzard, have their art teams give input on this part of the GDD.

Level descriptions should go into detail about the motivation for the scene and what the player gains or learns by playing it. They should also describe how this scene transitions to the next scene.

User Interface

The *user interface (UI)* description covers the onscreen buttons as well as the peripheral buttons or keyboard controls that the players use to:

1. Navigate (e.g., walk, jump, fly)
2. Control the PC (e.g., activate abilities, use weapons)
3. Orient themselves in the world (e.g., maps)
4. Manage inventory (e.g., equip weapons and armor, use items)
5. Interact with NPCs (e.g., fight, talk, trade)

6. Track PC status (e.g., health, magic, money, experience)
7. Use special items in the world (e.g., switches, doors, devices)
8. Set options (e.g., audio, video, button mappings)
9. Save/load games
10. Join or host multiplayer games
11. Chat with other online players
12. Get help or information
13. Pause or exit the game

The sniper rifle in *Half-Life: Counterstrike* has a specialized interface screen.

Some UI elements may be connected to player inventory items or abilities such as a compass, IR glasses, or sniper rifle. These special interfaces need to be described so that the artists and programmers can account for them while laying out the *graphic user interface (GUI)*.

In-Game Interface

Activities that occur frequently such as movement or weapon use should be mapped to the most easily accessible buttons on the controller or keyboard. Use standard conventions. If all other games in the same genre use the X button to fire a weapon then your game should too. Don't force players to relearn an interface just for your game.

Keep the onscreen controls or *heads-up display (HUD)* to a minimum. These should be elements the average player really needs to keep an eye on during normal gameplay, such as health. These are usually passive interface items, things that the player doesn't directly interact with. Active interface items are onscreen menus that the player interacts with to make choices during gameplay.

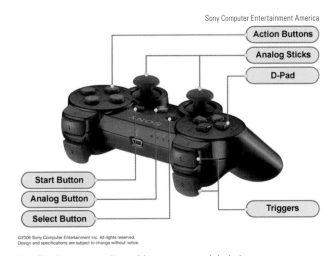

Sony Computer Entertainment America

©2006 Sony Computer Entertainment Inc. All rights reserved.
Design and specifications are subject to change without notice.

PlayStation 3 controller, with components labeled.

The GDD should contain a image that maps all of the controller or keyboard buttons to a specific action. If these are customizable, the default mapping should be indicated.

Sony Computer Entertainment America

Electronic Arts

Racing games have simple controls. *Gran Turismo HD* (left) uses transparent gauges for an unobstructed view of the road. By contrast, *The Sims: Open for Business* (right) uses a "dashboard" and icons to provide shortcut commands to the complex interactions of the game.

Diagram by Per Olin

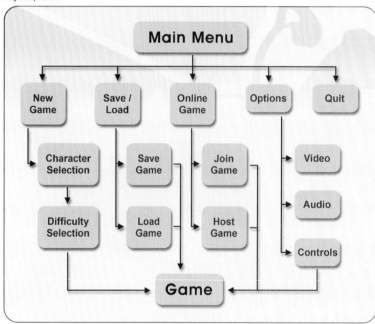

A simplified menu tree for the highest level of a game.

Menus

Most games have relatively thin *menu* trees. Nonetheless, the GDD should contain a flowchart of all menus and the inputs that transition from one menu to the next.

Keep menu hierarchy to a maximum of three levels. Games that are easy to pick up and play tend to put the shortcuts in the menu system so that players can get into games quickly. Some games start with the first level, then introduce a menu once the first level is complete. The important thing is to get the player to begin playing and making choices within the game as soon as possible!

Evolving and Targeting Your Game Design Document

The key difficulty in a GDD is not creating it; rather, it is updating it and spreading that information to the team. I have found that breaking things down into manageable chunks based on features, and using a Wiki format helps to make sure that the people that need to read different sections actually read it. Also, presenting elements can never hurt. Sitting all your level designers in a room and pitching the level design philosophy to them, and taking their feedback is much better than simply emailing out a level design document.

— *Christian Allen (Creative Director, Red Storm Entertainment)*

"No Plan Survives Contact with the Enemy" *

Any good document should be kept to its absolute minimum, and details should only be fleshed out during implementation. Our experience has been that too much time invested in documentation before implementation results in misdirection and wasted work. [Short documents] tend to focus more on the goals of a given system than anything else.

— *Starr Long (Producer, NCsoft)*
* Field Marshal Helmuth von Moltke

Graeme Bayless on Clarity in Game Documentation:::::

Graeme Bayless is the Director of Production for Crystal Dynamics, a division of EIDOS. Graeme has been directing computer game development for 18 years, and has been in game development for nearly 25 years. He has shipped over 60 games in his extensive career, and has worked on nearly every type of game… ranging from military simulations to action games, from RPGs to sports, and from interactive films to strategy games. Graeme has been a Programmer, a Producer, a Director, a Lead Designer, and even a QA Manager in his career. He has worked for such companies as Sierra, Sega, Electronic Arts, and now EIDOS. Graeme is a self-admitted gamer geek, and when he's not at work poring over management documents, he can be found playing nearly every type of game on the market. Beyond computer games, Graeme is a board/miniatures gamer, a movie nut, an avid reader, and an astronomy enthusiast. Graeme lives in Saratoga, CA with his incredibly patient wife and two giant puppies.

Graeme Bayless (Director of Production, Crystal Dynamics)

The most important aspect of any form of game documentation is *clarity*. The entire point of a design document, be it GDD, TDD, or Test Plan, is to clearly communicate to the reader the intent of the plan. For example, if you're writing a Game Design Document, you MUST include sufficient detail so that a programmer could take this document and make legitimate progress towards building the code to support the design vision… without ever speaking to the designer. No, this doesn't mean I support such… in reality, I feel communication between the disciplines is the key to success… but a GDD must have adequate detail to answer all of the key questions. A programmer or artist should be able to pick it up, read it, and learn enough to know what you're building and how you plan to do so. It should include sufficient detail to allow programming to make good memory maps, to allow art to properly plan on how to support the design goals visually, and so on.

All such planning documents have a few things in common… they get detailed enough to have real tangible facts in there… how many levels… how many characters… how will the gameplay flow… how many animations… how will audio be stitched together… etc. The goal of these documents is to provide real data, not just guesses. By the time a product enters main production, all this hard information should be real and on paper. An often overlooked component is the organizational aspect… some common system of allowing easy access to related topics. Additionally, I recommend having the documents be living documents… dead ones don't get updated, and become obsolete long before they get used. An active system like Wiki can really help design and planning documents become useful tools.

The GDD is the backbone of the game. It should contain the story elements, character descriptions, features, gameplay mechanics, level layouts, and user interface design. It may take many months and many revisions to complete the GDD. Once ideas are committed to printed word, further debate amongst the team leads to refinement. The next step is to define how the underlying game technology will work. We'll cover game architecture and performance goals in the following chapter.

:::CHAPTER REVIEW:::

1. Create a game design document (GDD) for your original game idea. How does the GDD differ from a concept/pitch document?

2. Create a branching script for a scene in your original game. Make sure that there are at least three possible dialogue choices that can be made by the player character per response.

3. Localizing a game for the German market has posed several technical and content-related challenges. Discuss what might need to be modified if you were to localize your game for Germany. How might this localization process differ for the Japanese and South Korean markets?

4

Technical Design

creating the blueprint for production

Key Chapter Questions

- Who writes the technical design document (TDD), and who reads it?

- What is object-oriented design (OOD)?

- What are some security measures that should be taken during production?

- What are some common risks the technical team faces?

- What is revision control?

The *technical design document (TDD)*—the plan for creating the game code—is usually written by the technical director or lead programmer. It describes all the software that needs to be written or licensed, the data to be stored and updated, and the tools required for the entire team.

The TDD is often written in parallel to the GDD, but it cannot be finalized until the GDD is complete and approved. The TDD should be reviewed by every member of the team, even the nonprogrammers, to ensure that nothing has been overlooked.

The subsections below describe the major topics that need to be covered in the TDD.

Architecture

The architecture section of the TDD describes all the software components of the game. This is the high-level technical overview of the game. It outlines the program flow and data relationships. Object/class definitions should be specified for object-oriented designs. All significant algorithms should be described, along with their source. The architecture should describe any novel approaches and reference any external white papers or technical documents that can provide more details. A picture is worth a thousand words. Visuals help clarify the architecture. Include Dataflow diagrams, state-action tables, or object-oriented design (OOD) diagrams.

:::::: Object-Oriented Design (OOD)

Diagram by Per Olin

Example of an object-oriented diagram (OOD).

Classic technical design breaks problems into a set of functions or procedures performed by the game program. Object-oriented design (OOD) is a design approach where systems are described as a collection of *objects* that act on each other. Objects are defined by their structure, the data they contain, and their behavior, the things they can do.

Objects are grouped into *classes* that share common structures and behaviors. Objects pass messages to one another requesting information or asking for an action to be performed. These actions are called *methods*. Each class of objects has a predefined set of methods that the objects will carry out. An example in graphics would be to create a class of graphic objects. Subclasses would be circles, squares, and triangles. Methods would be create, move, resize, draw, and destroy. In the classic approach a graphics routine would draw a circle. In OOD the circle would be asked to draw itself.

Coding Standards

Many years ago, games were written by a few programmers and sometimes only a single individual. There was little need to share code between people, beyond showing off a particularly clever algorithm to one's peers. Nowadays, games are composed of hundreds of thousands of lines of code written by teams of engineers. It is critical that the code be shared and understood by all engineers in the development team.

Development Systems

When we started work on the Amiga we had stone-age tools to use for development. Seriously, there were 10 software engineers banging on a single host computer! The hardware designers used pencils and erasers! There were no source-level debuggers, no performance analyzers, no graphics or audio editors. When we developed the Lynx at least we had a powerful development computer: the Amiga. Yes, we used the Amiga as our host system for all Lynx development; after all, the Amiga had the best graphics and audio at the time, and we preferred the Amiga development environment over the lesser computers then available. We started the 3DO using Amigas, but the demands of the system led us to adopting a wide range of development efforts on many different machines. Today, PS3 development is done on Linux, Mac and the PC, and I hope that someday we will use the PS3 to do PS3 development. The Lynx is the only machine I worked on that didn't have an operating system. The Lynx had a number of runtime libraries we created that developers could use if they wanted, but the developer could go directly to the bare metal if preferred. On the Amiga you weren't supposed to touch the hardware directly, but most everyone did anyway. The Amiga had no way to protect itself against the ravages of a program run amok. The 3DO and the PS3 both have built-in protections that keep a failing program from destroying everything.

— *RJ Mical (Senior Software Manager, SD Tools Group, Sony Computer Entertainment of America; Co-Creator of the Amiga, Atari Lynx, and 3DO)*

The *coding standards* section describes the conventions, guidelines, and style of the game that the programming team will follow. The goal is to make it easy for any programmer to maintain the code. Typical standards include the following:

1. naming conventions for variables and program modules
2. in-line comments and supporting documentation
3. information-hiding, or black box application programming interfaces (APIs)
4. reuse of code and data structures
5. style guides

Application Programming Interface (API)

An application programming interface (API) is a set of functions or tools that a software library or application provides for building programs. Utilities and procedures that are commonly used by all game programs are placed in a library for ease of maintaining them.

Trade-offs have to be made for speed vs. maintainability of code. An example of this is unrolling a loop for faster execution. Hardware may impose constraints that run counter to readability of code. Time-sensitive portions of game code are often written in assembly language.

Tools

Everyone on the development team uses tools to create assets for the game. Standard applications like Microsoft Word and Microsoft Excel are used to create dialogue scripts, asset lists, and documentation. Some common content editing applications and their uses include:

- SN Systems ProDG, used by console programmers to compile and debug software
- Microsoft Visual Studio, used by PC programmers to edit and debug software
- Autodesk Maya, used by artists for 3D modeling, animation, effects, and rendering
- Adobe Photoshop, used by artists for creating textures and 2D imagery
- Adobe Premiere, used by video editors for editing in-game movies
- Digidesign Pro Tools, used by audio engineers for multi-track composing, recording, editing, mixing, and mastering
- Microsoft Project, used by producers and project managers to track schedules and tasks

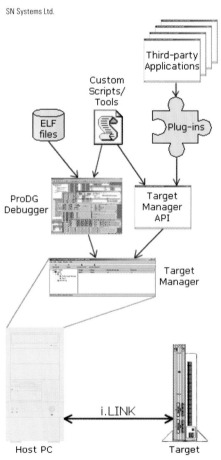

SN Systems ProDg is a compiler and debugger that runs on a PC attached to a development system, in this case a PlayStation 2 devkit.

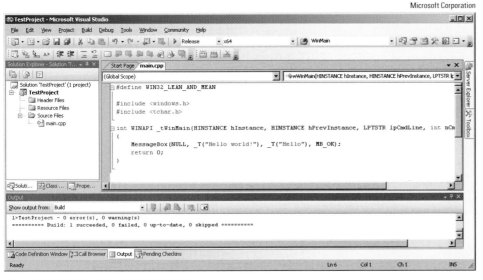

Microsoft Corporation

Visual Studio 2005 with code highlighted.

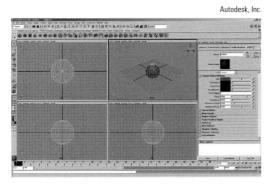

Autodesk, Inc.

3D model being created in Maya 8.0.

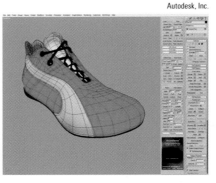

Autodesk, Inc.

3D model being created in 3D Studio Max 8.

Adobe Systems Incorporated

Adobe Photoshop CS2 in action.

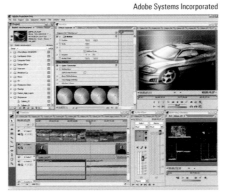

Adobe Systems Incorporated

Adobe Premiere interface.

Adobe Systems Incorporated

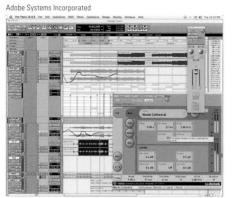

ProTools interface.

Microsoft Corporation

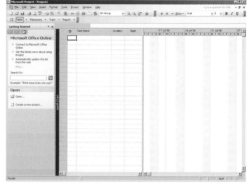

Microsoft Project interface.

:::::: *God of War:* Putting Tools
in the Hands of Art and Design

Sony Computer Entertainment America

The approach we have taken at Sony Santa Monica for the *God of War* team is to structure code and tools such that as much control as possible is directly in the hands of the art and design teams—which make decisions regarding placement of game objects and scripting of enemy behaviors, what loads when, what is visible when, what both front-end and in-game menus and other display elements look like (and how they behave), and much more. Only rarely does a programmer have to be involved in these tasks. Taking the programmers out of the day-to-day equation of the game production allows them to focus on the game infrastructure, optimization, tools, and all other critically important issues involved in an AAA game. Due to our approach, all our programmers are, in effect, technology programmers (including our gameplay programmers, since they create systems to be used by designers). Our approach also allows us to have a relatively small team of programmers compared to many other studios with a different approach to game making. However, due to our focus on technology, we employ only highly technical senior programmers—which is also a reason why we can get away with a smaller programming team than most.

— *Christer Ericson (Director of Tools & Technology,
Sony Computer Entertainment of America)*

Data are usually designed for efficient use by the proprietary software of the game. Conversion utilities are required to transform the data from a standard content creation tool into a form that is usable by the game code. Most of these utilities must be custom written by the development team.

Common external applications such as 3D rendering, video compression, and audio playback are available from third-party developers. By focusing on a single purpose, the developers of these packages can offer robust, time-saving solutions. Examples include:

- OpenGL, for 2D and 3D graphics application programming interface (API)
- Microsoft DirectX, for access to 3D graphics and sound hardware features on PCs
- RAD Game Tools Bink, for video compression and playback
- RAD Game Tools Miles Sound System, for audio compression and playback

© 1997–2006 RAD Game Tools, INC. © 1997–2006 RAD Game Tools, INC.

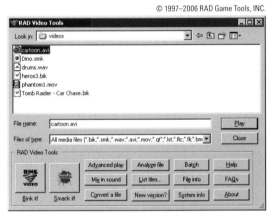 

RAD Game Tools Bink (left) is used for game video production and playback, while Miles Sound System (right) is used for game audio compression and playback.

Christer Ericson on the Traits of a Good Game Programmer :::::

Before joining Sony in 1999, he was a senior programmer at Neversoft Entertainment. Christer received his Masters degree in computer science from Umeå University, Sweden, where he also lectured for several years before moving to the United States in early 1996. Christer is an active participant in the game industry. His involvement includes serving on the advisory board for Full Sail's Game Design and Development degree program (since 2002) and on the advisory board for the GameTech technical seminars. Christer has lectured at both the Game Developers Conference (GDC) and SIGGRAPH. He is the author of *Real-Time Collision Detection* (Morgan Kaufmann, 2005).

When we hire programmers we primarily look for strong generalists with a solid understanding of computer architecture, low-level issues, math, and data structures and algorithms. With a small team it is important that we have multitalented programmers that are capable of working in just about any area. The low-level computer architecture skills we

Christer Ericson
(Director of Tools
& Technology,
Sony Computer
Entertainment America)

consider important because they form a solid basis for additional knowledge to be built upon. Unfortunately, many programmers have only a "black box" understanding of the machines they work on, leading to inefficient systems that waste valuable resources (be it memory or cycles), inevitably leading to problems further down the road and, ultimately, does not enable art and design to create the best game they possibly could. We do not care if people do not know the full semantics of certain C++ keywords or if they are not hip to the latest trend in software engineering; such skills are fleeting and the programmers we look for are talented enough that they can pick up such knowledge in a heartbeat if necessary.

Game Engine

Comprehensive *game engines* are also available for use in your game. These technologies provide state-of-the-art functionality for core game components. They can help a new game studio get up to speed with working prototypes that put them on a level playing field with more established studios using their own technology. This comes at a price. License fees range up into the hundreds of thousands of dollars and may include a percentage of revenue on your game when it is sold. It may be far less than the cost of creating this technology from scratch, but you should take care to ensure that the features offered by licensed code will support the design goals of the game. Some examples of licensed technology include:

- Epic's *Unreal 3*, for 3D game development. Includes graphics, networking, AI, animation, and content creation on PC and consoles
- *Havok*, for physics and collision of objects
- Criterion Software's *Renderware*, for 3D game development. Includes graphics, physics, AI, and audio

All licensed technology should be described, no matter how insignificant it is. Licenses need to be reviewed by publishers to assure ownership and compliance. Some third-party software that is free (freeware) actually has specific restrictions about use on products that are for sale.

BioWare Corp.

Electronic Arts

Electronic Arts

BioWare's *Mass Effect* (left) uses the Unreal 3 renderer; EA's *The Godfather* (middle) uses Havok for realistic physics; and EA's *Black* (right) uses Renderware for its 3D renderer.

Risks and Contingencies

Murphy's Law is certainly true of game development. The risk assessment section covers all the "what-ifs" of the project. This includes a list of continuous activities that must be undertaken to resolve technical risk in a systematic and structured way. In the contingencies section, every possible issue should have a trigger event and a proposed resolution. You won't catch all the problems that arise but you can minimize wasted time by actively searching for issues and defining a strategy for dealing with problems when they occur.

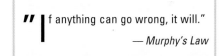

> "If anything can go wrong, it will."
> — *Murphy's Law*

Illustration by Ian Robert Vasquez

Include a disaster recovery plan. What happens if your building is destroyed? Most developers maintain offsite backups. Check these on a regular basis to make sure the data can be recovered. Establish plans for temporary work space and equipment rental.

Loss of Data

Always keep an offsite backup!

As part of risk mitigation, all data in a game should be backed up. Backup plans usually call for weekly backups of the entire set of assets and code. Incremental backups of just the items that have been modified are done on a daily basis. It's important to include assets in their raw form with the scripts and settings used to process them into the form used by the game. Next-generation games encompass up to 50 gigabytes of data in their final form and terabytes of raw assets. Backup to tape on next-generation games can take more than a single day to complete.

Assume 75% efficiency with your projects. If a task is estimated to take three days to complete, then schedule four.

Schedule Slips

Almost all projects fall behind at some point. Well-managed projects get back on course; poorly managed projects continue to slip until they miss their release dates entirely. The TDD should present the programming team's approach to slips in technical tasks. Some common tactics to prevent or overcome schedule slips include the following:

- Any major change in features or scope should result in a re-evaluation of the remaining tasks and a reprioritization. If the original release date needs to be met, then optional features and associated tasks should be cut if sufficient programming resources cannot be added to the project to complete tasks in their alloted time.

- Task scheduling shouldn't assume programmers are working at 100% efficiency. Estimates usually assume ideal conditions: no interruptions, perfect understanding of solutions, no mistakes. Good managers build in additional time to account for this.

- The time required to implement radically new or complex features is difficult to estimate. It is also difficult to assess the interdependencies with new features and other areas of the game program. If possible, work on this part of the code first so that there is time to make adjustments without slipping later on.

- The entire production pipeline should be reviewed when determining task priorities and order. Artists or designers may become stalled in their work while waiting for a critical component to be implemented in the game program or tools. As a result, these components may need to be completed early in the software development schedule.

Third-Party Technology Dependencies

Third-party technology can save considerable time and money over building proprietary systems. It also creates dependencies. Even if the programmers have access to source code for third-party technology—which is rare—they may not have the time or ability to make changes, fix critical bugs, or complete unfinished features.

When new platforms are introduced, the third-party vendors are racing to get their software done in parallel with developers trying to complete their games. Sometimes important features for the developer end up taking longer to add or work differently than expected.

The contingency plan should identify the features required and a desired time frame for their completion. This information should be discussed with the vendor and agreed to, with time to spare in case they fall behind. A secondary source should be identified in case the vendor falls too far behind or fails to deliver.

Security

Games are one of the most popular targets for software hackers. Computer (PC) games are particularly vulnerable. According to the Business Software Alliance, 35% of the software installed on personal computers worldwide in 2004 was pirated. The BSA also reports that for every two dollars' worth of software purchased legitimately, one dollar's worth was obtained illegally.

Pirate vendor in Brazil.

Many popular PC games are pirated over the Internet via warez sites, spam, auction sites, and peer-to-peer (P2P) systems. Despite state-of-the-art copy protection, many games can be downloaded for free within days after their commercial release. Billions of dollars are lost to piracy in an industry where most publishers are having a tough time staying profitable.

Computer games aren't the only targets. All game consoles and handheld gaming devices have been hacked. Some schemes are elaborate, involving chips that are soldered into the hardware to overcome security and regional encoding restrictions. Piracy isn't the only threat. Some hackers break games in order to cheat. Most popular online games employ game managers (GMs) that actively expel or ban players who cheat, since it can ruin the game experience for other players.

Security Policy

The TDD should describe the security policy for the game. Some typical components are described below.

Roles and Procedures

This section outlines the roles and responsibilities for the security team: programmers, community managers, IT. It also defines procedures for approvals.

Asset Classification

Game assets need to be categorized to indicate the degree of protection they require. This should include assets that are subject to license or copyright restrictions.

Asset Protection

Critical game components need to be encrypted. Products such as Macrovision's Safedisc provide copy protection and methods to thwart hacking. Extra steps must be taken during the creation of a product's gold master to include this copy protection.

Access Control

This is a description of the measures taken to prevent theft or unauthorized access. It starts with a description of the physical area where assets will be kept, how access is controlled, and how the area will be monitored. Network access control systems are described: source/revision control, network connections and protections, and access violation detection.

Compliance

Independent monitoring systems need to be established to verify that the security policy is being followed.

Revision Control

As previously mentioned, game projects consist of several hundred thousand lines of code. Hundreds of changes to the software take place on a daily basis. In order to keep track of the changes, all projects employ a *revision control* system. This system usually involves third-party software that manages files and directories over time. A tree of files is placed into a central repository. Special commands allow programmers to recover older versions of their code and data, and to examine the history of code changes.

A programmer must "check out" a particular file to have exclusive rights to modify the file. This prevents two or more programmers from editing the same file and creating potential conflicts. Once the changes are complete, the programmer tests them and then checks the file back in for the rest of the team to access.

The revision control system is the central player in the *build process*, which defines the steps necessary to create a complete snapshot of the game. Builds allow members of the team to play the latest version of the game while areas are still under construction or modification.

Weekly Builds

There should never be less than a weekly build, for various reasons. Build times should be optimized; a full build including code/art/sound should not take longer than 1–2 hours. There should be a no-art-sound build option so that only-code builds can be done, which should take no longer than 30 minutes. Think of the several weeks of overall project time that will be saved if these low build times are accomplished. Also, there should be a method whereby new art/sound can be 'dropped in' to an existing build to test it out in-game, without requiring a build. Don't forget to account for placeholder data in the TDD (textures, models, sounds, and associated filenames).

— *Frank T. Gilson (Senior Developer of Digital Games, Wizards of the Coast)*

Some common revision control systems include:

- Subversion (or SVN), free open source software
- Microsoft's Visual SourceSafe, best suited for small teams over LAN
- Perforce Software's Perforce, easy to use and relatively fast
- Avid Technology's Alienbrain, combines digital asset management (DAM) and software configuration management (SCM); powerful and pricey

The revision control system is usually integrated into the backup plan. It also serves as a critical component of the security policy by governing access to valuable source assets.

Ed Rotberg on the Elements of a Good Technical Design Document :::::

Ed Rotberg has been in the game business since 1978. He has worked as producer, designer, programmer, and executive management at various times in his career. He was one of the founders of Videa, which was eventually acquired by Bally Midway. His career has also included a two-year stint at Apple Computer. Ed has worked for Atari, Bally Midway, 3DO, THQ and Silicon Entertainment. His credits include: *Atari Baseball, BattleZone, Star Wars, Blasteroids, S.T.U.N. Runner, Shuuz, Steel Talons, Guardians of the Hood, Snake Pit, Station Invasion, IMSA Racing (M2), NASCAR Silicon Motor Speedway, High Heat Baseball 2002, MX Superfly,* and *WWE CrushHour.*

The initial TDD that is submitted at project start should only be considered a rough, first draft. Not until the rewrite that will happen after

Ed Rotberg (CTO, Mine Shaft Entertainment)

pre-prod should these documents even begin to be considered development "bibles." In fact, the post pre-prod rewrite of these documents along with the budget and schedule should be one of the most important milestones for the entire process.

Since each game is different, so will the TDD vary in layout and presentation. However it is critical that these documents remain in sync with one another to avoid the mayhem and chaos that would ensue should they fail to remain well connected.

The elements of a good TDD include:

■ Identification and description (including block diagram) of the major components of the runtime software.

■ Staffing requirements for the software team, including primary areas of responsibility for each individual.

■ Definition of the minimum platform requirements for this title.

■ Identification of risk areas in the development process, whether they be in software development, graphics, audio, asset acquisition, obtaining tools, or staffing. This also includes any new technology that will be developed specifically for the title. Wherever possible, details about the proposed approach to solve the problems listed in this section and mitigate the risk should also be included.

■ Minimum performance requirements for the title and some indication of how this will be monitored and what tools will be used for profiling.

■ For most titles it is important to identify what units of measurement for distance will be used in the title and how the mapping will be done from the art tools to the software. This should include expected world size.

■ Details of the asset processing pipeline to be used for 3D graphics, 2D graphics, audio, video, and other assets. This should include details of the actual flow of assets from the artists' station to the final product.

■ Identification of tools to be used in the development of title for software development, graphics creation, video and audio creation. This will include vendors for purchased tools as well as identification of tools that will need to be created in house and/or developed by outside contractors. It is critical that the tools for source code version control and asset management be detailed here. It is also helpful to specify early on what bug tracking system will be used.

- Description and specification of any middleware used by the titles, including justification for the choices made, and the benefits entailed by their use.

- Coding standards to be used by the software team. This includes documentation standards as well as what coding techniques (such as error handling) will and will not be allowed. Any testing procedures, such as test drivers for libraries, and automated build schedules should be listed. This may also include the required use of coherency checking tools such as Lint or dependency verification utilities. All of this needs to be enforced!!

- Standards to be used with software version control and asset management, including version labeling standards.

- Asset naming conventions used by the team. Again, these need to be enforced.

- Details about major data structures and file formats used by the game.

- Breakdown of each of the major components of the runtime software into individual libraries and models.

- Descriptions of the general interfaces between the libraries and modules of the game. This is a section that will need to be kept updated continually throughout the development process.

- A thorough detailing of the memory management used in the game, including memory tracking tools and memory leak detection tools/ techniques. Details about anticipated memory requirements for each part of the game, including code, audio buffers, graphics data, text, screen buffers (including depth buffers), stack, and other data. Again it is helpful if this section be kept current throughout development.

Artificial Intelligence

The behavior of all NPCs is controlled by the *artificial intelligence* (AI) software. Their actions, from choice of movement to choice of dialogue options, are all determined by code. The degree to which players suspend their disbelief and immerse themselves into a game is directly related to the quality of the AI. Every

Players are accompanied by AI-controlled squad members or bots in *Half-Life: CounterStrike - Condition Zero*

year games hit a new benchmark in visual realism, yet AI remains primitive by comparison.

Behaviors

AI is complex software that must incorporate specific details about the game design, the environment, and the expected behaviors of the NPCs. AI code can easily consume more than its fair share of CPU bandwidth as it tries to come up with believable behaviors. Next-generation game platforms should provide more processing power to help make AI more realistic. Nonetheless, programmers often find that they must devise shortcuts and cheats to get AI to perform in a believable manner without crippling the performance of the game.

Pathfinding

Pathfinding involves specialized AI algorithms used by both PCs and NPCs to determine which path to take as they move throughout the game world. Most games use the A* search algorithm to calculate the shortest path from point A to point B, without bumping into walls or going too far.

A* Search

The A* search algorithm finds the shortest path to a goal state using a *heuristic*. A heuristic is a way to solve a problem that sacrifices a degree of accuracy in favor of faster calculation. The A* search will always produce a path from one point to another. It delivers the best path for the time allotted for the search.

Firaxis Games Inc.

In *Civilization IV*, units move in logical formations.

The effort required to implement and tune good pathfinding systems is usually underestimated when schedules are being prepared. A great deal of development time goes into optimizing and debugging pathfinding systems. Collision issues can arise with multiple movers, and testers should have access to scripts that can create and move large numbers of items in the game so that they can observe these problems.

Good AI provides authenticity and replayability. AI systems should avoid cheating, such as giving the AI access to more information or faster response time than a human opponent. AI will see dramatic improvements in years to come as processing power increases and players demand more realistic AI behavior.

Physics

All 3D games are simulations of 3D worlds. They may have fewer actors and things to bump into and break, but they must provide believable interactions. *Physics* code is found at the core of every major game, from simple collision detection to more advanced hair and cloth simulation. Your TDD needs to describe each physics subsystem and how it interfaces with the rest of the game. Physics subsystems include rigid body dynamics, soft body dynamics, fluid dynamics, collision detection, hair and cloth simulation, and finite-element fracturing.

Sony Computer Entertainment America

Heavenly Sword has sophisticated physics that allows the PC to smash people into objects and sweep debris into enemies.

AGEIA offers PhysX™, a software engine and dedicated hardware processor for handling the multitude of calculations necessary to simulate real-world physics. Just as video card manufacturers moved PC game consumers to 3D hardware accelerated games, AGEIA hopes to move us to hardware physics acceleration.

As characters and environments reach new levels of visual realism, so will physical interaction. Players will be less forgiving of past flaws or limitations in the physics of games. Physics should directly contribute to improved gameplay, since it adds time and often license costs to develop and test. Also, consider "alternative" physics that can be used to create excellent gameplay situations (e.g., light gravity, sticky walls).

AGEIA Technologies Inc.

AGEIA PhysX processor acceleration card for the PC.

Input/Output (I/O)

One of the core technologies for every game is the input/output of data. Console and PC games store most of their data on optical media. Elements that require fast access, such as the current level being played, are loaded into random access memory or RAM.

Media Formats

The target platform determines the storage and delivery media for your game. The TDD needs to specify the media format and describe how data should be stored and retrieved. Current optical media options include the following:

- *Blu-Ray Disc*: Named Blu-Ray for their unique blue-violet laser. A single-layer disc can hold 25 GB, enough for over two hours of HDTV or more than 13 hours of standard-definition TV. Dual-layer discs can hold 50 GB. Engineers estimate the potential maximum transfer rate at over 288 Mbps. This standard has been adopted by Sony for the PlayStation 3. It is backward compatible with DVD.
- *DVD-ROM*: Storage capacity (single-layer/dual-layer): 4.7 GB/9.4 GB. Data transfer rate (1x): 11.08 Mbps. Used by game consoles and computers.
- *CD-ROM*: Storage capacity (single-layer): 700 MB. Data transfer rate (24x): 3.6 Mbps. Used by computers.
- *UMD*: Storage capacity (single-sided, dual-layer): 1.8 GB. Data transfer rate: 11 Mbps. Used in the Sony PSP handheld.

Current optical game options include the Blu-Ray disc (left) and UMD (right).

The days of cartridge-based game systems are over. All major home consoles now accept some sort of optical disc media.

Streaming

Game software is delivered on high-capacity optical media, downloaded from the Internet, or, for cell phones, transmitted via wireless signals. As the data are being retrieved, something must be displayed to provide feedback. Otherwise, users assume that the game has crashed or a connection has been lost. Older games simply displayed a load screen, forcing players to wait. Newer games actually begin the game in the foreground as they continue to load data in the background. Game data are interleaved with music on the disc so that the soundtrack continues uninterrupted.

This process of storing data in interleaved form and retrieving it continuously is called *streaming*. It allows players to traverse endless 3D spaces and move from one level to the next seamlessly. The TDD must take into account the transfer rate of the media and impose constraints on level designers so that streaming can deliver data fast enough to keep up with the player's actions. Use streaming for installs in order to ensure that the game is played as soon as possible

Some games provide a "load bar" (*Neverwinter Nights* shown) that gives players some indication of the waiting time before the next level is available.

Hardware Considerations

Getting access to next-generation console development systems or *devkits* may be tricky for a first-time developer. That's why many developers start by creating games for the PC. If you do manage to work on a console, your hardware considerations are much simpler. The hardware has few options beyond peripherals and memory cards. PC developers, on the other hand, must determine their target configuration. This is an especially tricky balancing act. You don't want your game to appear outmoded on the latest hardware, and you also don't want to lose out on sales because only the most up-to-date systems will run it. Many developers start out by programming games on the PC because it is relatively inexpensive and easy to work on.

Most consoles such as the PlayStation 3 (shown) have development systems that connect to a PC.

Minimum Specification

All PC games include a minimum hardware requirement on the box. For planning purposes, you should usually target the top-selling high-end machine available on the market two years earlier than your anticipated release date. By that point, prices are low enough that many consumers will have upgraded. The *minimum specification* typically lists the required processor type, minimum processor speed, memory size, hard drive space, and supported video cards.

Sony Computer Entertainment America

PlayStation 3 cell processor.

Multiprocessor

The Sony PlayStation 3 (PS3) has a Cell Processor PowerPC core with seven CPUs. The Xbox 360 has three symmetrical IBM cores. For target platforms with multiple processors, the TDD should cover how these processors will be used. How will tasks be split across processors and how is communication between tasks handled? PC games also need to take into account multicore processors and be able to run on such systems (even if these processors are not leveraged for performance), since the more hard-core and tech-savvy players who own these systems will be vocal online if they cannot play your game!

Performance Goals

Wherever possible, quantify the expected performance of the game under normal conditions. Items to specify include:

- frame-rate (average, minimum, and peak)
- polygons per second (transformed, textured, and lit)
- maximum memory usage
- maximum load times
- maximum CPU load (per code module)
- compatibility (drivers, failsafes, fallbacks)

Profiling routines and third-party performance monitors should be utilized frequently to check current status against the goals.

Multiplayer and Internet

Gaming is often criticized as an antisocial activity, but online multiplayer gaming is a high growth area. *World of Warcraft* boasts over seven million subscribers playing on nearly 200 servers. Players chat with each other, trade gear, and form clans to battle monsters and complete quests.

Revenue from online games in 2005 was $1.15 billion, according to PricewaterhouseCoopers LLP. NPD estimates that more than 25% of console games sold in the United States in 2005 had online capabilities.

The TDD needs to consider all multiplayer interactions to define the communication protocol and establish constraints for the design. For instance, players of real-time strategy (RTS) games may be limited in the number of simultaneous units present on the battlefield.

Courtesy of Blizzard Entertainment, Inc.

Courtesy of Blizzard Entertainment, Inc.

World of Warcraft (action screen [left] from *The Burning Crusade* and server selection screen [right] shown) is the most successful massively multiplayer online role-playing game (MMORPG) to date.

Communication protocol needs to be defined. Will the architecture be client/server or peer-to-peer? Each has its own benefits and weaknesses. Client/server is more stable, less prone to hacking, and requires fewer messages (Internet traffic) than peer-to-peer. However, it requires a larger post-release investment in dedicated servers, and it is more complicated to implement than peer-to-peer. A game demo should be discussed in the TDD, along with the different likely beta phases (such as closed beta1, closed beta2, and open beta).

Multiplayer games require rigorous testing under a variety of conditions. You should conduct an online beta test period in order to work out the issues before selling the game. Many publishers fear that this may taint customer perceptions or lead to piracy. However, any multiplayer game that expects a community larger than 50 players can't be tested in the traditional manner. It must be tried by hundreds or, better yet, thousands of players with good reporting processes. The TDD should provide hooks for testing and procedures for managing the test process.

There are many questions that need to be asked and answered in the TDD:

- How many players will be supported?
- How will matchmaking take place?
- What happens when someone drops out of a game?
- How will latency or lost packets be dealt with?
- How will cheaters be detected and dealt with?
- Will there be support for clans, observers, and tournaments?

Multiplayer games generally enjoy a longer market life than solo play experiences. This is largely attributable to active online communities of players. The support of these communities requires coordination between marketing, customer service, technical support, and product development.

BioWare Corp.

Even the aliens have noticeable facial expressions in *Mass Effect*.

Graphics

The flashiest part of the technology is the portion that deals with getting pixels on the screen. The *graphics* system deals with creating and manipulating graphic objects, displaying objects, particle effects, lighting, textures, and managing user interface elements. A great deal of the TDD should describe the various graphic systems and define the data to be shared among them.

Artists and producers need to know the technical requirements for models and textures, while programmers should understand how the art assets will be used, as well as the degree of freedom the player has over the camera view.

The 3D Pipeline

The TDD should describe the 3D pipeline used to get objects onto the screen with each frame. Most games use the same basic pipeline with game-specific optimizations.

Diagram by Per Olin

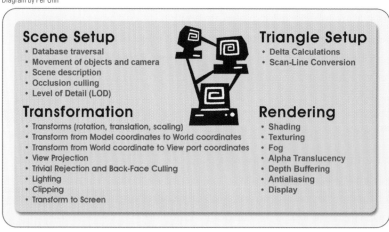

Scene Setup
- Database traversal
- Movement of objects and camera
- Scene description
- Occlusion culling
- Level of Detail (LOD)

Triangle Setup
- Delta Calculations
- Scan-Line Conversion

Transformation
- Transforms (rotation, translation, scaling)
- Transform from Model coordinates to World coordinates
- Transform from World coordinate to View port coordinates
- View Projection
- Trivial Rejection and Back-Face Culling
- Lighting
- Clipping
- Transform to Screen

Rendering
- Shading
- Texturing
- Fog
- Alpha Translucency
- Depth Buffering
- Antialiasing
- Display

A high-level outline of a typical pipeline involving scene setup, transformation, triangle setup, and rendering.

In the early 1990s, games implemented the 3D pipeline in software. Scenes were crude by today's standards, since the CPU had to do all the work. Now, much of the pipeline is handled by hardware, and 3D graphics cards accelerate transformation, lighting, and rasterization (rendering). This makes it possible for photorealistic scenes containing millions of polygons.

User Interface

The user interface includes all feedback given to the player during the course of game. From health bars to maps, from menu buttons to options screens, the TDD specifies the system for layout and editing of the interface. It also includes a description of the input mechanism—such as a keyboard, mouse, controller, or specialized peripheral. If the input mechanism is not already defined in the GDD, cross-referenced diagrams for each input device and their respective key/button mappings should be included in the TDD.

Art Tools

Various tools are required to create art assets or convert them into a form readily usable by the game. These include:

- Level editors
- Particle effects editors
- Geometry and/or scene converters
- Animation and object viewers

Programmers consult with the artists and designers to determine the functions needed by the tools and the optimal interface.

Sound

The TDD describes how music and sound effects will be encoded, stored, retrieved, and played in the game. This includes:

Microsoft Corporation

- Architecture (OpenAL, DirectSound, EAX)
- Encoding (MP3, AAC, WAV)
- Quality/Noise reduction (Dolby, THX)
- Sample rate (48kHz/1.14Mbps)
- Stereo vs. mono

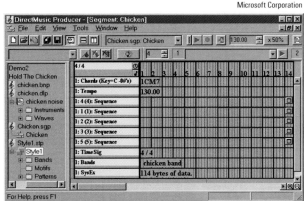

Games require hundreds if not thousands of sounds, from second-long sound effects to minutes-long musical soundtracks. The TDD should contain specifications for sound and estimates for memory and storage requirements.

Many excellent programs such as DirectMusic Producer are available for sound composition and editing.

The accompanying table outlines the uncompressed size of a 60-second sound sample at various resolutions and sampling rates.

Content from "Tricks and Techniques for Sound Effect Design" by Bobby Prince, presented at CGDC in March 1996. Diagram by Per Olin

Type	Mono	Mono	Stereo	Stereo
Resolution:	8 bit	16 bit	8 bit	16 bit
Sampling Rate				
44.1k	2646k	5292k	5292k	10584k
22.05k	1323k	2646k	2646k	5292k
11.025k	661.5k	1323k	1323k	2646k
8k	480k	960k	960k	1920k
7k	420k	840k	840k	1680k
6k	360k	720k	720k	1440k
5k	300k	600k	600k	1200k

Storage requirements for one minute of sound.

Localization

The TDD needs to identify the target territories and describe any issues or constraints for each. For instance, PAL is higher resolution (576 horizontal lines) than NTSC (480 horizontal lines), but NTSC updates the onscreen image more frequently than PAL (30 times per second versus 25 times per second). This affects the visible area on the screen as well as synchronization of sound and animation.

Games that compose text on the fly by inserting descriptive adjectives, such as "the bronze sword of fire," need to be reworked. Most Latin-based languages distinguish between masculine and feminine nouns and order their adjectives differently. Some languages (such as German) are more lengthy than English, and literal translations can run outside the boundaries of the screen or onscreen buttons. The TDD should describe the tools and procedures for isolating and updating the assets that need to be localized. Constraints need to specified, such as maximum character counts, safe areas for display, characters tied to movement, key positions on the keyboard (e.g. W,A,S,D), text embedded in graphical images, and differences in legal or technical nomenclature.

Nintendo

Text strings should be stored in separate files to ease localization (*Fire Emblem* shown). Never embed onscreen text in the code!

Research and Development

Chances are that one or more unique aspects of the game will require *research and development (R&D)* before they can be implemented. The TDD needs to identify the general approach and list related technologies for each element that requires R&D. Sufficient time should be allotted for engineers to arrive at a workable solution.

Design features and market events may require additional time for R&D. Revolutionary new features such as speech recognition need time to be implemented and refined before they can become part of the game. New console introductions also require more work, since game programmers have to make assumptions based on theoretical specifications and development hardware that is subject to change prior to release.

Technical Design Review (TDR)

Once the TDD is complete, it should be reviewed by senior engineers and technical directors as part of the *technical design review (TDR)* process. One or more of the reviewers should have expertise in a given field and not be a member of the development team. This is the time for objective feedback. It is better to hear about problems now before any code is written rather than months later when architectural changes are painful and costly.

Illustration by Ian Robert Vasquez

A typical TDD may be over a hundred pages. Reviewers should be given ample time to read the TDD and do their own research. Typically the review process is two weeks. The reviewers meet with the technical director on the project and the software engineers responsible for each major area. The goal is to make sure the plan is solid, so encourage the participants to ask tough questions and expect logical answers.

The outcome of the TDR should be a consensus that the TDD is sufficiently thorough and sound to proceed with production. If not, the authors need to address areas that are weak. The TDR should be confined to reviewing the technical plan, not the overall merits of the game design. This is handled during the green light meeting. The TDR should take place before the green light meeting so that the technical issues have all been worked out beforehand.

Prototype

The creation of a prototype or product vision demo is invaluable. It lets designers test their concepts before all the game code is written and all the assets are cre-

Sony Computer Entertainment America

ated. It establishes goals (visual, performance, sound) for the rest of the game. It gives publishers and marketers tangible proof of concept. Most importantly, it gives the team something to play with and help determine priorities for the rest of the game. If a prototype is contemplated, then the description of features to be implemented should be included in the TDD

flOw was prototyped in Flash on the PC.

> I prototype every concept I can, constantly. If the concept itself fails miserably I still have intimate knowledge of why it failed and what could have made it better.
>
> — *Jeff Stewart (Game Designer, Petroglyph Games)*

Prototyping Guidelines

It is my opinion that a game is made or broken in pre-production. If you exit your pre-production phase without a full understanding of what lies ahead, you are destined to hit a brick wall at high speed… and trust me, that hurts. Prototyping is a fundamental part of pre-production. It's a chance to test your assumptions, and see the results. It is necessary for a publisher to see what they are investing in, and it is necessary for the team itself to rally around. Prototyping also takes many forms. It isn't just building the proverbial "vertical slice." It also can take on smaller forms. The idea of rapid-prototyping to prove concepts can be equally beneficial, particularly early on. For example, one of my development teams is currently using a board game as a prototyping mechanism to see some of the game mechanics in action. This prototype will never have a life outside of the pre-production phase, but it has already proven invaluable to the team for illuminating issues that would otherwise not have been seen until they required reworking—thus saving the team both time and money.

> — *Graeme Bayless (Director of Production, Crystal Dynamics)*

Early, rapid, and constant prototyping is rule #1 with me. I believe it is the only way to make games that are truly fun, engaging, and have the right "feel." With all of the games I have directed, we build something playable as quickly as possible and start playing it daily. You quickly learn what works and what doesn't, and the experience serves as a catalyst for generating improvements, new kinds of game mechanics, and other enhancements to the actual game experience. Another very important effect of continuous prototyping is the ongoing engagement of the whole team in the process. Everyone plays the game, and therefore knows what game they are making, how all the parts fit together, and what the end goal is. Also, everyone gives feedback on the game which invariably results in new and useful ideas. I call this process "evolutionary game design." It is a process of constant and rapid build/test/review cycles and is extremely effective.

— *Mike Booth (Chief Executive Officer, Turtle Rock Studios)*

We try to do an early prototype of how one portion of a key game segment will look and feel as part of the preproduction process. This forces you to confront all the problems that completing one game segment requires you to figure out how to handle. Prototyping is the only known cure for "that'll-be-no-problem-itis" (also called "assumption consumption"), the most dangerous disease a producer can catch from team members. Some people have 1,000 excuses why *they* don't need to do prototypes, none of which should be listened to.

— *Don L. Daglow (President & CEO, Stormfront Studios)*

Everything important and/or unique in a game must be prototyped. Prototyping is an attitude more than a process, which is building material with a pre-understanding that it is intended to be discarded. This is often a difficult hump for people to get over, particularly artists for some reason. But every aspect of the game's movement, its art style, its camera system, animation, combat. . . . All of these elements MUST be prototyped before being committed to the design.

Prototyping allows a few things which cannot be done otherwise. First, it allows you to be scientific. You can test one element of the game at a time, in relative isolation, and see if it works. It's brutal to play through a completed level and just say "that sucks" and not have a clear idea why. Proper prototyping prevents this.

Also, prototyping can negate a lot of dependencies. If the technology, or the staff, or the style, or the story, or whatever is not ready yet, the team can still make forward progress because it's not trying to solve the game holistically, it's just digging at a specific element. This can keep things progressing in the early stages.

Finally, prototyping produces what is in effect the real game design: an interactive prototype is always superior to any document in communicating what the "look and feel" of the final game will be. No game should enter full production without this in place.

I have lately taken to structuring the prototyping (or pre-production) phase in terms of a list of questions to be answered. I actually write out these questions and post them in a conspicuous place. In my current project, the list ran to over one hundred specific questions to be answered during pre-production. Many of them are obvious (such as "how high does the character jump?") but thinking in terms of questions helps to focus the prototyping efforts, and gives everyone a clear sense of what has been achieved in the prototypes. The list of questions has to be a living document—answering one question inevitably reveals new questions—but the objective is to actually eliminate this document by the end of pre-production.

— *Michael John (Lead Designer, Method Games)*

Ghost Recon Advanced Warfighter: Customizing the Prototyping Process

Courtesy of Ubisoft Entertainment

We have implemented a new map prototype process to enhance gameplay and minimize production risks. Due to our production pipeline, and especially on next-gen consoles, our maps are huge and very complex. By prototyping maps early in our last-gen engine (or in a current engine for newer maps), we are able to play them quickly—finding key problems in concept or layout that raise red flags, as well as evaluating the fun factor. Making these changes early on, the rough prototype saves time and sweat later when the maps go into full production. This especially helped the multiplayer maps on Ghost Recon Advanced Warfighter—because it was our first title on the Xbox 360, there was enough risk in development without having to worry about needing to change the maps around at the last minute! Other elements, such as controls, movement, and various gameplay features all go through at least some level of prototype to evaluate fun, risk, and potential problems.

— *Christian Allen (Creative Director, Red Storm Entertainment)*

John Ahlquist on Prototypes :::::

John Ahlquist developed the tools and engine for Electronic Arts' *Command & Conquer: Generals - Zero Hour* and *The Lord of the Rings: Battle for Middle-Earth*. John currently runs Ahlquist Software—developing game software for a variety of clients. John previously worked for Altsys/Macromedia on Aldus FreeHand and was one of the creators of Macromedia Fireworks. Prior to Macromedia, John spent seven years working at Texas Instruments, programming Integrated Circuit CAD tools in the Design Automation Department. He is a second-degree black belt in Tae Kwon Do and has been playing video games since *Pong*.

John Ahlquist
(Founder, Ahlquist
Software)

I recommend that you always prototype games. The best games have been prototyped on several levels: first on paper with a written description of the game, and next on a tabletop with placeholders ranging from paper cutouts to scale models. Once the game engine is running, prototyping in a holodeck (simple empty level with a floor, perhaps four walls and a few props) lets artists and programmers evaluate and develop animations, AI behaviors, and effect sequences. Finally, I consider Alpha the final prototype; in a perfect world the dev team will have time to revise the Alpha twice to produce the final game. It doesn't often happen—but in my mind, it is the goal. Prototyping early and often is an important ingredient in a quality game.

The main goal of the TDD is to provide a written plan for implementing the design. Once a project is green-lighted and production begins, the information in the TDD gets outdated. It can become a full-time job for someone to update the TDD to reflect reality. Many established studios start out with well-defined TDDs but then, over time, fail to keep them up to date. This obviously doesn't stop good games from being published but it does make it more difficult to familiarize new programming team members with the plan.

The next chapter covers the essential documentation tools of the art and audio teams: the art style guide and sound design document.

:::CHAPTER REVIEW:::

1. Create a technical design document (TDD) for your original game idea. How does the TDD differ from a game design document (GDD)?

2. Choose three of the tools discussed in this chapter and research how each of them is used in the game production process. How does each tool relate to the project's content and the process itself, and which team members normally use them?

3. Why is prototyping such an important process in game development? In what ways can it be implemented successfully? What steps would you take to prototype your original game?

CHAPTER

5

Art & Sound Design

giving the game shape and emotion

Key Chapter Questions

- What are the components of the *art style guide (ASG)*?

- What are the stages in the *art production pipeline*?

- How and when do game artists utilize various *shading* techniques?

- What are the components of the *sound design document (SDD)*?

- How are *sound effects*, *music* and *dialogue* integrated into a game's sound design?

This section delves into two additional design documents: The art style guide (ASG) and the sound design document (SDD). These are not as widely used as the GDD and TDD, but they are gaining popularity as some next-gen teams take on Hollywood-style production values and methods.

Art Style Guide

The *art style guide* (ASG) describes the artistic approach for the game by identifying key art assets and establishing standards for art development. Games are their own worlds and they need to have a unique look. Some games, such as *Alien Hominid*, are highly stylized; others, such as the *SOCOM* series, are more photorealistic.

© 2004 the Behemoth

Sony Computer Entertainment America

Alien Hominid (left) uses a bright colors and cel-shaded style to convey its playful design, while *SOCOM III* (right) goes for photorealism in its lighting and textures to portray its serious subject matter.

The art director needs a well-established style guide to communicate the vision to the team. This is especially true for next-gen games where artwork is produced by large teams, sometimes approaching 100 or more.

:::::Art Jobs Overseas

© 2006 Indiagames

Emperor Ashoka is one of the first games produced entirely in India.

As next-gen games demand more visual assets, many developers are turning to overseas companies to take on a portion of art creation. India and Eastern Europe are popular locations due to their lower labor costs and growing base of skilled 3D modelers and animators. Differences in time zone, language, and culture increase the need for an all-encompassing style guide.

The ASG is created by the art director and used as a reference for the artists and animators on the project. Artists respond best to visual imagery. The guide should be short on words and long on images, including:

- Sketches and concept drawings
- Storyboards
- Color palettes and texture samples
- Digital photos of objects and environments
- Reference images or links to other games and other media including films, magazines, and websites

Mood

Each area of the game has a particular *mood*. This feeling is reinforced by the visual design. Light, color, and texture create a mood and help to tell a story. You can create dark and scary scenes by using a single light source such as a candle, campfire, or lantern. Cheery scenes, on the other hand, usually have lots of light and bright colors.

Courtesy of Ubisoft Entertainment

Sony Computer Entertainment America

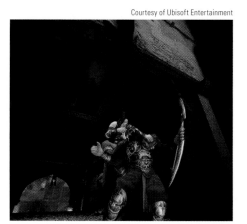 

Prince of Persia: The Two Thrones (left) contains dark chambers to create a sense of mystery and foreboding, while *Neopets: The Darkest Faerie* (right) contains open, sunny worlds to encourage kids to explore at their own pace.

The mood should match the design. If the mood or an area doesn't support the action that occurs within it, a player's suspension of disbelief is broken.

THQ Inc.

Warner Bros. has a very detailed style guide to ensure that *Scooby Doo! Unmasked* looks the same in all media.

Palette

Most delivery platforms are capable of displaying millions of colors. Some handheld devices and mobile phones are limited to an 8-bit palette or 256 colors. Even where this is not an issue, the style guide should include palettes for the major areas of the game. These indicate the colors that should be used to achieve the mood for each area. Licensed products may have a specific palette to be used for the characters of the game. This is to ensure that famous characters like Homer Simpson or Scooby Doo are consistent from cartoon to game.

Also consider whether the game will be viewed on an NTSC or PAL television set. Certain colors bleed or cause artifacts when they appear next to each other. Text that is legible on a PC monitor can be difficult to read if the text color is incompatible with the background.

Characters

Concept drawings should be included for the major *characters* in your game. These include both player characters (PCs) and non-player characters (NPCs). Show various poses and clothing options. For characters that need to be exact in all respects, the images should show multiple views: front, side, back, signature pose, and an action move. Include color images to establish proper color for hair, eyes, skin, and clothing.

Art by Mark Soderwall

Character concept drawings, such as these created by art director Mark Soderwall, should show multiple views and poses.

If the characters are based on real actors or licensed characters, reference photographs and images should be included in the style guide. Next-gen games require close-up views and realistic skin textures. These are best conveyed with photographs.

The game characters in *Harry Potter and the Goblet of Fire* need to match the likeness of the actors in the film.

Environments and Objects

Each major *environment* in the game should be described in the art style guide. Reference images (photographs, drawings, concept art) should be included to give a visual depiction of each environment. Overhead maps should indicate landmarks and points of interest during gameplay. Images of objects should be shown from different angles with player character silhouettes for proper scale. Define a world coordinate system to be used by all artists on the project so that all objects will be appropriately sized when imported into the game world.

World Coordinate System

Let's say that 1,000 world coordinate units = 10 feet in the real world. By convention, the lower left corner of a 3D space is X=0, Y=0. Human characters should be 600 units tall (maximum Y coordinate) and 200 units wide (maximum X coordinate). The modeler creates a space 600 tall and 200 wide to create the character. When it is placed in an environment, it will be scaled properly.

Sample Scenes

Sample scenes should be modeled, textured, lit, and rendered to indicate the target resolution, quality, and style of the final game. These images should represent what the game will look like when it is being played. They serve as benchmarks for the team. Model detail and texture resolution should be as accurate as possible; otherwise, the benchmark images may exceed the capabilities of the game software or delivery platform.

This medieval village from *Neverwinter Nights 2* is an example of a safe area where the player can rest, buy and sell goods, and gain information from villagers.

Image from a *Killzone* cinematic showing art direction and visual goal for the game.

Warcraft III: The Frozen Throne uses a control panel with icons for unit actions.

Guitar Hero II has an interface that looks like a guitar fret.

Icons

User interface options usually have onscreen buttons or indicators. These are portrayed as symbols or icons that represent an action or attribute. The style guide defines a consistent look, size, and position for the icons. The style of the icons should be consistent with the art direction for the game. Avoid embedding text in interface art, since most games are localized to different languages.

Menus

The game design document (GDD) should contain a flowchart of menus for the game. The art style guide expands on this by defining the look of the menus and buttons. It also provides information about transitions and animation. Menus usually have animated parts and may include streaming video for background visuals. The interface *is* the game for *Guitar Hero,* where players see a steady stream of cues.

Asset Lists and Dependencies

After reviewing the mission or level descriptions from the GDD, the art director or producer creates a list of visual assets for the game. This includes characters, creatures, buildings, vehicles, landmarks, props, signs, terrain, foliage, special objects, and effects.

Diagram by Per Olin

Asset ID	File	Description	Resolution	Anims	Scene / Mission	Dependencies	Clearance
100	TANK01	Medium Battle Tank Model	LOW	8	1+	0	n/a
101	TANK20	Heavy Battle Tank Model	LOW	8	3+	0	n/a
200	BRIDGE01	Trestle Bridge Model	HIGH	1	5	0	n/a
220	TUNNEL01	Tunnel Opening	HIGH	1	5	200	n/a
303	TRAIN44	GE AC4400 Locomotive	LOW	8	5	200	Release on file: GE
501	FXCAN01	Tank Firing FX anim	LOW	120	1+	101,102	n/a
515	FXTRN01	Train Explosion	LOW	240	5	303	n/a

Sample art asset list for a scene in a military game

The target resolution should be indicated. In some cases, models at different resolutions, low and high, may be required for viewing at distance and close up.

The list should indicate where each asset will be used, along with any interdependencies (e.g., train, trestle bridge, tunnel opening, and explosion effects are all required for the bridge explosion). During the scheduling phase, the asset list becomes a task list, since each asset is assigned to one or more artists for completion.

Real-world objects and characters should be noted so that legal clearances can be obtained. This process can take months and may require a substitute if permission isn't granted.

Art Production Pipeline

Art typically goes through the following stages:

1. Description – text describing character
2. Concept drawing – pencil sketch of character
3. Storyboard (Cinematics) – pencil sketch panels (3) showing character firing a gun in a scene
4. Placeholder art – human model with no textures (FPO)
5. Modeling and animation rigging – human wireframe with IK skeleton
6. Texturing – textured human model
7. Shading – shaded model
8. Lighting – lit model
9. Animation – moving model with constraints
10. Effects – flames/smoke particles added

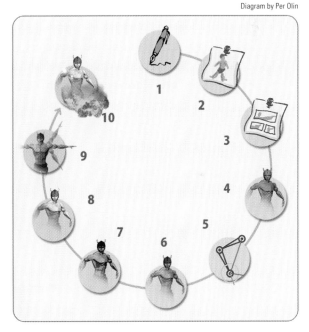

Diagram by Per Olin

A typical art production pipeline showing the various stages for the creation of an object in the game as described in this section.

Description

Art is initially described in the GDD. More detailed descriptions may appear in the style guide. It is the responsibility of the art director or producer to identify all the art elements needed for the game. If descriptions are inadequate, they need to be defined. Nothing is more painful for an artist than to throw away weeks of work because the art doesn't fit the game's needs.

Art by Mark Soderwall

Concept Drawings

Major objects such as characters, creatures, vehicles, and buildings should have concept drawings. These are reviewed by the art director and the game designer prior to modeling. In the case of licensed properties, these may require licensor approval, which can take 2-3 weeks, so it's important to schedule sufficient time to allow for review and changes.

Set of concept drawings showing detail progression, created by art director Mark Soderwall.

Storyboards

Cinematics and in-game *cut-scenes* are described via *storyboards*. These panels should match the aspect ratio of the target platform. Each panel is a scene from the script showing the characters, action, and camera movement (e.g., pan, zoom, and tilt). The dialogue and scene numbers should be excerpted from the script for reference. Since the storyboards are derived from the script, the script must be finalized before the storyboards are.

Sony Computer Entertainment America

Shot 01G

NARRATOR: ...it would finally come to an end.

Shot 01H

NARRATOR: Death would be his final escape from madness.

Shot 01I

Dominus' POV slamming down towards rocks.

Cut to black.

Storyboard panel from *God of War*.

Storyboards lack timing information that is critical for pacing. An *animatic* is a movie that incorporates frames from the storyboard and/or wireframe models synchronized with a scratch soundtrack. The soundtrack includes a read-through of the script and some sound effects and placeholder music. The animatic allows you to work out timing issues.

Placeholder Art

Art by Jason Bramble

Complicated objects or scenes may have associated placeholder art so that programmers and designers can get a mission running and playable while waiting for the final art to be completed. This may involve only simple spheres or cylinders, or, in the case of characters, a single untextured human figure. Some artists use a texture containing the phrase "FPO" to indicate that the model is for placement only. This avoids confusion among reviewers when there's a mixture of final art and works-in-progress.

Simple placeholder art can be used in a game while the final art is being completed.

Handling Placeholder Art and Sound

Placeholder art (models/textures) and sound should be strongly differentiated from actual game assets by content and filename. The game should auto-insert placeholder assets for missing game assets, especially to prevent crashes. The game should call out (onscreen and debug log) when it uses all placeholder assets so that they can be removed/replaced. Much of this is a TDD issue.

— *Frank T. Gilson (Senior Developer of Digital Games, Wizards of the Coast)*

Modeling

Once concepts have been approved, the modeler creates a 3D model of the object. This is typically done using off-the-shelf tools such as Maya or 3D Studio Max. Models may be defined using *spline curves* or as *polygonal meshes*. A spline curve defines the control points for a curved surface and the type of line connecting the points. The surface is filled in during rendering time. This representation is easily

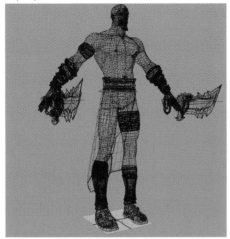

Wireframe model of Kratos from *God of War*.

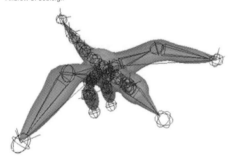

Simple model of a bird showing the animation rigging (black lines).

scaled to various sizes and levels of detail without altering the geometry. A polygonal mesh defines a surface as a network of patches, usually triangles. Increasing the size of an object requires that more triangles be added to its surface. It's important for the modeler to know the target resolution so that each object has the ideal number of vertices. If a model is too complex, it will slow down performance and may have to be simplified.

Animation Rigging

Once the model is complete, it is rigged for *animation*. The rigging is an internal skeleton that defines where joints will bend and how far they can bend and turn. The animators will refine this later as they create detailed movements.

Texturing

The *texture* is the skin of the 3D model, a 2D bitmap image that is mapped onto the surface of the 3D model. Complex objects, such as characters, are composed of multiple textures. The regions where textures meet are called *seams*. A lot of effort on both the programming and art sides goes into making the seams realistic.

The resolution requirements for each model dictate the texture size. The individual pixels in a texture are called *texels*. The highest resolution texture ratio is one texel per pixel on the screen.

Texture size affects the details within each object of the game and the surrounding environment. The higher the texture size, the more details you can see. Memory limitations prevent artists from using high-resolution textures on everything. Trade-offs must be made so that the overall scene looks convincing. Typical textures are 256×256. High-resolution textures are 1024×1024 or greater. Compression can be used to fit more textures into memory.

The art style guide should contain sample textures for game environments and objects, and guidelines for texture resolution. Characters and items that the camera needs to zoom in on should have high-resolution textures if possible. Small props and items seen from a distance should have lower-resolution textures.

Mipmaps

Mipmaps are alternate, lower-resolution versions of a texture. The process of wrapping an object with a texture, lighting it, shading it, and then drawing it on screen is handled by a *renderer*. During gameplay, the renderer switches the texture to an alternate mipmap to reduce rendering time and artifacts. Filtering is also employed to reduce aliasing.

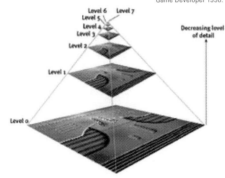

Sample of mipmap images.

Baked Lighting

Sometimes the shadows and highlights are drawn into the texture. This saves time for complex light and shadow calculations during gameplay. This technique, called *baking*, is usually used only when the lighting for a scene is fixed and the object doesn't move. Typical applications are buildings for real-time environments.

Shading

Shading determines how an object reflects light. Techniques include:

- Flat shading
- Bump mapping
- Normal mapping
- Parallax mapping
- Cel shading

In *Star Trek Online,* the running lights on the ships are baked in; they're part of the light maps and not calculated in real time.

Flat shaded model of Kratos from *God of War*.

Flat Shading

The simplest shading technique is known as *flat shading*. Objects that are flat shaded have no texture. A single color is applied to each polygon of the model, and shade is determined based on light sources. This results in an unrealistic, segmented model. Most games use more sophisticated techniques likes bump mapping, normal mapping, and parallax mapping.

Bump Mapping

The *surface normal* is the vector perpendicular to a surface or face at any point. In *bump mapping*, the surface normal for each polygon is perturbed using a texture map (bump map) prior to lighting. This results in a more detailed surface without changing the underlying geometry. It can give the appearance of depth or texture to an otherwise smooth surface.

Normal Mapping

Normal mapping is similar to bump mapping, but it actually replaces the normal rather than just perturbing it. A high-resolution version of the model is often used to generate the normal map, which is then applied to a lower-resolution model.

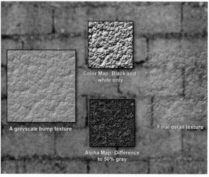

A gray scale bump map is used to create an alpha blended detail texture.

Normal mapping gives the appearance of rich detail without actually modeling it in *Quake 4*.

Parallax Mapping

Parallax mapping alters the appearance of the texture as the camera changes position. This is accomplished by using a height map to displace the texture coordinates so that the texture occludes itself. Otherwise-flat surfaces appear to have more depth and realism.

Cel Shading

Cel shading is a specialized shading technique that makes 3D objects appear like hand-drawn cartoons. It is utilized to give games a comic book or cartoon look. *Ultimate Spiderman* includes comic book frames and action overlays to support this style. This creates a greater connection to the original comic license. Games such as *Viewtiful Joe* and *Alien Hominid* use this style to buck the trend of hyperrealism.

Shading is an efficient way to bring detail and character to a scene. Realism or style is accomplished using software algorithms rather than geometry.

Realistic water surfaces in *Pacific Fighters* are actually "visual tricks" using parallax mapping.

Ultimate Spiderman has a cartoon look despite being 3D. This is a example of a cel-shaded character.

Viewtiful Joe has a playful, hand-drawn look.

Lighting

Light sources must be specified for each scene in the game. There is an overall *ambient light* source that is applied to all objects during rendering. Ambient light doesn't create shadows, since there is no direction associated with it. The artist defines both the brightness and color of ambient light.

Courtesy of Ubisoft Entertainment

The lighting and visual effects in *FarCry Instincts* make the jungle come alive.

Directional lights have uniform intensity and direction. They do not have falloff. These are used to simulate sunlight and may be used as the key light for a scene.

Point lights emit light from a single point in all directions. Examples include candle flames and light bulbs. Like ambient light they have a brightness and color, but include a falloff or range.

Spot lights are a conical beam of light. Examples include headlights and searchlights. They may be static (fixed position) or dynamic (moving).

Animation

University of Cambridge

A wireframe model showing a simple walk cycle.

Once objects have been rigged with a skeleton and joints, the animator creates the various *movements*. Each movement is described in an animation list. Storyboards are used to show the key frames of the movement. Some movements like walking or running are looped so that they repeat; these are called cycles. Character movements must blend together so that the transition from a walk to a run to a leap is smooth and natural looking. When characters are standing still they need to have idle motions. These may be simple movements such as fidgets, head turns, or arms crossing. This motion keeps the character from looking rigid and fake. Signature moves are used to give a character more personality or to distinguish one character from others. In fighting games, the signature moves are associated with special attacks or kills.

Sony Computer Entertainment America

Flowing hair and intense particle effects are trademarks of *Heavenly Sword*.

Special Effects

Special effects are applied last. These include flowing hair, flaming torches, billowing capes, and smoking shotguns. These require extra processing power so they are usually reserved for special characters and "money shots." The effects help sell the realism of a scene.

Video Resolution and Aspect Ratio

The *video resolution* is the actual number of pixels—horizontal by vertical—that can be displayed in a single frame. Video resolution determines the level of detail for the scene.

The *aspect ratio* defines the ratio of image width to height. *High-definition television* (HDTV) supports a widescreen aspect ratio of 16:9. The highest standard, 1080p, is 1920 x 1080 or about 2.07 million pixels per frame. Most CRT monitors have an aspect ratio of 4:3, however, most 17" PC monitors can support 1920 x 1080p.

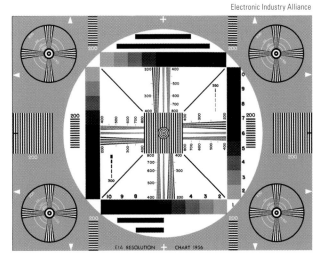

Electronic Industry Alliance

EIA 1956 standard test pattern for video resolution.

Video resolution must be considered in the style of the art. Low-resolution displays will not be a good match for photorealistic imagery.

The art style guide should contain a storyboard template that matches the aspect ratio of the target platform. Camera placement and environment layout should take into account both aspect ratio and resolution. Close-ups will look jagged in low resolution. Panoramic shots are well suited for 16:9 aspect ratio.

Diagram by Per Olin

Platform	Maximum Resolution
PlayStation 3	1920 x 1080
Xbox 360	1920 x 1080
PlayStation Portable	480 x 272
Nintendo DS	256 x 192
PC (high-end videocard)	2560 x 1600
NTSC TV	640 x 480
PAL TV	768 x 576

This table summarizes the maximum resolution for various platforms.

Diagram by Per Olin

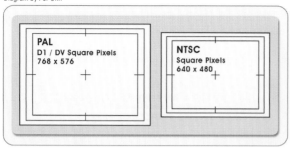

PAL
D1 / DV Square Pixels
768 x 576

NTSC
Square Pixels
640 x 480

Older televisions crop the edges from the screen, so important images need to stay within the safe area.

Safe Area

Both NTSC and PAL TVs contain a portion of the screen that may not be viewable. The *safe area* is the area of the television picture that can be seen on all TVs. Older TVs have a much smaller safe area than newer flat panel and LCD TVs. It is important to place onscreen text and user interface items within the safe area so that they can be seen completely. All storyboards in the ASG should include the safe area and any margins reserved for letterbox.

Sound Design Document

Games would be pretty boring without audio. Sound is used to give positive confirmation of player actions. Even the first *Pong* game had a simple "bleep" sound effect as the paddle struck the ball. Sound evokes emotion. Fast-paced music reinforces the intensity of battles and races; players can be scared by suspenseful music leading up to a surprise.

The sound designer needs to determine the style of the music for the game, which parts of the game should have music, and how sound transitions throughout the experience. The sound design document (SDD) needs to describe the elements of music and sound that will be needed for the game.

Aaron Marks on the Importance of an Audio Plan :::::

Aaron Marks
(President, On
Your Mark Music
Productions)

Practically falling into the game industry seven years ago, Aaron Marks has amassed music and sound design credits on touch screen arcade games, class II video bingo/slot machines, computer games, console games—and over 70 online casino games. Aaron has also written for *Game Developer Magazine*, Gamasutra, and Music4Games.net. He is the author of *The Complete Guide to Game Audio*, an expansive book on all aspects of audio for video games. He is also a member of the advisory board for the Game Audio Network Guild (GANG)—and he continues his pursuit of the ultimate soundscape, creating music, and sound for various projects.

Historically, audio is the last asset to be completed in the game development process, and it's often almost an afterthought. Creating a game is a very dynamic undertaking, and plans continuously change. Having at least a solid idea about how much music is needed, how many different themes are desired, what objects will require sound effects and how dialogue will be involved in the story is a huge step in the process. By the end of the production cycle, most of it will have changed entirely but knowing this going in will still allow the audio content creators to be gainfully employed and able to meet their milestones despite the evolving requirements.

I work better when I'm brought in early, as part of the team and as part of the decision making process. And when this happens, I feel the game is better for it. Being hired in the last two weeks of a game and coming into it completely cold will almost guarantee one third of the game experience is going to suffer. Having a plan early on is the key.

Sound Effects

Sound is every bit as important as gameplay and art. Good *sound design* enhances the game by giving it emotional depth. Many studios have full-time sound designers who work alongside game designers, software engineers, and artists to create sounds that correspond with the action on the screen. While much of their time is spent creating sound effects, they may also compose music or record voice-overs.

Every interaction between the characters and their environment and between the player and the interface is reinforced by *sound effects*. From footsteps, to explosions, to button clicks, games have literally thousands of sounds. The sound designer defines a list of all sound effects in the game and where they are intended to be used. The art asset list is a good place to start, but many more sounds need to be created.

Sound effects can help give direction to a player in areas that would otherwise be confusing. The groan of a beast behind a locked door or the dripping of water in a dark basement both provide hints to the player. Keep in mind that sounds take memory space and may require processing power if they are to be blended or positioned in 3D space. The sound design defines the quality of the sound effects by describing the compression scheme to be used.

Sound effects are emitted from an object or character in the game or from an invisible source. They have range and may have a 3D volume. Some

Bungie Studios

Halo 2 won the award for best sound design from the Academy of Interactive Arts and Sciences.

games describe the materials for surfaces and objects so that the sound effects can be altered accordingly. For example, horse hooves in mud vs. concrete or metal bar vs. baseball bat against a steel door. Sound effects are blended in real-time so that they can be heard over the soundtrack.

© (P) 2004 Microsoft Corporation

Legendary composer Danny Elfman wrote the theme for *Fable*.

Soundtrack

The *soundtrack* is the underlying sound throughout an area or sequence in the game. It may be a musical score or a collection of ambient environmental sounds. Orchestral soundtracks are gaining popularity in games. These are composed, arranged, performed, and recorded in the same manner as theatrical scores. Games may require many more hours of music than movies. Soundtracks are stored on the game's media, usually DVD, and streamed from the disc during gameplay.

The sound designer or audio director needs to describe the various soundtracks and where they will be used. Mood and tempo should match the look and pacing of the game. The design should also note where soundtracks need to be looped or blended into each other. Some games have dynamic soundtracks that switch the music to match the tempo of the current game action.

Adaptive Audio

Some sound designers create *adaptive audio* that changes in response to player actions. This form of sound design requires more technical design so that the audio transitions properly as the player makes choices or moves about the environment, often changing direction and backtracking. Composers working with adaptive audio often write several versions of a particular musical cue, each of which can be triggered by a particular player action; each of these versions blends in seamlessly from the cue that came just before it. Think of adaptive audio as story branching with sound!

WAV vs. MIDI

WAV files are premixed sound effects or soundtracks. They are linear and not adaptable, although game software can select and transition between WAV files to produce adaptable results. The quality can be exceptional, since these sounds are recorded and mixed using standard methods.

MIDI files are more adaptable because each individual note can be manipulated on the fly during run-time of the game. MIDI soundtracks in older games tend to sound alike. Newer games have customized instrument banks to create more variation.

Voiceover

The sound designer or producer is responsible for identifying voiceover needs. Just like sound effects, the sound designer must work out the quality level of the voice. Voiceover is usually streamed so memory usage is not as big an issue. After reviewing the script, the sound designer creates a list of characters and lines. Some parts are minor and a single voiceover actor may be able to play two or three different characters. The next step is to cast the various characters. This can be handled by auditioning talent or enlisting a casting agency. Typical recording sessions take two to four hours per actor. There are two or three takes for each line so that the sound designer has a few choices; sometimes all of these takes are utilized within

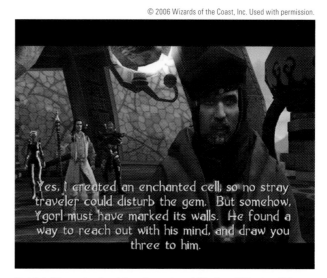

Patrick Stewart voiced the character of Khelban "Blackstaff" Arunsun in *Demon Stone*.

the game for variety, especially if character dialogue (such as a greeting) is triggered each time the player bumps into a particular NPC. Remember that dialogue can be nonlinear, and it does not appear only in cinematics! Be sure to contract ahead for pickup sessions to occur later in the project so that lines that need to be altered or redone can be recorded without delay.

Art & Sound Design: giving the game shape and emotion

chapter 5

Outsourcing Localized Dialogue

Games that rely heavily on vocal elements will require extensive rework, which can become a little tricky. Unless your sound designer understands the localized language, you'll end up outsourcing the entire project to a company who does, which is usually a company within the country you are localizing to. They will be responsible for translating scripts, hiring new actors, recording sessions, editing the final audio and possibly having an involvement with the implementation of these new assets. No matter how well they may speak English and understand what you wish to accomplish, there are always unexpected roadblocks because of the language barrier; finding a third party who can review the work and give an unbiased opinion is an essential addition to the process.

— *Aaron Marks (President, On Your Mark Music Productions)*

Main characters are often played by well-known screen actors or voice talent. These actors are contracted separately and may require special sessions to work around their busy schedule. The cost for famous actors is lower than that for films but it is on the rise as games gain popularity. If you intend to use the actor's name to promote your game, even if it is just on the box, you will need to contract for those rights separately from the performance rights.

The SDD is as vital to a quality game as the GDD, TDD, and ASG. Sound designers need a game that is near alpha, with all animations complete, in order to create the best synchronization between sound and action. Unfortunately, this is an area that is often shorted when games run behind schedule. Allow sufficient time for sound design and don't let other aspects of the production rob that time.

Localization and Dialogue

Localization usually involves substitution of the voice tracks. Once the script is recorded, the sound designer should provide the asset ID, length, and dialogue for each line spoken. Character descriptions and sample recordings also help the localization team to properly cast their actors.

L.A.S.T.

Late audio sounds terrible (LAST) is an acronym that most sound designers use to remind their producers to plan ahead for sound.

It's important for artists and sound designers to know "the hook" for the game, the one special element that sets a game apart from every other game. It is embodied in the high concept and USPs, and it is also reinforced by the game design, art, and sound. Visuals and sounds that fail to support the design create discontinuity, breaking a player's suspension of disbelief. A 3D model may look stunning by itself, and a soundtrack may be memorable when played, but if these elements don't fit the game, they will wreck the experience for the player. Producers should involve artists and sound designers in the planning process. This ensures continuity, and it also enhances the end result. Game designers benefit by collaborating with programmers, artists, and sound designers. This creative feedback results in better games.

The next chapter deals with the final step in the preproduction planning process. This is where producers pull the various plans together and formulate a tactical plan for developing the game.

1. Create an art style guide (ASG) and/or a sound design document (SDD) for your original game idea. What are the unique components of these documents?

2. How are modeling, texturing, and animation techniques used in game art? How are music, sound effects, and dialogue used in game audio?

3. In what ways can art and audio enhance mood, increase immersion, and provide feedback to the player?

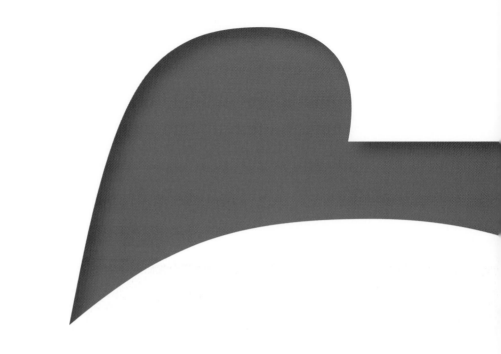

CHAPTER

6

Production Plan

bringing order to chaos

Key Chapter Questions

- What are the components of a production plan?
- What are the various roles and responsibilities of the development team?
- What are the different forms of testing and when should they take place?
- Why are scheduling and budgeting important?
- What are the key parts of a budget?

The final stage of pre-production is the creation of the production plan. This document is the "owners manual" for the project management of the game. It provides the final reality check before the game goes into production. Could this game actually get done on time, on budget, *and* provide a return on investment?

The purpose of the production plan is to show that the game can be built on time and follow the game design document (GDD). In addition, there should be sufficient analysis to support the proposition that the game can be produced within budget and provide at least its target return on investment.

The production plan is authored by the producer of the game. It consists of a staffing plan, project schedule, budget, and financial analysis. The game design document (GDD) describes what the game is. The technical design document (TDD) describes how the game is built. The art style guide and sound design describe how the game will look and sound. The production plan describes the strategy for developing the game.

Phases of Game Development

The accompanying table outlines the various activities associated with bringing a game from concept to completion. The column labeled Primary indicates the persons responsible for overseeing and approving an activity. The Secondary column shows the people responsible for contributing to the activity.

As you can see, the producer oversees all phases—but team management is shared with the directors and leads for each discipline. Programming, art, design, sound, and testing managers need to have good "people skills," and a general awareness of each discipline and how they depend upon one another.

::::: *NFL Street*: Avoiding the Death March

Electronic Arts

One of the best experiences of my career was on the first NFL Street game. We had a difficult challenge in that we not only had to build a plan to deliver a great game on time, but we had to do so while building a prototype that would convince the executives that the game was worth doing. This created some really interesting challenges for planning, not the least of which was that we needed to do the opposite of what you normally would do... we actually pushed some of our riskiest components to the back of the schedule and frontloaded our high-visual impact components instead. This allowed us to get a fully playable and polished-looking game up and running fairly early (months before alpha), which allowed us to actually get approval to finish the game. The costs were real... we had to scramble at the end with the high-risk elements we'd left until late... but I was blessed with such a strong team that we were able to pull it all together and deliver a great game... on-time. All through this project, we stayed on top of the planning well enough that we never had the team enter a death march, and we were able to see every risk coming and properly adjust to meet it.

— *Graeme Bayless (Director of Production, Crystal Dynamics)*

Concept	Primary / Approver	Secondary / Contributor
High concept, premise, game description, USPs	Design Director	Designers, Writers, Producer
Edit/format proposal, estimated budget and schedule	Producer	Associate Producers
Concept art, storyboard(s), presentation (Powerpoint slides, reference video and images)	Art Director	Artists
Review of concept, interactive mockup	Technical Director	Programmers
Pitch to publisher/management	Design Director, Producer	Art Director, Technical Director

Pre-Production	Primary / Approver	Secondary / Contributor
Game Design	Creative Director	Designers
Technical Design	Technical Director	Programmers
Art Style Guide	Art Director	Artists, Animators
Sound Design	Audio Director	Sound Designers
Production Plan	Producer	Associate Producers

Production	Primary / Approver	Secondary / Contributor
Naming conventions, asset database	Programming Lead, Art Lead, Design Lead, Sound Lead	Programmers, Artists, Designers, Sound Designers
Engine code, Game code, Tools, Installer (PC), Security / Encryption, Multiplayer code	Technical Director, Lead Programmers	Programmers
Concept sketches, 3D models, Textures, Lighting, Scene descriptions, Storyboards	Art Director	Artists
Code/asset revision control and build procedures, Software task schedule	Lead Programmer	Associate Producer, Programmers
Concept sketches, Scene descriptions, Storyboards	Art Director	Concept Artists, Illustrators
3D models	Lead Model Artist	Model Artists
Textures, Bump maps, Normal maps	Lead Texture Artist	Texture Artists
Shaders	Art Director	Lead Artist, Lead Programmer
Lighting	Art Director	Lead Artist
Character and in-game object animation	Lead Animator	Animators
GUI / Menus	Art Director, Design Director	Interface Designer, GUI Artists, GUI Programmer
Character / Enemy / NPC designs ' Balance	Design Director	Character / Unit Designers
Missions / Levels	Single Player Design Lead, Design Director, Art Director (for look)	Level Designers, Artists, Programmers (for special scripting)
Multiplayer maps and Multiplayer balance	Multiplayer Design Lead, Design Director	Designers
Voice-over (V/O) script	Design Director, Audio Director	Writer, Designers
Music soundtrack, sound effects	Audio Director	Sound Designer, Musicians, Composers
Cinematics	Cinematics Director, Art Director	Model Artists, Animators, Artists, Sound Designers, Video Editors
Schedules, Tracking, Status Reporting, Interdisciplinary Communication, Milestone Preparation, Contracts, Team Management, "Firefighting"	Producer	Associate Producers, Lead Programmer, Lead Designer, Lead Artist, Lead Animator, Audio Director

Post-Production (Beta to Release)	Primary / Approver	Secondary / Contributor
Bug fixing	Producer, Lead Programmer	Programmers, Designers, Artists, Sound Designers
Quality Assurance Testing	Q/A Director	Q/A Testers
Gameplay Testing	Producer, Design Director	Gameplay Testers, Associate Producers
Localization	Producer, Audio Director (V/O), Lead Programmer	Associate Producers, Sound Designers, Programmers, Artists (for text embedded in textures and GUI)

Activities associated with bringing a game from concept to completion.

Staffing Plan

Both the GDD and TDD should provide enough information to determine the scope of the project. This will, in turn, dictate the size of the team necessary to produce the game. The staffing plan provides an estimate of staff size, by role, throughout all phases of production. Typical projects start with a core team for concept development. Once a project is green-lighted, the team expands to complete the GDD, TDD, art style guide, sound design, production plan, tools, and possibly a playable prototype.

	Concept			Pre-Production					Production			
	Jan 06	Feb 06	Mar 06	Apr 06	May 06	Jun 06	Jul 06	Aug 06	Sep 06	Oct 06	Nov 06	Oct 06
Producer	1	1	1	1	1	1	1	1	1	1	1	1
Assistant Producers	1	1	1	2	2	2	2	2	3	3	3	3
Associate Producers									2	2	2	2
Design Director	1	1	1	1	1	1	1	1	1	1	1	1
Designers	2	2	2	5	5	5	5	5	8	8	8	8
Technical Director	1	1	1	1	1	1	1	1	1	1	1	1
Software Engineers	2	2	2	5	5	5	5	5	10	10	10	10
Art Director	1	1	1	1	1	1	1	1	1	1	1	1
Artists	3	3	3	5	5	5	5	5	15	15	15	15
Audio Director	1	1	1	1	1	1	1	1	1	1	1	1
Audio Engineers				1	1	1	1	1	2	2	2	2
Q/A Director, Testers									1	1	1	1
Staff Headcount	13	13	13	22	22	22	22	22	44	44	44	44

Headcount excerpt from a staffing plan.

The *staffing plan* lists the full-time staff required. This staff may be augmented by third-party contractors. Some contractors are project duration employees who work on-site using studio resources under the direction of studio personnel. These project duration employees should be included in the staffing plan. External contractors are hired for a specific deliverable and they work in their own facility. These external contractors should appear in the budget and their deliverables in the task list.

Labor is the largest expense on a project, so the staffing plan provides the first estimate of the overall project cost. The next steps are the task list, schedule, and finally the budget. There is a lot of back and forth between these steps, and you should expect to revise the staffing plan to fit the needs of the schedule and budget.

Schedule/Budget Mismatches

Dealing with schedule/budget mismatches is unique to each project. Factors such as the publisher, market conditions, and team morale dictate what type of response to take. If the game turns out to be a bad idea, kill it as early as possible. If the game is harder and more expensive to make, time to start selling to the publisher again.

— *Rich Adam (CEO, Mine Shaft Entertainment, Inc.)*

Roles and Responsibilities

At this point, we should cover the various roles and responsibilities of the development team. Each team member has one or more responsibilities. Good teams are versatile but understand and respect the need to have well-defined roles.

Producer and Management Team

Project leadership is provided by the *producer,* who is the information conduit between the production team and the publisher. Producers report progress and follow up on issues as they arise. They are also responsible for getting the game done on schedule, within budget, and as close to the vision expressed in the GDD as possible.

In large projects, there may be additional associate producers (APs) to oversee specific areas of production. Typical areas of specialization for APs include art production, level design, localization, online/multiplayer interface, cinematics, audio, and licensor/publisher communications.

Design Director and Design Team

A producer is not responsible for designing the game. This is the job of the *design director.* Other positions with similar responsibilities include creative director, game director, or lead designer. The design director holds the vision of the game and is the principal contributor to the GDD.

EA's *Madden* series (*NFL 07* shown) is tightly managed to ensure release at the beginning of each year's football season.

The design director is the person the team goes to for additional information as the game is being developed. This last point is important. Some designers make it up as they go along, resulting in costly overruns and unpredictable quality. Other designers rigidly follow the GDD even when actual implementation turns out to be less than fun to play. A good design director has a solid plan but knows how to make changes to improve the game.

Design directors are responsible for making the game fun. They may oversee the design team, although this task is sometimes handled by an assistant producer, depending on the management abilities of the design director. In large projects, the design director should not be bogged down with administrative duties but should still have the respect of the team when it comes to making creative decisions.

Core Responsibilities of the Producer

While the role of producer does differ from one company to the next, there is a core set of responsibilities that seem to be universal... producers, simply, are "the glue". They facilitate... they communicate... they track... they push and prod... they scrounge resources... they look ahead when everyone else is looking down... they cheerlead... they smooth feathers... and a variety of other short descriptors that touch upon the same basic thing. Also, much like glue, a great producer is invisible... doing their fantastic work behind the scenes, and making everything run so well that you hardly know they are there. I guess the best way I can describe the job of a producer is this... they are responsible for making everyone else more effective. If a game project went well, you can be assured there was a great production team at work. If a project met deadlines and/or didn't require a multi-month death march... you can be certain a great production team was somewhere in the mix. Producers generally don't create the content... they support the work of those who do, and make it easier for them to do so. I guess you could take a twist on the old adage and say that behind every great artist/programmer/designer is a great producer. While those great creative people can make content without producers, they rarely can do so as effectively and painlessly as when they are properly supported.

— *Graeme Bayless (Director of Production, Crystal Dynamics)*

The producer of a video game has too many hats to wear them all effectively. Therefore, the producer must build a management team to share the broad spectrum of work that faces a game producer. The producer must be able to sell the game to a large and diverse constituency. First, the manufacturer and publisher must approve the game. This is a massive sales effort that most projects do not survive. Once approved, the game must be staffed. The producer must hire the senior managers for each of the disciplines required for the product. I have always had a large say in every hire for the projects that I have produced. The leads are part of the process, but I like to architect the team I work with. Minimally this is programmers, designers, and artists. Other specialists might also be needed such as writers, live action film expertise, physicists, etc. Each of these team members must also be sold on the vision for the game. Each of these disciplines breeds tendencies toward certain personality traits. These diverse personalities are not always congruous. The producer must be VERY good at managing personalities to keep the team a team. In addition, my experience has taught me that people with large talent frequently have large personalities. Again a personality management challenge. The vision for a game is constantly under attack from multiple fronts. Budget miscues, personnel issues, creative interference from publisher-management-licensor-tester-spouse, technical barriers, unrealized fun factor in feature X, market competition, neutrino storms, etc., any and all of these can crop up at any moment. Dealing with these factors and making decisions to protect the core fun, and the creative vision of the game is what great producers manage well. What a great producer does is to create a shared vision amongst a diverse set of constituencies, and motivate those people to agree to work together to create that shared vision.

— *Rich Adam (Chief Executive Officer, Mine Shaft Entertainment)*

Some design directors may contribute aspects of the game's implementation directly, or, as in large projects, they may review and provide direction to the team on an ongoing basis. The design team consists of level designers, scripters, interface designers, writers, researchers, and game tuners.

Level designers create the levels or missions in a game. They use licensed or proprietary level editors to build the environment by placing objects created by the art team. Sometimes they also utilize programs such as 3D Studio Max and Maya to integrate assets. They create the boundaries for the level and establish what is in it.

Sony Computer Entertainment America

God of War has won many awards for game design.

Scripters define the behavior of NPCs and specify events for a given level. They either write code, like programmers, or use a proprietary game editor to create game logic. They define what takes place in a level.

Interface designers work closely with artists and programmers to define the control scheme for the player. This includes defining onscreen buttons and menus and the flow of control in the game. They map controller buttons to game functions. Interface designers also provide feedback systems for the player. Feedback may be:

- Visual: onscreen status information, e.g., health meter, overhead map
- Auditory: sound effects accompanying player input or actions
- Touch: vibration of the controller

Writers and researchers provide dialogue and background information, respectively. This gives the game depth and authenticity.

Game tuners adjust the pacing and difficulty of the game. They may do this by editing parameters such as enemy toughness or frequency. They may also alter the placement of NPCs and obstacles. They often observe potential customers during gameplay focus testing to identify areas that are counterintuitive or overly difficult to play.

Technical Director and Programming Team

The *technical director* (TD) is the chief architect for the game. TDs author the TDD and oversee the software development team. The TD's responsibility is to build the game and deliver a final product that is high quality and follows the requirements set forth in the GDD and TDD. Quality games have responsive performance and are relatively bug free.

Illustration by Ian Robert Vasquez

Sony Computer Entertainment America

Resistance: Fall of Man is a launch title. Much of the design had to be completed prior to final specification of the PlayStation 3 hardware.

Game software is often leading edge and requires specialists who stay abreast of the latest technology in their respective areas of knowledge. Depending on the size of the project, there may be one or more lead software programmers for specific areas of the game. Typical areas of specialization include networking, artificial intelligence (AI) and path finding, physics, 3D rendering and shading, lighting, animation, sound, streaming, interfaces, database, security, and tools.

Tools are especially important. Even if your team licenses its development tools, you will probably have to create software to facilitate getting the art or design elements into the game engine. Some developers have their own proprietary tool suite and game engine. Large developers usually have a dedicated R&D team that continuously improves the tools and game engine by adding features and optimizing performance.

Programming Team: What Do You Look For?

When we hire programmers we primarily look for strong generalists with a solid understanding of computer architecture, low-level issues, math, and data structures and algorithms. With a small team it is important that we have multitalented programmers that are capable of working in just about any area. The low-level computer architecture skills we consider important because they form a solid basis for additional knowledge to be built upon. Unfortunately, many programmers have only a "black box" understanding of the machines they work on, leading to inefficient systems that waste valuable resources (be it memory or cycles), inevitably leading to problems further down the road and, ultimately, does not enable art and design to create the best game they possibly could. We do not care if people do not know the full semantics of certain C++ keywords or if they are not hip to the latest trend in software engineering; such skills are fleeting and the programmers we look for are talented enough that they can pick up such knowledge up in a heartbeat if necessary.

— *Christer Ericson (Director of Tools & Technology, Sony Computer Entertainment of America)*

Art Director and Art Team

The *art director* oversees the visual aspects of the game. Like lead designers, art directors may manage the art team or they may provide guidance and leave the administrative work to an associate producer (AP). The art director is the principal author of the art style guide and is responsible for the look and visual style of the game—everything from interface to character animation.

Sony Computer Entertainment America

Shadow of the Colossus has a spiritual undertone that is evident in its style.

Like the TD, the art director is supported by a staff of artists who specialize in creating visual assets for the game. These typically include modeling, texturing, animation, interface, camera and lighting, environments, characters, cinematics, and tools. The art team works closely with the design team to create the game. Sometimes artists are part of the formal design team, especially when it comes to level building (environments), scripting (camera placement), and character interaction (animation).

Art is the largest component of next-generation games. Art groups tend to be larger than the rest of the development team, and art production is usually the critical path for completion.

Overseas Outsourcing

In an effort to reduce costs and lower risk, some developers have outsourced portions of the art to third-party contractors in lower-cost areas such as Eastern Europe and Asia. This requires increased communication and possibly bilingual APs, with constant monitoring for continuity and consistency.

Illustration by Ian Robert Vasquez

Audio Director and Audio Team

The *audio director* handles all the audio for the game, including sound effects, music, and voice-over/dialogue. Some studios hire an outside contractor to serve as audio director. Audio directors are sometimes referred to as audio managers; when there are several management positions on the audio team, the manager is second in command. Almost all studios

Sony Computer Entertainment America

The *Ratchet & Clank* series (*Ratchet: Deadlocked* shown) is well known for high-quality sound and voice acting.

use third-party contractors to design and supply some aspect of the game's sound. For that reason, a good audio director needs to maintain a network of skilled musicians, composers, sound designers, and recording houses.

The audio director needs to fully understand how music and sound is to be used in the game—including any technical constraints—and translate this knowledge into direction for audio professionals who may have little or no experience in crafting sound for games.

Communicate Often!

As an audio contractor, it's very important to keep your sounds fresh and reinvest income in what are often expensive sample libraries. On a particular project, I wanted to go all out and spent several hundred on a new sound library and about two weeks doing field recordings. I had been told all along that the project was set in present day, and I wanted to do the music and sound effects right. I was almost finished with the project, had 20 minutes of some great music done, and had the various sound effect elements ready to go. What could go wrong? Well, when the sample artwork was finally sent my way, I was horrified to discover that the game was now taking place in the 1920s! What happened to "present day"? Unfortunately, all I got out of the producer was, "Oh, I'm sorry, I thought I told you." Needless to say, the sample libraries I had purchased were useless, the sounds I had recorded were useless and the music I completed was useless. Over a month of work was shot and, worst of all, I had about a week left to meet my milestone— all with 20 minutes of new music and new sound effects yet to do. Lessoned learned: Communicate often with the producer!

— *Aaron Marks (President, On Your Mark Music Productions)*

The QA Director and Testing Team

The *quality assurance* (QA) *director* develops the testing plan and manages the testers for a game. For most developers, quality assurance testing is handled by a publisher. There are different forms of testing for various stages of development:

- Playability testing is performed by people who match the target customer profile but are unfamiliar with the game. Designers conduct these tests on a regular basis once there is a playable version of the game. One goal is to identify areas that are confusing or too difficult for average players. However, even a logical and straightforward game can be "bad"; playability testing ultimately focuses on ensuring that the game's "fun factor" is present.

■ Focus testing is, again, performed by target customers and may broaden to other groups. This testing is conducted by marketing to determine which aspects of the game are most appealing. This helps to guide positioning of the game.

■ *Quality Assurance testing* is performed by experienced testers. The goal is to find repeatable issues in gameplay and classify those issues according to severity. This testing is conducted by a testing group that is independent of the development team. It usually begins after the Alpha milestone has been reached. More about this in Chapter 7.

■ *Regression testing* is performed by the QA testing team. It is used to verify that past issues have been dealt with as reported by the development team.

■ *Format testing* applies to console games. It is performed by a hardware manufacturer's verification testers. It is used to ensure that the game meets all guidelines and standards required by the hardware manufacturer. This certification is required before a gold master can be released to manufacturing.

■ *Compatibility testing* applies to PC games. It is performed by a publisher or independent company to determine whether the game has any issues running on a particular hardware configuration. PCs offer many options for processors, graphics cards, sound cards, and motherboards. The permutations are endless, so most games are tested on popular PC brands and configurations that meet or exceed the minimum specification requirements for the game

Larger development studios have their own QA testing and it is becoming more vital to bring testing closer to the development team. Once the team has a playable build, testers check it for bugs and provide playability comments to the designers. Developers working under milestone contracts for third-party publishers need to verify that milestones are fully playable to ensure full payment for their deliverable.

No game is 100% bug free. Members of the QA team have a responsibility to report all issues

Courtesy of Blizzard Entertainment, Inc.

Blizzard makes frequent updates to *World of Warcraft: The Burning Crusade*. Each patch must be thoroughly tested to ensure that it works as intended and doesn't introduce new issues.

and offer their opinions about the overall quality level of the game. It is the producer's job to determine when testing and bug fixing should be concluded.

Flexible Staffing

Since labor is the biggest cost item for a game, accurate staffing can save thousands of dollars. Beyond the leads, it is very difficult to predict when to bring additional staff onto the project or when to take them off. It's better to hang on to people longer than needed than to risk losing them before their work is done.

Project Schedule

The GDD and TDD establish the project objectives. Producers and directors then define the major categories of work required to achieve those objectives. These categories are further broken down into individual tasks. Finally, task dependencies are identified and priorities are established to form an optimum schedule.

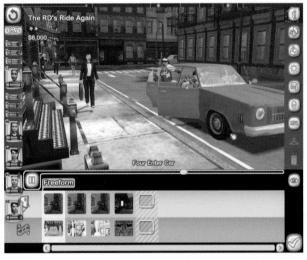
© Lionhead Studios Limited

The Movies simulates the planning that goes into creating scenes for a film.

Everyone on the team should have input into the task list. This ensures that the people performing the work feel a responsibility to stay on schedule. Tasks need to be realistic and achievable. Tasks that involve unknowns should have adequate research and development time. High-risk tasks should have less risky, alternative solutions.

The process of task definition can be top-down, bottom-up, or a combination of both. Top-down planning works when the project leadership has a good grasp of all that needs to take place to get the game done. Innovative games that are using radically new technology or unproven game mechanics may require some degree of bottom-up planning. In this case, individual components of the game are described as tasks—and then the project leadership pulls them back into a cohesive master task list.

Task Length

If a task takes less than a day to complete, it should be included with a group of similar tasks of short duration. If a task takes more than five days to complete, it should be broken into two or more smaller tasks.

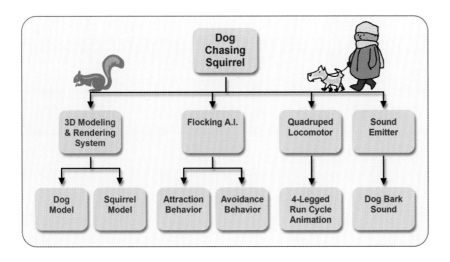

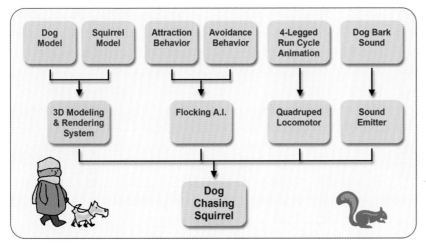

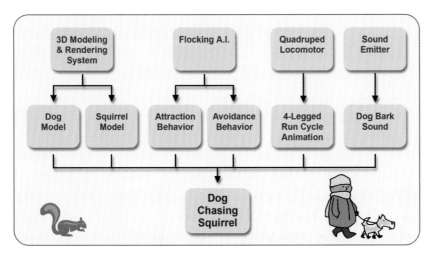

The above flow diagrams show three different approaches—top-down (top), bottom-up (middle), and hybrid (bottom)—to implementing a "dog chasing a squirrel" moment in a game.

It's tricky to determine how detailed to be when creating task lists. If you get too detailed, the list becomes quite large and difficult to grasp. It also makes the team members feel as though they are being micromanaged. On the flip side, if the tasks are too broad it is hard to determine dependencies and track progress.

Michael Booth on Effective Production Schedules :::::

Michael Booth (CEO, Turtle Rock Studios)

Michael Booth started his career in the game industry by "taking a semester off" from graduate school in 1995 to develop a game on his PC in the spare bedroom of his home. Five years, three cross-country moves, and starting and selling his first company later, that game was released in 2000 under the title *"Nox"* by Westwood/EA to commercial and critical success. While at EA, Michael acted as Technical Director on *Nox Quest, Red Alert II: Yuri's Revenge,* and *Command & Conquer: Generals.* Desiring to return to the creative atmosphere of smaller development teams, Michael founded Turtle Rock Studios in early 2002. Shortly thereafter, he began discussions with Valve, the developers *Half-Life 2* and *Counter-Strike.* Valve's "Steam" digital distribution system sounded extremely promising for small independent game developers, and Valve was interested in Michael's expertise in AI and game design for their *Counter-Strike* franchise. The result was *Counter-Strike: Condition Zero, Counter-Strike: Xbox* and *Counter-Strike: Source.* This collaboration remains ongoing; Turtle Rock Studios is currently deep into development on its first original game title using Valve's Steam and Source technologies.

Good plans and schedules must be high level, lightweight, and easily modified to reflect the actual state of the development project. I view them as tools to make sure we know what game we are building, and that everyone has a general sense of where we are going and what things will looks like when we get there.

Highly detailed plans and schedules are worse than useless. Not only do they cost a great deal of time to construct and incur a lot of "meeting overhead," they are almost always out of sync with the project the moment they are finished. This results in management having a distorted view of the project's state. Decisions are then based on these assumptions, and "crunch time" is usually the result.

Also, nothing kills creativity like a meticulous schedule with hour-by-hour prioritized task lists. If you need that kind of certainty, you shouldn't be in the game industry.

Starr Long on Creating a Production Plan :::::

Starr Long has been in the business of making games for over 12 years. Along with Richard Garriott, he was the original project director for the commercially successful *Ultima Online*. Starr worked his way up through the ranks of Origin Systems, starting in quality assurance on *Wing Commander*, *Ultima*, and many other titles. He was Producer on *Ultima Online 2*. He also worked with Richard Garriott on *Tabula Rasa* for the Korean online game giant NCsoft, creators of *Lineage*, the world's largest online game.

Starr Long (Producer, NCsoft)

In creating a production plan, we first list bullet points of all the features and content [associated with the game]. Each item is prioritized 1, 2, or 3 based on how important it is to the shipping product. From there the design team creates 1–2 page scope documents that describe and outline the goals of each feature or piece of content. Inside these scope documents each subitem within any given system is also prioritized. From those documents the team then provides estimates that we plug into the MS Project Server schedule. At this time we use the prioritizations to determine what items are in or out of the schedule. To keep things on track we have a policy that if a person's bug count goes over 10 or their scheduled tasks slip by more than a few days then they go into overtime and/or we rescope/redesign their tasks based on our prioritizations to fit within our budgeted schedule time.

Tasks

Each *task* in your production schedule should consist of the following components: name, description, start date, due date, time estimate, dependencies, and person(s) assigned.

Name

The task *name* uniquely identifies the task within the overall project schedule. It is usually a single name or short phrase. Examples include "Animate Harry's broom" or "Owl concept art."

Diagram by Per Olin

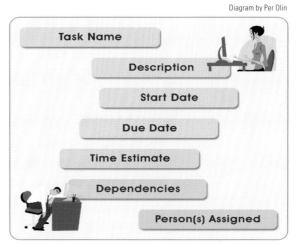

Each *task* contains a name, description, start date, due date, time estimate, dependencies, and person(s) assigned.

Production Planning Starts in Pre-Production

All of the production planning takes place, for the most part, during the pre-production phases of development. We break up our pre-production into three discrete phases… concept, pre-visualization, and demonstration. Each phase is completed with a formal review of specific deliverables and a "greenlight" into the next phase (assuming it passes muster). During the concept phase, the project not only performs brainstorming on game concept components, but looks at focus testing and market analysis to evaluate the validity of the game concept. During pre-visualization, the work focuses on setting the visual bar so that the product can be visually understood by not only the team but the executives. Finally, the demonstration phase focuses on building a playable component of the game "in-engine". All through this process, the planning documentation is being created, so that at the conclusion the team can move into our first production phase… the building of a "vertical slice". During this phase, planning has largely given way to execution, but mostly from the standpoint of verifying validity of assumptions made during pre-production. Once the vertical slice is complete, full production begins and the focus shifts entirely to execution of plan.

Schedule overruns and budget shortfalls come when assumptions made are incorrect. This can happen because you had to make "guesses" (which is common when you're pushing the boundaries of technology) or because you have inexperienced teams making those planning analyses. In order to combat this, I prefer to build in time for those surprises… while I cannot say for certain whether any given surprise will come, I can say that there will be surprises. If the game is riskier, I build in more such time. If I do this properly, I very rarely get surprised by overruns or shortfalls.

— Graeme Bayless (Director of Production, Crystal Dynamics)

Description

The task *description* provides more detailed information about the task. For the first example above, "Animate Harry's broom" expands to "Add control points and squash/stretch to broom take off. Do roll, dive, crash, swoop, glide, and stationary states. Apply bristle shader and magic sparkle particle effects to broom."

Start Date

If the task needs to begin on a particular *start date*, this needs to be noted. For example, voice recording sessions for "name" talent need to be scheduled around the availability of the actor. They are often scheduled months in advance and the dates are inflexible.

Due Date

If the task needs to be complete by a particular *due date*, this needs to be noted. For example, game demos for trade shows like E[3] need to be ready in advance of the show. Often the final milestone of the game, the gold master date, is determined early on, before all of the tasks have been determined. This isn't just because some unknowing executive is trying to place unreasonable demands on the team. It can arise out of an attempt to hit the holiday season, coincide with the launch of a new hardware platform, or simply bring in revenue to keep a publisher's cash flow positive.

Time Estimate

Most projects get into trouble when it comes to *time estimate*. Optimists tend to drastically underestimate the effort required to complete a task. Some producers actually double every estimate to give themselves breathing room. Others assume that the team is *sandbagging* (being too conservative about its abilities), and they cut the estimate by 25% to make sure everyone is working hard. Both strategies can lead to problems by tricking producers into thinking they have more time than what is reflected on the schedule.

If an estimate looks suspiciously long or short, then challenge it. Ask questions until you feel satisfied that the person performing the task has a good grasp of what to do. Build in some padding when unknowns are involved, like integrating a new technology. Include checkpoints to detect when a task is running behind and establish fallback plans if a task needs to be simplified or cut.

Allow for thinking time and breaks. People should not be scheduled 100% of their time. Project managers outside the game industry assume 75% of the workday is available for task work. Some game producers assume that teams will be in "crunch mode" working 12-hour days in order to hit a due date. A better approach is to remove tasks or add resources to ensure that a due date can be reached by staff working a normal eight-hour day. That doesn't end crunch time; it just saves it for when the unforeseen happens, as it always does, and the extra effort is needed to handle a crisis.

Dependencies

List all *dependencies* (other tasks that depend on this task). Some may require full completion before the task can begin. For example, "Animate Harry's broom" requires that "Model Harry's broom" is done. You should also list the things that this task requires in order to begin or complete. You'll need to make a second pass to accurately list the dependencies by name once all the tasks are defined.

Person(s) Assigned

The persons assigned are responsible for completing the task. They should understand the task and give input on the description, time estimate, and dependencies. It's important to have someone assigned to each task before laying out the master schedule.

As you lay out tasks and dependencies, you'll encounter conflicts. Inevitably people will have gaps between tasks or they'll be tasked with simultaneous items. Unfortunately there isn't a good automated method for correcting this. The producer needs to manually assess the task list and make adjustments.

Expect the Unexpected

There is no real magic here. I lay out all of the tasks in Project, make preliminary resource assignments, and see where the calendar says we will finish. The thing I have done in the past few years that has improved my accuracy is to add a line item to each feature called "Problem Solving" and I assign some time to that to allow for dealing with unanticipated technical or design issues.

— *Rich Adam (CEO, Mine Shaft Entertainment, Inc.)*

Be Proactive

I try to detect schedule overruns and budget shortfalls as early as possible so that they make the least possible damage. I work with relatively short build cycles throughout the project. So we are always on top of things. Weekly progress meetings. Which tasks and features have been completed, which tasks are outstanding? The feature list and task lists are open for alterations at the start of every cycle.

— *Jesper Sorensen (Business Unit Manager & Game Director, ncom.dk)*

Don't Forget Pre-Production

We do a "pre-production" phase for all of our games. From the results of this pre-prod, we get enough information to be able to create a much more accurate schedule and budget, including staffing requirements. We feel that pre-prod is a critical step in the game development process. If done properly, it can drastically reduce the false starts and dead ends often encountered to actual development. As a result, we have had a very strong record of delivering product on time and in budget.

— *Ed Rotberg (Chief Technology Officer, Mine Shaft Entertainment)*

Master Project Schedule

The *master project schedule* pulls all elements of the project schedule together. Usually the technical director (TD) maintains a software schedule, and the art director keeps an art schedule, and the design director tracks a mission design schedule. The producer needs to see the whole picture and how the various activities of the entire team interrelate.

Most producers use Microsoft Project to assemble the master project schedule. This software has many useful features and some, like resource leveling, that just don't work for game production. Microsoft Project is the most popular software for project management, so it is the best one to learn first. The following figure shows part of the master schedule for a game.

Microsoft Corporation

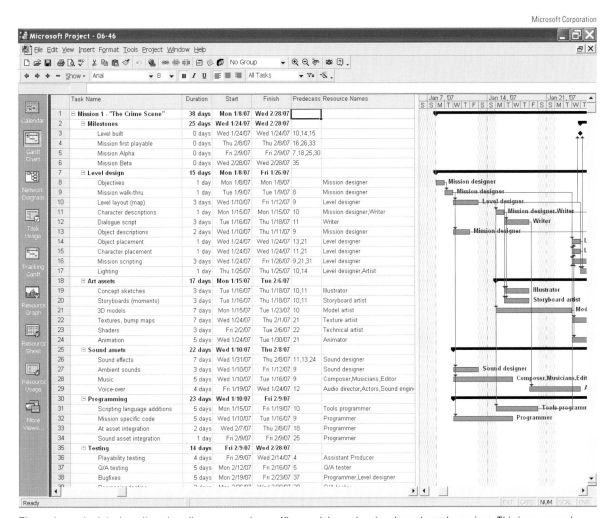

The project schedule describes the milestones, tasks, staffing, and dependencies throughout the project. This is an example from Microsoft Project for a single mission in a game.

Enter the information for each task. Don't plug in start dates unless they are required dates. The same goes for completion dates. In both cases, you will have to set the constraints "must start" and "must finish," respectively. Don't forget to enter the dependencies (predecessors). This will help sort out a logical order for the tasks.

Start with the Big Picture

Look first at the overall timeline and then work with your leads to drill down what can get done well within that timeframe. Overruns and shortfalls can be handled with pro-active management. Pay attention to your group—and if you have a good sense of the pulse of the project, you can solve problems before they spin out of control.

— *Drew Davidson (Director, Entertainment Technology Center, Carnegie Mellon University)*

Setting Up Your Master Schedule

Start from the top down. You have pre-production, production, and post-production phases. Now, break them down. Use a good piece of scheduling software as a tool, but don't let it straightjacket you. Understand how the platform you are developing for constrains your process. Look to identify risks so you will be able to make management aware of what could conceivably take longer and cost more than anticipated. If these risks cannot be covered (extra time and money will not be there), then you can't take them.

— *Frank T. Gilson (Senior Developer of Digital Games, Wizards of the Coast)*

Milestones

Milestones are specific points in the schedule where various components are integrated and something demonstrable is created. Milestones should be entered into the schedule, usually every 4–6 weeks. Remember to include integration and testing time to make sure the milestone is fully functional and meets your publisher's expectations.

Some key milestones include:

- Production Begins
- First Playable
- Alpha
- Beta
- Release Candidate
- Gold Master

These milestones are covered in more detail in the next chapter.

Iteration After Iteration

The biggest difference between standard software development and game software development involves iterations. Elements of game software go through many iterations to get them right—and the newer/riskier a piece of a game is, the more iterations it invokes. A producer needs to be aware of a "bad" iteration cycle, where improvements are not actually occurring.

— *Frank T. Gilson (Senior Developer of Digital Games, Wizards of the Coast)*

Budget

The *budget* lists all the costs associated with developing a game. It is typically broken down into monthly increments. Detailed budgets may show weekly expenses, which are used during actual production for fine-tuning cash flow.

The categories of the budget are divided into two parts: fixed costs and variable costs. *Fixed costs* are expenses that are incurred every month, such as salaries and rent. These items don't change from month to month. *Variable costs* are items that change from month to month. They include payments to short-term contractors, capital expenses (equipment), travel and entertainment (T&E), and software license fees.

Microsoft Corporation

	A	B	C	D	E	F	G	H	I	J	K	L
1					Concept			Preproduction				
2	Labor			Unit Cost	Jan-07	Feb-07	Mar-07	Apr-07	May-07	Jun-07	Jul-07	Aug
3	Producer		$183,333	$8,333	1	1	1	1	1	1	1	
4	Associate Producers		$175,000	$5,000	1	1	1	1	1	1	1	
5	AssistantProducers		$150,000	$3,333				1	1	1	1	
6	Design Director		$166,250	$7,917	1	1	1	1	1	1	1	
7	Designers		$825,000	$6,250	2	2	2	5	5	5	5	
8	Technical Director		$201,667	$9,167	1	1	1	1	1	1	1	
9	Software Engineers		$1,080,000	$6,667	2	2	2	5	5	5	5	
10	Art Director		$157,500	$7,500	1	1	1	1	1	1	1	
11	Artists		$1,368,333	$6,250	3	3	3	5	5	5	5	
12	Animators		$443,333	$5,833				3	3	3	3	
13	Audio Director		$140,000	$6,667	1	1	1	1	1	1	1	
14	Sound Engineers		$167,917	$5,417				1	1	1	1	
15	Total Salaries	$5,058,750	Headcount	13	13	13	26	26	26	26	26	
16	Employment Taxes & Benefits	$2,023,500										
17	General & Administrative	$758,813										
18	Travel & Entertainment	$75,000										
19	Furniture & Equipment	$500,000										
20	Software	$100,000										
21	Media	$6,000										
22	Shipping	$10,000										
23	Insurance	$60,000										
24	Licenses	$150,000										
25	Contract Services											
26	Story & script		$150,000									
27	Voice recording		$150,000									
28	Cinematics		$1,000,000									
29	Music & SFX		$300,000									
30	Motion capture		$250,000									
31	Total Contract Services	$1,850,000										
32												
33	TOTAL BUDGET	$10,592,063										

Sample Excel budget spreadsheet for a two-year, 50-person project.

Budgets are typically broken down into five or more categories:

- Salaries
- General and Administrative
- Research and Development
- Licenses
- Travel and Entertainment

The Power of Excel

Do not underestimate the power of Excel—not only as a production planning tool, but for almost everything! On one project, we only had so much memory for words on a handheld educational toy, so we used Excel to track memory usage character by character. It was tight enough that someone on the team wrote "Who go moon?" in reference to Neil Armstrong.

— *Drew Davidson (Director, Entertainment Technology Center, Carnegie Mellon University)*

Salaries

Salaries tend to be the largest component of the budget. Monthly payroll costs are derived directly from the headcount staffing plan. You can either use actual salaries for existing staff or estimate a monthly cost per person by averaging the actual and estimated salaries for the entire team and dividing that by the total headcount. Be sure to include other payables, including benefits (insurance, 401k, etc.) and taxes.

Contractors

Many developers keep a core staff of full-time employees and then hire outside *contractors* for the duration of the project. They may also subcontract to outside companies to create some of the assets, usually artwork and 3D models.

Contractors or Employees?

Some job functions are considered *non-exempt,* which means that workers are entitled to overtime pay if they exceed a certain number of hours per day. Long-term contractors may, in fact, be considered employees, and state labor laws may require that you pay benefits and withhold taxes. If contractors work on-site and have no other clients for a long period of time, there's a good chance that they should be converted to employees.

Some developers hire project duration staff. These are specialists that sign on for a single project or for a specific component of the game. This works in areas where there is a supply of talented independent contractors.

General and Administrative (G&A)

Fixed costs known as *general and administrative* (G&A) costs are necessary to run a studio but not directly attributable to production salaries. They include items such as salaries for administrative staff, rent, taxes, equipment depreciation, insurance, telecommunication charges, utilities, postage, and media. G&A costs are usually apportioned to a project according to the monthly staff headcount.

Research and Development (R&D)

Research and development (R&D) expenses include one-time costs that a project incurs to create assets (programs, art, sounds) for the game.

Voiceover and Onscreen Recording

Actors are needed to record voices for characters in the game and in cinematic sequences. Most actors belong to a union, either the Screen Actors Guild (SAG) or the American Federation of Television and Radio Artists (AFTRA). Before you can work with members of these unions, you need to be a union signatory, which means agreeing to follow the terms and conditions of the union for hiring, recording, and paying talent. You may also enlist a third-party agency to act as signatory. The base fees for union members and the minimum session time are not negotiable. "Name" talent will charge a premium over and above the base fee. In addition to the actor's fee, the union will include benefits and union fees.

You can work with non-union actors, but the quality of the performances might be inconsistent. It's also okay to save money by having employees do scratch tracks or the occasional one-liner. Bear in mind that union talent cannot work on projects that are "nonunion."

Vivendi Universal Games

50 Cent Bulletproof features a high-quality rap soundtrack and voiceover by the artist.

In addition to talent fees, voiceover costs include fees for casting, directing, recording or filming, editing, media, and delivery of the recorded assets. These are usually budgeted in the month that the recording session takes place.

Sony Computer Entertainment Inc.

Rogue Galaxy tells a deep story with stunning movies.

Cinematics

Most games have one or more pre-rendered *cinematics* or movies. The opening screen and backstory (intro) are displayed in a high-quality, cinematic video clip. These can range in length from a few seconds to a few minutes. Producers usually budget based on the number, length, and complexity of each video sequence. Games that have a large number of cinematics employ a video director.

Get Three Bids

For any major expense, such as cinematics, always get a few competitive bids. If there is a wide variance, ask questions of each vendor to determine the differences in quality or satisfaction guarantees. Ask for a "not-to-exceed" bid to avoid costly overruns and incidentals.

In addition to 3D modeling and rendering, the costs for cinematics include script (writers), storyboards, editing, soundtrack, and encoding (video compression). A large number of companies serve both the film and game industries, so the best value for the dollar is usually available from third-party vendors.

Music and Sound Effects

Music costs include composition, arrangement, directing, performance, recording, mixing, editing, encoding, and media. If you plan to record a live orchestra, talent and union fees will apply as well. If the musicians are performing licensed music, you'll need to secure both mechanical and performance rights to the score and songs.

Sound effects are created using synthesized or sampled sounds. Larger studios employ full-time sound designers to custom craft sounds for the various actions in the game. Many audio production companies offer a wide range of services including talent casting, soundtrack composition, and sound effects design.

Game soundtracks might be recorded in a studio by a live orchestra (Ron Jones, left) or in a home studio (Aaron Marks, right).

Writing

Writers are generally hired on a per project basis. They create scripts for cinematics and in-game dialogue and also develop story outlines, character descriptions, plot points, and backstory. They may be subject matter experts engaged to do research for the game, especially if the game depicts modern or historical events, involves actual people, or references detailed scientific knowledge. Game writers may be staff or contract employees. Scriptwriters are usually contractors and they are paid by the number of pages they write.

Illustration by Ian Robert Vasquez

Licenses

Software tools and third-party game engines have one-time cost for acquisition plus annual maintenance fees for updates and support. These fees may be charged for each workstation as a site license or on a project use basis. Examples of per user licenses include Maya, Perforce, and Alienbrain. Examples of project use include Unreal, Bink, and GameSpy. You can reflect these in the budget in the month they are due or amortize them throughout the year.

Licensed software can save a lot of time and allow your programmers to concentrate on game-specific code. It can also create uncertainty in the schedule if the licensed software is undergoing development.

Epic Games, Inc.

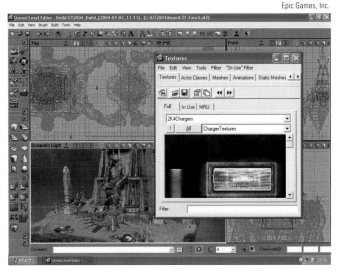

Epic licenses its Unreal tools for developers making primarily first-person shooter (FPS) games on PCs and consoles.

Production Plan: bringing order to chaos   chapter 6

Travel and Entertainment (T&E)

Travel and entertainment (T&E) expenses include airfare, taxis, rental cars, mileage reimbursements, tolls, parking, lodging, and employee meals while they are on business trips. Development studios need to budget enough to cover trips to publishers when pitching a concept and semimonthly trips for design discussions and milestone

Illustration by Ian Robert Vasquez

reviews. Be sure to include industry conferences and the occasional business opportunity that requires travel. If you employ subcontractors overseas, plan on 2–3 trips annually to check up on their progress and working conditions.

Entertainment covers meals with guests, usually prospective business partners. It is also common practice for studios to cater employee dinners when projects involve late hours and weekends. These are called "crunch-time" meals. Your accountant can provide you with guidelines for classifying entertainment expenses.

Budget as Benchmark

It's difficult to increase a budget once it's been agreed to. Some projects simply can't afford to run over budget. Take the time to analyze the data and make the best estimate you can. Allow for some contingencies, but avoid the temptation to grossly overestimate the budget. The budget is one of the benchmarks for determining the overall success of a project.

Financial Analysis

The *financial analysis* looks at the cost of the project and compares it to the expected return on investment. Publishers, investors, and developers look at the

Illustration by Ian Robert Vasquez

bottom line to guide their decision to make a game. Every production plan should include financial analysis to show that the project can be profitable for all concerned.

The following subsections describe each element of the ROI. Development deals vary widely as do publishers' terminology and definitions. The basic concepts here cover most situations. Some elements may be eliminated or hidden in actual agreements. Consider that ROI elements associated with mobile, casual, and web games—and online games with subscription fees and digital object sales—will differ.

Diagram by Per Olin

Retail Price		$49.99			
Average Wholesale Price		$32.00			
Hardware Manufacturer's License		($7.00)			
COGs		($2.75)			
Distribution Fees		($0.50)			
Net revenue per unit		$21.75			
Units Sold		300,000	600,000	1,200,000	2,400,000
Gross Receipts		$6,525,000	$13,050,000	$26,100,000	$52,200,000
Development Costs		($8,000,000)	($8,000,000)	($8,000,000)	($8,000,000)
Return Reserves	10%	($652,500)	($1,305,000)	($2,610,000)	($5,220,000)
Net Receipts		($2,127,500)	$3,745,000	$15,490,000	$38,980,000
Licensor Royalties	3%	$0	($112,350)	($464,700)	($1,169,400)
Developer Royalties Net of Advances	12%	$0	$0	($1,858,800)	($4,677,600)
Marketing		($1,000,000)	($2,000,000)	($5,000,000)	($9,000,000)
MDF, Commissions	5%	($326,250)	($652,500)	($1,305,000)	($2,610,000)
Net Revenue		($3,453,750)	$980,150	$6,861,500	$21,523,000
Return on Investment		0.0%	5.4%	23.5%	43.5%
Break-Even		489,379	545,244	712,840	1,015,996

This table outlines a simple return on investment (ROI) and break-even analysis for a game. The amounts are for example purposes only and do not necessarily reflect a typical game.

Units Sold

The *units sold* component of your financial analysis represents your best guess of how many units a game will sell at a given price. Simple models shown in the sample spreadsheet use an average wholesale price. Other models use three wholesale pricing tiers: full price, discounted (greatest hits), and value (heavily discounted). The wholesale price is the price paid by retailers to distributors for a game, not the price paid by consumers.

Most game industry professionals use industry data such as TRSTS, NPD, or PC Data to look at historical sales for competitive products and arrive at a prediction for future sales. These sources don't offer much help when looking at revolutionary new

IP, but they give some indication of consumers' past appetites for certain genres of games. Unfortunately there are no public databases for development and marketing budgets, since these can have considerable impact on a game's success.

NPD Group

TOP 10 CONSOLE GAMES, JUNE 2006

1) New Super Mario Bros. (DS, Nintendo)
2) Grand Theft Auto: Liberty City Stories (PS2, Rockstar/Take-Two)
3) Brain Age: Train Your Brain in Minutes a Day (DS, Nintendo)
4) Cars (PS2, THQ)
5) Hitman: Blood Money (Xbox 360, Eidos)
6) Cars (Game Boy Advance, THQ)
7) FIFA World Cup 2006 (PS2, Electronic Arts)
8) Big Brain Academy (DS, Nintendo)
9) Hitman: Blood Money (PS2, Eidos)
10) Cars (GameCube, THQ)

TOP 10 PC GAMES, JUNE 2006

1) World of Warcraft (Blizzard/Vivendi)
2) The Elder Scrolls IV: Oblivion (2K Games/Take-Two)
3) Guild Wars Factions (NCsoft)
4) The Sims 2 (EA)
5) Heroes of Might & Magic V (Ubisoft)
6) The Sims 2: Open for Business Expansion (EA)
7) Age of Empires III (Microsoft)
8) Rise of Nations: Rise of Legends (Microsoft)
9) Star Wars: Empire at War (LucasArts)
10) Civilization IV (2K Games/Take-Two)

Source: NPD Group

Publishers and retailers watch the monthly top-seller's data provided by NPD Group (June 2006 results shown).

Manufacturer's License Fee

The *manufacturer's license fee* is charged by console game manufacturers for each disc or cartridge made for their platform. Consoles are proprietary devices and games need to be encoded to run on them. The fees charged help manufacturers defray the cost of the console hardware, which is usually sold to the consumer at a loss. There is no fee for computer (PC) games.

Cost of Goods Sold (COGS)

Cost of goods sold (COGS) is the actual manufacturing cost for each individual boxed copy of a game. It includes manufacturing fees (except licenses), jewel case, game manual, and box. This is typically $1.75 to $3.00 per unit.

Distribution Fee

In order to get your product onto the retail shelves, you must pay a *distribution fee* to a distributor, which gets the boxed copies from a warehouse and stocks them on a retailer's shelves. It's impractical for publishers to maintain relationships with smaller retailers. Distributors represent multiple publishers to a network of retailers. Their fees range from 5–15% of gross receipts.

Development Costs

The *development costs* represent the total cost of game development, including all advances paid to the developer and all external R&D costs. Unless otherwise specified, development costs are considered to be an advance against the developer's royalty. The *publisher G&A* represents the overhead costs incurred by the publisher. These costs include administrative costs and quality assurance testing, and they are often treated as development costs.

Return Reserves

Publishers manufacture and ship as many units as they think the market can sell within a reasonable time frame. Sometimes too many units are shipped and a portion must eventually be returned or sold at no profit. Publishers account for this by allocating a percentage of revenue to *return reserves*, which can range from be 10–20%. Royalties are not paid on these units until they are deemed liquidated, usually six months to a year after initial manufacturing.

Net Receipts

The definition of *net receipts* varies. In most cases, gross receipts are the wholesale sales price minus manufacturer's license fee, cost of goods, and distribution fees. This result is then multiplied by the units sold. Net receipts are the gross receipts minus the development costs and reserves. Royalties are typically based on net receipts.

Licensor Royalty

Some games are derived from an existing license. Games based on movies, comic books, and even other games pay a *license royalty* for each unit sold. If the licensor received any upfront payment or a guarantee, it is deducted from the royalty receipts.

Developer Royalty

Game developers hope that their games will become best-sellers and bring in additional profit in the form of royalties. These royalties are paid to the developer once the publisher has recouped all of its costs, including any development costs advanced to, or paid on behalf of, the game developer. Internal studios, owned and operated by a publisher, don't receive royalties but they may have a profit-sharing program for their employees. These funds can be estimated in the same manner as royalties.

Marketing

There should be a projected *marketing* budget for the lifetime of the game's sales. This may be a fixed amount or a percentage of the overall development budget. Publishers reserve the right to increase or decrease the budget depending on how the game is perceived as it nears release, or how well it is selling at postrelease. The *marketing development fund* (MDF) includes monies allocated to promote a game for a specific retailer, such as ads taken out in a local newspaper advertising a game in the Best Buy flyer. Commissions (usually 3–5% of net receipts) are paid to sales-people for selling the game.

The Limitations of Financial Analysis

A strong financial analysis can provide comfort that, in an objective world, money can be made on your game. The reality is that many other factors determine success, including:

- passion of the team
- lack or weakness of competition
- no disruption in the market, e.g., new technology
- cash flow of publisher and/or developer

Jesper Sorensen on the Production Planning Process :::::

Jesper started his career as a consultant and project manager within the traditional software development industry. Prior to his position at ncom.dk, he worked as a game project manager within News Corp's Digital TV subsidiary NDS. He has produced 16 games, primarily targeted toward children.

I handle each game project as a stone mason handles a stone. Each raw stone is different and so is each game project. Each budget, team and overall vision will vary. I have seen multiple projects fail in the game and software industry because they had to follow one development methodology dogmatically. You cannot make a 6-½ foot Venus of Milo out of a two foot stone. This means that project planning is always a combination of a top down and bottom up process. However, the combination is never the same.

Jesper Sorensen (Business Unit Manager & Game Director, ncom.dk)

The feature list is always a team effort with the project manager at the end of the table having the final call. We always look at features first. We make a list of features and have them prioritized according to the overall vision.

Since it is a team effort, commitment to the feature set is strong. Then I have the feature set approved and possibly altered by the publisher. It is a ping-pong session going back and forth. When the feature set is in place, it is time to break it down into task lists that each team member can work by.

I have the production team break these features into tasks with time estimate—most often using the Wideband Delphi method. Letting team members do their own time estimation is a good way to get real commitment to time estimates. You are more obliged to meet a target you have put up yourself than a target put up by your boss or another person.

After the original time estimates are done, I have the time estimates sanity checked by peers who don't know the original estimates. Since there more often are more features and task than there are time, I cut at the low end of the feature list and upwards until the game is within the budgetary limitations. The final overall sanity check is against historical data. I find a previous game that has the same scope and compare it with this new project. By that point, the initial project plan with Gantt charts writes itself.

The Role of the Producer

The producer is responsible for evaluating on a constant basis the scope of the game, from the earliest design through the final gold disc, and ensuring the title meets its release date and budget requirements. Every milestone is composed of thousands of tasks, each the responsibility of an individual team member, and all tightly interconnected. The production pathway must be designed, tasks prioritized and assigned correctly, and potential roadblocks identified and solutions found. On collaborative efforts involving team sizes required by next-generation development, continuous and effective communication is essential; the producer must facilitate this through the department leads to individual developers, in both directions.

Creating and maintaining a schedule would seem to be the paramount duty of the producer. Far more important, however, is managing a team of talented, passionate, and experienced developers. No game design remains unchanged from initial concept to the retail shelf, and each decision is affected by creative, technical, and scheduling forces. Conflicts naturally arise. The leads are expected to present their opinions and provide a solid argument for them. The producer is expected to understand all ideas have value, and to make sure each is heard. Once all options have been discussed and evaluated, a final decision must be made. While the producer is responsible for the schedule and budget of the production, the creative lead is responsible for providing the best gameplay experience possible. Each consideration carries equal weight, and the decision eventually reached during discussions between the two must attempt to satisfy both.

These decisions are not made on a whim, and the studio is not a dictatorship. A good artist, programmer, or designer is valued at the Santa Monica Studio not just for their talent but also for a passion for their work. This same passion can lead to conflict if a team member feels their voice is not heard or their opinion is dismissed. Each person on the development team carries a huge amount of responsibility to the product and to his or her teammates. As such, any change of direction needs the buy-off of all team members involved, who must pursue the new goal with the same energy they would any other task. Keeping the team motivated, focused, and communicating is the most intangible and essential part of the producer's job. Simply taking a great game idea designed by a strong lead designer and tossing it to a bunch of talented developers won't result in an exemplary title. Understanding the dynamics of the team, the strengths and weaknesses of each person, the pitfalls that inevitably come during a long and highly collaborative production—these are the abilities a producer at Sony is required to demonstrate every day. When a triple-A product is on the shelves, and more importantly in Playstations around the world, only then has a producer done their job.

— *Shannon Studstill (Director of Production, Sony Computer Entertainment of America)*

You know how to create the game design document (GDD), technical design document (TDD), art style guide (ASG), sound design document (SDD), and production plan. Now you have all the elements necessary to go into production. The next chapter gets into the actual management aspects of game development.

:::CHAPTER REVIEW:::

1. Create a production plan for your original game idea. What are the roles and responsibilities of the game producer and members of the production team?

2. Is it possible to balance time, money, and quality? Which of these elements are you personally most likely to emphasize or de-emphasize, and why?

3. Develop a test plan for your original game idea. How will you ensure that your game will be virtually bug free, logical, usable, and accessible—while maintaining the "fun factor"?

Part III:
Management
& Production

Team Management

communication, objectivity, and leadership

Key Chapter Questions

- What are the five stages of group development?

- What is a *post-mortem* in game production?

- What are some effective techniques for running a production meeting?

- What is *feature creep* and how can it affect a project?

- What are some major project *milestones*?

Your project has made it through all the phases of pre-production; you have a clear vision and a plan to realize it. During the production phase, the producer's role is to organize the team and keep the project on track. At this point, the team grows in size and the majority of the team members are new to the project and each other. The first job facing the producer is team management.

Not all development groups are teams, but teams have historically performed more effectively than isolated individuals. Mature teams are organized, with strong leadership, efficient processes, and distinct roles. They can adapt to the inevitable changes and challenges of game development without chaos, drama, or long delays. It's the producer's job to assemble and guide the staff to become a real *team*.

Five-Stage Team Management Model

Diagram by Per Olin

Forming	uncertainty about the group's purpose and structure
Storming	intragroup conflict
Norming	close relationships and cohesiveness, accepted behaviors and goals
Performing	fully functional, high task performance
Adjourning	focus on disbanding (temporary groups)

In 1965, Dr. Bruce Tuckman published his four-stage "Forming, Storming, Norming and Performing" team development model. In the 1970s, he added a fifth stage, "Adjourning." This model has been quoted in many project management texts (notably in Stephen Robbins' *Organizational Behavior*), and it is easily adapted to game production teams. The accompanying table describes each of the five steps.

Let's take this model and apply it specifically to the game industry.

Forming

The group is newly formed. Goals are unclear. This stage happens at the beginning of a project when the core team is selected and the GDD is being drafted. Many game developers have loosely defined responsibilities so there is often confusion over design direction. This stage ends when individual members are beginning to think of themselves as part of a group and the design begins to take shape.

Storming

Members struggle over roles and leadership. There may be infighting and petty rivalries. Game producers may find it difficult to decide when to be assertive and when to let the team resolve issues alone. New producers may lack respect from the team and other members may try to take control. Once a hierarchy is established and the design goals are set, this stage ends.

Norming

Friendships and mutual respect begin to develop. Cross-discipline understanding begins to occur. This is most clear in development teams when artists and programmers begin working together without continual prodding from producers. This stage ends when clear goals and expectations for behavior are established. This usually occurs near the end of preproduction.

Performing

Politics are over and now the group is concentrating on getting the work done. This usually happens when the bulk of the staff has been hired and the production has delivered a few milestones. Most development teams have a few strong contributors, and by this stage they no longer feel the need to prove themselves to the rest of the group. The processes and roles are well defined. Individual ego has given way to the general sense of camaraderie. Despite the long hours worked together, team members actually enjoy each other's company and tend to socialize with each other. This stage ends once the project reaches the beta milestone.

Adjourning

The focus of the team is on completing the work and wrapping things up. Some team members are excited and race to the finish line. Others find it hard to relinquish the project and sometimes put the schedule at risk by introducing new features or reworking completed tasks. The end of this stage should be punctuated by a post-mortem.

The Post-Mortem

Successful teams look at their mistakes and figure out ways to correct them on future games. It has become common practice for developers to host post-mortem meetings after a game ships (or is cancelled). The best rule of thumb to follow is to identify what you did wrong and what you would change in the future. Don't go in with a list of things that everyone else did wrong. Chances are they are already aware of it and your axe-grinding will only serve to create an atmosphere of accusation rather than problem solving.

This five-stage model seems to fit most permanent teams, although some dysfunctional groups may not go through all the stages until they complete a few projects together. The important thing to keep in mind is that all teams go through conflict at the beginning when roles and goals are not well defined. Leave plenty of time in pre-production to account for this. Once performing stages are reached, everyone is working at maximum efficiency.

Accountability

Now that production is under way, the producer needs to establish clear reporting lines and *accountability* among the team members. Someone needs to ultimately be responsible for the execution of every task. Other team members may be identified to provide support in the form of precursor tasks or information. Finally, every task also needs someone to review the task and approve of its completion.

For example, let's say that the end goal of a particular set of tasks is to create the behavior of a character. In this case, the artificial intelligence (AI) programmer has the responsibility for implementing that character's behavior, while an animator has a linked responsibility to complete the character's animations so that this behavior can be observed by the player. In this example, the lead designer must review and approve of the character behavior.

Documentation

The game design document (GDD), technical design document (TDD), art style guide, sound design document and production plan are living *documents*. They should be updated to reflect changes as they occur during the course of production. Procedures need to be established to review, approve, and distribute these amendments to the rest of the team.

Processes and procedures that arise during the course of production should be carefully documented so that new team members will follow them. An example would be documentation for using a proprietary level editor. Make sure team members include rationales for all document changes (required before the document will accept the change) and allow for communication tools such as online threaded discussions.

Wiki

A *wiki* (Hawaiian for "quick") is a website that allows users to edit content quickly. It provides for standard templates and links to other pages within the site. Wikis are growing in popularity among game developers to create "living" online documentation.

> The simplest online database that could possibly work.
>
> — *Ward Cunningham, inventor of the first wiki, WikiWikiWeb*

Meetings

Most people hate *meetings;* game developers are no exception. Anything that takes away from the fun of creating something or threatens to throw you behind schedule is considered a waste of time. Unfortunately, with big teams, the only way to effectively communicate across multiple disciplines is in a meeting.

There are some simple rules to follow to make meetings productive, efficient, and useful for everyone.

Ian Robert Vasquez

- *Invite* only the people who need to be present. As a courtesy, you might cc people who might have an interest. You might have too many people at the first few meetings. People just like to make sure they aren't missing anything important. The meetings will quickly settle down to a reasonable size.
- *Use tools* such as Microsoft Outlook Calendar to manage meetings. Remember that some people never check their calendars, while others live by them.
- *Remind* people the day before, and again 15 minutes before the meeting starts.
- *Set a time limit* for the meeting. Usually one hour is the maximum.
- *Establish an agenda* for the meeting. At the beginning of the meeting, write the agenda items on a whiteboard with a time limit for each item. If you run over your time limit, drop a lower priority item and save discussion of it for another day.
- *Schedule the meeting before or after lunch,* but avoid early morning or late afternoons. Many developers are night owls, and the unofficial hours for developers are 10:00 a.m. to 7:00 p.m. Some developers are single parents and may need to leave by 5:00 p.m. to pick up their kids from day care. If you must meet over lunch, have food brought in.
- *Nominate a note taker* who will be responsible for recording and distributing the meeting "minutes." This is a good job for an assistant producer.
- *Write down action items* and assign someone to be responsible for each item. At the beginning of the next meeting, review action items from the last meeting. Update the status. If something lingers on the list for more than two meetings, call a separate meeting with just the parties involved and press for resolution.
- *Avoid tangents* and too much detail. Keep track of the topic being discussed. Recognize when the conversation is going off topic or has become too detailed. Schedule a smaller group to work out details separately.
- *Avoid repetition* and redundant commentary. In a large meeting, there is always one person who has nothing to contribute beyond repeating what someone else has said. Don't be insulting, but be firm and ask for comments to be on point and additive rather than repetitive.

- *Summarize* the meeting before it ends. Set aside five minutes at the end of the meeting to make sure everyone doesn't run off before you get clear agreement on issues and accountability for action items. Make sure that a written summary ("meeting minutes") is sent to everyone after the meeting so that no one forgets what was discussed.

A few well-run meetings will earn the respect of the team. You won't have trouble getting people together once they realize that you aren't going to waste their time.

Monitoring

The producer needs to *monitor* and report on progress. If production lags or goes awry, it's the producer's responsibility to take steps to bring it back on track. One way to check progress is to review the schedule with the team leads by conducting formal reviews once a week until the game reaches Alpha, and more frequently after that. Longer intervals (monthly) don't provide enough information to properly track progress, and shorter intervals (daily) don't allow enough flexibility to shift tasks without constant rework of the master schedule. Weekly monitoring should include a formal full build and basic run-through.

Status Reports

After each weekly meeting, the producer should prepare and distribute a status report consisting of a list of action items by the date each item was first entered and the current status. Once an action item is completed, it drops off the following week's report. Action items can be grouped by functional area (e.g., software, art) or by individual. This report serves as a chronology of events and keeps the team focused on addressing issues before they become major obstacles.

Galactic Buccaneer
Status Report for week of March 12, 2007
Producer: Lisa Abarta

KEY	Project Start	Preproduction Start	Production Start	Alpha	Beta	Format Q/A	Gold Master	Release
DATES	01/02/07	04/02/07	09/10/07	06/04/08	08/05/08	09/01/08	09/22/08	10/21/08

Status:
- Design session covering pirate attacks and their effect on the game economy.
- Starship pathing is partially functional.
- Development kits received.

Action Items

Date	Status	Description
02/23/07	Done	Integrate missile tracking system.
03/02/07	In Progress	Art asset list for missions 1-7.
03/09/07	In Progress	Review Technical Design Document first draft.

Sample weekly status report. This one shows key dates and tracks action items.

All Talk and No Action

We've all been in meetings where great ideas were suggested or problems were identified, yet somehow nothing ever gets implemented or fixed. This is usually because no action items were recorded and no one was assigned to deal with them. This simple process can make the difference between success and failure on a game.

Task Assignments

Simply giving the team a schedule and task list is not sufficient, especially when production first begins. The master schedule can be overwhelming for most teams, so producers need to dole out assignments in smaller pieces by establishing goals at the beginning of the week and showing the tasks that need to be completed for the next milestone. This makes goals more attainable and provides a feeling of satisfaction every week when objectives are reached.

Galactic Buccaneer			
Weekly Task List		12-Mar-07	
PERSON	**ROLE**	**DUE DATE**	**TASK**
Duke	Concept Artist	15-Mar-07	Concept sketches of squirrel ships
Lisa	Producer	15-Mar-07	Review art task list for missions 1-7
Robert	Writer	16-Mar-07	Character descriptions for invasion sequence
Lisa	Producer	16-Mar-07	Upgrade Maya license for Helen
William	Level Designer	17-Mar-07	Rough map of jungle planet
Bonnie	Technical Director	20-Mar-07	Specification for object database
Chris	Modeler	21-Mar-07	Harvester model
Robert	Writer	22-Mar-07	Review dialogue for mission 1
George	Art Director	23-Mar-07	Review level layout for mission 1
John	Programmer	23-Mar-07	Harvester logic for mission 1
Helen	Animator	23-Mar-07	Pirate fighting moves

Example of a simple weekly task sheet.

Change Requests

There will come a time in every project when a significant change needs to be made. Games, especially those containing original intellectual property (IP), are creative endeavors, and you have to accept that the design that everyone envisioned at the outset may require modifications as the product begins to take shape. Give your designers some room to make mistakes as they push to try new things.

> I f you want to add something, then tell me what I can cut.
>
> — John Hight

Change Request

Project: *Galactic Buccaneer*

Date: March 12, 2007

Requestor: Lisa Abarta, Producer

ITEM:
Add squid monsters to ocean world invasion.

IMPACT:
The squid monsters were not part of the original design. This change will require the following:
- Concept, modeling, and animation of the squid monsters. Estimate 10 person/days
- Special case tentacle code: Estimate: 5 person/days
- Design integration into ocean world missions. Estimate: 3 person/days
- Sound effects for squid monsters. Estimate: 1 person/days

NOTE: The manatee monster will be dropped, saving 5 person/days.
Total impact: 14 person/days

COST:
Additional resources will be added to stay on schedule.
Contract services: $1000/day x 14 days = $14,000

APPROVED

_____
Executive Producer

_____
Publisher

Sample change request, which includes the impact and cost of the change and requires formal sign-off.

This doesn't mean that the design should be completely organic and the schedule should slip constantly until the team is exhausted or the funds run out. The producer needs to be the steady hand. If a major change is contemplated, call together all the leads and estimate the impact on all areas. Get input from objective parties, marketing, and upper management to determine whether the change will improve the potential sales of the game. Once the cost of the change is understood in terms of time and resources, look for areas of the game to simplify or remove. This may sound narrow-minded, but it is the best way to keep the game on schedule and the team focused on quality rather than quantity. It also avoids the phenomenon called "feature creep."

> Let's save that for the sequel.
> — *Tactful producer, when faced with feature creep*

Feature Creep

Feature creep occurs when staff members perform independently and not as part of a team. Individuals begin to embellish on the design by extending beyond the original specification. This can produce desirable improvements—but, more often than not, it creates overly complex gameplay and a lack of continuity throughout the game. Feature creep most likely occurs because people want to leave their mark on the game. Most team members fancy themselves as designers and, once they get hold of an area of the game, they like to improve on the plan. Most games that run late or require excessive "crunch time" are victims of feature creep. This is solely the fault of the producer, who must be objective and, even at the risk of bruising a few egos, stand up and say "stop."

> Avoid feature creep by starting with a conservative plan and keeping the development team involved to resolve dependency issues.
>
> — *Jeff Stewart (Game Designer, Petroglyph Games)*

Diagram by Per Olin

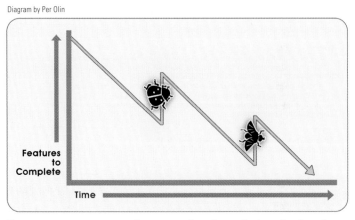

Feature creep can cause projects to run late due to the introduction of unexpected tasks.

Avoiding Feature Creep

Feature creep is inevitable in any software project. The key is to keep an accurate schedule so you know where you are in the development process. You also need to identify the most important tasks and features first, and complete them. . . . It is important to realize up front that you are going to run out of time, and plan to drop features at the appropriate time. There should be a number of such checkpoints. If you cannot figure out how a feature should work in pre-production, it is unlikely that you will be able to build it in production—so it should be dropped. Any features not completed by Alpha should be dropped, since finishing out the existing features and polishing gameplay always takes more time than you have from Alpha to Gold anyway. Getting started on a feature that cannot be completed is a waste of time, and it makes the project late. It should be avoided.

— John Ahlquist (Founder, Ahlquist Software)

Feature creep is a constant battle for anyone who values shipping games on time. It amounts to battling the urge for perfectionism in favor of expediency. Even in the most schedule-free game, feature creep can cause the introduction of new bugs and balance issues late in the process and must be avoided. A favorite phrase I use with my colleagues (and they frequently use with me) is "next game". That simple phrase is a reminder that just because an idea is a good one, doesn't mean it belongs in this game, at this time. The other way to battle all of these issues is to have a solid preproduction and prototyping phase. If there is a need to add a feature late in a game's development, you probably have a failed development whose seeds were sown many months before.

— Michael John (Lead Designer, Method Games)

I am open to new features that improve the game, but they should have a very good reason for getting in there. Since the team has been part of the original feature list and time estimates they also know that if new features have to take priority, other features have to be cut. I make this obvious for both the development team and the publisher at the start of each project and have them commit to it.

— Jesper Sorensen (Business Unit Manager & Game Director, ncom.dk)

Build in adequate time for change and polish. In specific, when planning projects I build in chunks of "change time", which then get allocated to specific tasks as those changes come up. If nothing changes, worst case I can bring it in early. However, since you always have changes, this time rarely goes unused… and though you may end up exceeding this time buffer, it still allows you to deal with the unexpected. Simply put… plan for the unexpected, because while you cannot predict the specifics, you can predict that it will come in some form.

— Graeme Bayless (Director of Production, Crystal Dynamics)

Slippage

Slippage is such a chronic problem in the game industry that many people just take it for granted. History has already shown that developers and publishers who combat this issue and learn to ship their games on time are, on average, more successful than those who do not.

Slippage usually happens when everything is going along as planned, but then things begin to slow down. Eventually, momentum stalls and the team is putting out fires and not forging ahead. Feature creep causes slippage, but there are many other ways it can occur, including the following:

- Incomplete design or planning, such as jumping into production too early ("We didn't think about that.)
- Design that exceeds the capabilities of the team, technology, or target platform ("We've optimized everything, and we just can't get the framerate we need.")
- Poor interdisciplinary communication ("But I needed it this way!")
- Starting the integration process late and discovering that things don't link up properly ("Let's build everything first then put it together.")
- Insufficient quality assurance during early production ("We'll fix the bugs after we hit Alpha.")

Producers have to look ahead and recognize when the actions of the team may lead to problems down the road. Tackle the tough problems first. Don't put them off until later in the schedule. At that point, too much has been invested and you may end up throwing more effort into an inferior approach. Remember this: Shipping a bad game on time won't make it better, but shipping a good game late may cost you sales.

> **A** late game is only late until it ships, but a bad game is bad forever.
>
> — *Game industry saying*

Milestones

As mentioned in the previous chapter, *milestones* are specific points in the schedule where various components are integrated and something tangible is created. Most publishers expect to receive a milestone every 4-6 weeks so they can track progress.

Diagram by Per Olin

Early milestones in the schedule contain updates to the design, art content, and various software modules. Some software is playable, although in stand-alone programs with placeholder artwork.

Regular Builds

"Disciplined" studios have a build process in their technical design reviews (TDRs), and they begin making daily builds as soon as the first bit of game code is written. Team members test their changes in a local copy of the daily build and then check revisions into a source control system such as Perforce. If somebody breaks the build, a programmer (usually a lead) works out the issues, and the newly checked-in item either is corrected or reverts to the last known safe state. This process provides the team with a continuous update on the current state of the game, and it reduces the chaos of integrating everyone's work for regular milestone deliveries.

First Playable

First playable is the point at which a playable version of the game can be delivered, usually on DVD, to the publisher. It is a snapshot of the game: a single mission or level that shows the intended game play. It may have placeholder art and sound. If placeholder art is used, you should include a rendered scene, or mock-up, showing what a final game screen should look like. These rendered scenes establish the goal for the look of the game long before the game technology is in place. The technical director should be consulted when the scenes are being created to ensure that the artwork matches the projected capabilities of the game.

Alpha

Alpha signals the point at which all content is now in the game and all features are fully implemented. There may be considerable tuning and debugging to follow, but no new features or content will be added after this point. Some content may be replaced in response to quality concerns, and features may be adjusted as well. The producer needs to hold the line and scrutinize tasks carefully to ensure that no new features or content are being created after Alpha.

It's also up to the producer to keep the team honest. Many good people fool themselves and others into thinking their game is at Alpha when, in fact, it isn't. The producer needs to conduct a complete review of the Alpha candidate and get sign-off from the various directors and leads that no new work needs to be added.

Quality assurance testing of the Alpha milestone focuses on reporting playability issues and bugs that impair a player's ability to complete the game. The Alpha milestone is not expected to be bug free. All placeholder art and sound should be replaced with final assets.

Beta

Beta is the point in the production process where all content is locked. Content cannot be changed or replaced. From Beta until completion, only bug fixes take place. Some bug fixes may require that content be altered or removed. In this case, the producer must approve of this alteration. The goal of Beta is to create a stable release candidate. As with Alpha, it is up to the producer to decide if the game has reached Beta. If the game isn't ready for content lock, the producer needs to determine what steps are required to get to Beta.

Tuning Game Difficulty

QA testers and development team members are much more adept at playing the game than the average consumer. If they tell you the game is too hard then it probably is. If they tell you it is too easy, get a second opinion by organizing play tests with average consumers who have never seen the game. Most consumers complain that they were unable to finish a game they bought because they got stuck or the game got too difficult. They paid $50 or more for the game; why shouldn't they be allowed to finish it?

The Beta milestone should be fully playable and relatively bug free. No bugs should prevent a tester from playing the game from beginning to end. Quality assurance testing now focuses on finding all bugs in the game. Some tuning is expected, but this should be fine-tuning of difficulty to suit the market. Adjustments may include:

- Lowering (or increasing) the amount of damage that an enemy can take before succumbing to a player's attacks; the speed of an enemy may be altered as well
- Reducing (or increasing) the number or frequency of enemies, traps, or obstacles in a given area
- Adding (or removing) power-ups, money, weapons, armor, or other types of rewards in a given area

Release Candidate

The *release candidate* is the first build of the game that the development team feels could go to manufacturing. At this point the game is assumed to be bug free. All bugs reported by quality assurance testing have been either fixed or waived. The producer is the final authority in waiving bugs. Producers should exercise judgment before waiving a bug. Although producers have a responsibility to ship products on time, they have an even greater responsibility to deliver a stable, high-quality product to consumers. The release candidate undergoes a complete round of testing, with testers playing the game from beginning to end, and checking both alternate pathways and player choices. All bugs reported fixed by the team are regression tested to verify that they are fixed in the release candidate. First priority A-bugs are dealt with immediately, and a new candidate is placed into testing. Once all bugs have been verified as fixed or waived, the candidate goes to *format* testing or, for PC games, *compatibility* testing. It is very wise to pre-format or pre-compat test (console/PC) before you get to this stage, perhaps by doing a dry run toward the end of Alpha and/or in Beta.

Gold Master

Format testing is performed by the console hardware manufacturer to ensure that the game is fully compliant with all technical requirements of the console. Manufacturers certify every game released on their consoles to guarantee consistency of interface and quality of their catalogs. Once a game has passed format testing, it is certified for manufacturing. This final build is called the *gold master*. For PC games, compatibility testing is performed instead of format testing to ensure that the game works on a wide variety of PCs.

Localization

Most games are released in multiple territories, sometimes simultaneously. The milestones for localized versions of the game lag behind the primary language. By Alpha, the script is in final form and casting for voice talent can begin in each territory. By Beta, the script has been recorded and all game text is locked. Each territory can complete translation and voice recording. Once the gold master is reached for

Nintendo

the primary language, Beta testing can take place for each territory. By this time, text and voiceover should be fully translated, recorded, and integrated back into the game. All artwork that needs to be altered for local language and culture has been changed. There may be multiple release candidates as bugs specific to the territory are encountered. These bugs are mostly errors in text or voice integration—but there are differences in the way in which consoles and PCs work in each country.

Many games, such as *The Legend of Zelda: Four Swords Adventures*, display translated text to accompany voiceover during cinematic sequences.

Frank Gilson on Managing the Development Team :::::

Frank T. Gilson (Senior Developer for Digital Games, Wizards of the Coast)

At Wizards of the Coast, Frank T. Gilson manages game design and development in the R&D department. Frank was a producer at Atari's Santa Monica, CA office—managing aspects of third-party development, contracting with talent (such as composers and writers), and overseeing external development. Prior to working at Atari, Frank was Associate Producer at Blizzard for *Warcraft III: Reign of Chaos* and the *Frozen Throne* expansion. He also worked in quality assurance as QA Technical Engineer (*Diablo 2*), QA Lead Analyst (*StarCraft: Brood War*), and QA Analyst (*StarCraft* and *Mac Diablo*). Prior to joining the game industry, Frank was a graduate student at UC Irvine in Mathematical Behavioral Sciences, studying formal models for economics, voter choice, and psychology.

In practice, the producer on a project is rarely in a position of power with respect to hiring or organizing the structure of development teams. Rather, the producer must be the glue between all the teams. I like to see each team have a competent lead. This person should have mastered his or her subject area, be a good manager, and be a 'passion driver' for the project. Various tools that improve communication and productivity certainly apply to the teams that work on game production. You need to organize and tie together e-mails, work documents, schedules, tasking, meetings, and more into a cohesive whole. A work in progress database with appropriate cross links is very valuable. Look to the lead for a team if the team is failing. This person is the captain of that ship, and responsible for its work output and morale.

Leadership

Producers may not be the vision holders, but they are the leaders. It's up to them to constantly foster communication and understanding among the group. They hold all team members accountable for their contributions and give each the opportunity to succeed. Producers don't just hire and manage a staff; they build a team. Many producers are the formal supervisors of the associate or assistant producers rather than any of the other development team members. Also, producers generally do not sign any checks, which can be a challenge sometimes!

Diagram by Per Olin

In his book *Winning*, Jack Welch describes the necessary characteristics of a good leader as the 4 Es:

- Positive *Energy*. Enthusiastic, not complainers.
- Ability to *Energize* others. Inspirational.
- *Edge*. Ability to make tough decisions.
- *Execute*. Ability to get things done.

Who wouldn't want to work with a producer who exhibited these traits? Producers who come to work each day and honestly conduct themselves with the 4 Es will have the respect of their teams and the faith to complete their projects. In addition to the four Es, honesty and adaptability are essential traits.

Honesty

It is critical that producers be *honest*. If you don't know the answer, admit it and find out. Good leaders are authentic and don't pretend to be something they're not. Once you're comfortable being who you are, you will be comfortable leading others.

Adaptability

Producers need to manage a wide group of people with varying degrees of experience and ability. This requires that you *adapt* your leadership style to fit the situation. Seasoned professionals are more like peers. They may require little or no supervision. Producers need to get status updates but rarely hand out assignments to these people. Team leads are skilled at their craft but may require coaching in their management abilities. The remainder of the staff is focused on the current assignment and requires a steady stream of task assignments. New hires need to know the processes and need regular communication until they get up to speed.

Accomplishments and Objectives

Accomplishments and objectives are usually discussed during annual performance reviews but should be applied throughout the production process, from action items in weekly status reports to task lists in the schedule. Objectives need to be clearly understood and, once completed, accomplishments should be recognized. Encourage team members to set their own objectives, taking care that they are in sync with the overall objectives of the project. Don't be shy about acknowledging when an objective has been met. Sometimes this simple feedback motivates the team more than anything else.

Conflict

Conflict can arise over tasks, procedures, or personalities. Task and procedure issues can be worked out through negotiation by bringing interested parties together and

Illustration by Ian Robert Vasquez

discussing an accommodation or compromise. However, personal conflicts are tougher, and they usually result from misunderstandings. Producers should try to mediate in order to clarify each side's perspective. Many producers try to avoid conflict. This is a mistake. Healthy conflict can lead to new ideas and avoid *groupthink,* where logical solutions are discarded in favor of popular ones. If your game just isn't fun or lacks something, try to bring different people together and encourage them to challenge the assumptions made about the game.

The "Small Team" Advantage

I prefer smaller teams of highly talented people as opposed to large assembly line teams. I require discussion and interaction between everyone on the team, and I encourage autonomous decision-making and responsibility. The development director has final decision-making authority with respect to the overall project goals, but that tends to be more "pointing the ship thataway" as opposed to micro-managing every small decision.

— *Mike Booth (CEO, Turtle Rock Studios)*

Optimizing Teamwork and Synergy

I tend to structure my teams to optimize teamwork and synergy. This takes on many forms... first, I believe in a peer-management system... where each of the primary disciplines (Art, Programming, Design) is led by a lead/manager, and this trio works together as a team to resolve 95% of all conflicts or difficulties... referring to their Senior Manager to resolve the 5% they cannot resolve without that help. I also physically mix disciplines in seating... I like to see cross-discipline teams formed to take on chunks of the game, and I seat them to maximize communication. This "pod system" approach gives these sub-sets of the team maximum ability to own their portion of the game... which leads to higher levels of commitment and quality from those teams. Regarding my management techniques, I am a firm believer that the role of management is one of facilitation. Simply put, my job is to provide an environment where talented people can be successful. I try to identify obstacles before they become barriers, and eliminate them before the team hits them at speed. I am also a firm believer in delegation and ownership... I want to let the team own their title, and the respective disciplines feel ownership and responsibility for their parts. The peer structure mentioned above helps with this... peer pressure can be a wonderful thing when properly directed. As for my own specific touch, I focus my attention on the 30,000' view, allowing the team to drill into the details. That way, I remain far enough distant to keep perspective, and can use that perspective to remind the team of things they may be too close to see. When a team begins to fail, I take measured steps to rectify. I will start out by identifying the areas of difficulty, usually through more direct observation and/or much more frequent updates. As the information is exposed, I will be able to ascertain at least some of the potential issues... and I'll start taking incremental steps towards fixing them. For instance, let's say that one problem is a discipline lead who is failing as a leader... I will start out by trying to give direct leadership support while simultaneously seeking to get training/mentoring to that lead. If this is unsuccessful, the support will become more directive, with specific goal-setting. If this still fails, I will potentially make a change... better a short-term pain than a long-term failure. Note that team failures are rarely failures of a team... but rather failures in leadership.

— *Graeme Bayless (Director of Production, Crystal Dynamics)*

At Stormfront Studios, the producer is the overall manager of a game project, and is responsible for the quality and timeliness of a project as well as completing the game on budget. To achieve these goals the producer leads a team of leaders from each of the four creative disciplines: game design, art, audio and technology. It's his or her job to focus and organize the efforts of those creative leaders and their teams to make the project successful. Disciplines with smaller headcounts will have a single leader and a small team reporting to him or her. Larger teams may have several leads for different sub-groups reporting to the discipline's project leader, each with several people reporting to them. At Stormfront, we work by managing to objectives. Each individual and team define (or are assigned) the key next steps they have to follow on their project, and we then track when those key steps are completed. When teams get off-track, the biggest key is to catch it fast, so the problems get addressed immediately rather than having time to grow. This is why tracking weekly progress asset-by-asset is so critical.

— *Don L. Daglow (President & CEO, Stormfront Studios)*

We have four main departments: programming, art, design, QA. Each of those departments has a lead who reports directly to the producer. Within each department there are sub-leads for various areas such as world-building, missions, animation, environmental art, interface, server, etc. We use various techniques to manage the team. They include daily reports from every team member that are rolled up into departmental dailies that are sent to the whole team. We use Microsoft Project Server so each person can keep their schedule up to date themselves. We also use checklists for every part of the game and we try to always be signing off something as complete.

— *Starr Long (Producer, NCsoft)*

Christian Allen on Empowering Development Teams :::::

Christian Allen
(Creative Director, Red
Storm Entertainment)

Christian's most recent project at Red Storm Entertainment is *Tom Clancy's Ghost Recon Advanced Warfighter* (Xbox 360). He grew up in Eagle River, Alaska. He served four years in the Military Police in the Marines, mainly at MCAS El Toro. After finishing his tour in 1999, he returned to Alaska—serving on the Air National Guard with the 176th Security Police, and working for the State of Alaska as a Child Support Enforcement Officer. Later, he worked in IT & Communications for the Department of Emergency Services. Christian started making mods for the *Rogue Spear* series in 1999—and, in 2001, he decided to make a career change and get into the gaming industry. He moved from Alaska to Arizona and attended the Art Institute of Phoenix. During this time, he also joined the Army National Guard—serving with the 855th Military Police Company. In 2002, Christian was hired by Red Storm Entertainment as an Assistant Game Designer. Since then, he has worked on a variety of military-themed first person shooters in several roles—from scripter, to weapon designer, to lead designer, to creative director. He lives with his wife of over 10 years, Angeline Fowler, and his daughter, Isabel.

Our teams at RSE are broken up in the classic manner, with Art, Engineering, and Design sections. As a Lead Designer, I have tried to foster a sense of ownership with the Designers and Scripters that work for me. I generally try to identify different areas of the game, and put one of the team members in charge of that section. With oversight, I try to empower them to take "their" part of the game and make it the best it can be within the scope of the project. I have found that this really motivates people, as well as identifying potential future leads among the team. Two of the Designers that have taken up this role under me have gone on to become Lead Designers.

When things are failing on a team, one thing we have done in the past is to use the "strike team" organization. Generally, when gameplay features are not panning out, and we don't want to cut them, bringing in fresh eyes from different disciplines can quickly help to turn them around. This hasn't always been a perfect solution, but it definitely helps to bring in people from various disciplines to attack the problems from other angles.

Rich Adam on Working with Small Scale Teams :::::

Rich Adam has been in the game business for 26 years. He has worked as producer, designer, and programmer at various times in his career. His work has included a six-year stint pioneering the product development for all of the interactive television programming at Interactive Network. Prior to forming Mine Shaft, Rich developed games at Atari, Bally Midway, Electronic Arts, THQ, and Silicon Entertainment. His game credits include *Missile Command, Gravitar, Empire Strikes Back, Trivial Pursuit, Dungeons & Dragons, John Madden Football, PGA Tour Golf, NASCAR Silicon Motor Speedway, High Heat Baseball 2002, Pac-Man Bowling, Pro Series Golf, MX Superfly,* and *WWE CrushHour.*

Rich Adam (Chief Executive Officer, Mine Shaft Entertainment)

We are a small shop, so our teams are small and we share the same facility. However, even small teams seem quite large when you take into account the middleware, the platform API, and contractors that are used in development. So even in a small scale team there is quite a bit of choreography that goes on to keep things on track. For every person we have on staff working on a project, we probably have 10–20 people who are working on subsystems that have schedule dependencies. Increasingly these non-staffers are working on a different continent or hemisphere. This is a complex problem, compounded by the fact that the ultimate product completion condition is subjective—is it fun?

We use weekly meetings as a formal method. But these meetings rarely happen as we are constantly discussing and iterating the design/implementation as a result of trying to make a feature work, so a formal meeting in-studio would be redundant. I guess this means that we are very open and loud about what we are doing every hour of every day. Our culture does not encourage going into a cave and creating a feature solo.

This is not true of external relationships. We have weekly conference calls with our publisher to communicate status and needs. For outside development groups, the weekly meeting is an effective method for staying in sync. We typically prefer Tuesday as the sweet spot in the week to conduct this communication. The standard tools MS Project and Excel for tracking schedules and budgets are sufficient for staying on top of the work.

I have not had much experience with failing teams. My experience is that teams generally do not fail. Flawed designs or concepts, or external factors tend to be the cause of project failures, not the teams. However, if a member of the team is creating disharmony or causing a significant negative impact on the project, I will design and implement an exit plan for that individual. This must be done decisively and expediently.

Shannon Studstill on the Importance of Communication : : : : :

Shannon Studstill (Director of Production, Sony Computer Entertainment of America)

Receiving her degree in cinematography from the AFI in 1994, Shannon Studstill was well-poised to begin her career at the start of the modern era of interactive entertainment development. She combined her artistic background with strong organizational and managerial abilities to ship two PlayStation titles as an Art Director. In 1998, she was approached by Sony Computer Entertainment of America (SCEA) in San Francisco and offered the position of lead artist. When Sony wanted to establish a new development studio in Los Angeles, they turned to Studstill to head the art department. As Director of Art for the Santa Monica Studio, she was responsible for building and organizing the art team. As the studio geared up for production on its first title, *Kinetica*, it became apparent to Sony that Studstill would best serve the Santa Monica Studio as producer for the game. Continuing a pattern she'd established at every stage of her career, Shannon shipped *Kinetica* on time and on budget. The Santa Monica Studio was growing, and so were Studstill's responsibilities. She was now evaluating all production processes and schedules while managing productions across the studio. These skills made Shannon the ideal person to assume the role of Director of Internal Development. It was with her production oversight that the studio began work on the game that would become the best-selling *God of War*, on which Studstill would again serve as producer. Working closely with game director David Jaffe, Shannon oversaw the project from initial conception to final product. Sony's largest-budget game to date, the title hit the shelves in late March 2005 to great critical acclaim and financial success. Studstill is now the Executive Producer for the God of War franchise, overseeing the development of future God of War productions on all platforms. She continues her role as Director of Internal Development, supporting PS2 and next generation PS3 titles that are developed internally, along with PSP and mobile productions that are developed externally through the Santa Monica studio. Shannon lives on the Westside of Los Angeles with her husband, an executive producer for a well-known Santa Monica commercial visual effects company, and their young daughter.

There is no team structure that will work for all projects, just as there is no formula for creating a successful new title. Building the right team for developing a game can be as challenging as designing the game itself, and as important to the success of the title.

Once the core group has been created and prototyping has begun, a production team can be assembled to start the high-level planning for the project, ensuring the team has a solid set of goals and time to meet them. This team can include a senior producer, producers, associate producers, assistant producers, and possibly a production assistant. In addition, department leads, frequently drawn from the core prototyping teams, begin assembling their individual teams. Of course, this loose outline is filled only with painstaking care, as strengths and weaknesses of team members must be evaluated and production roles properly assigned.

If there is one aspect of team management we at the Santa Monica studio stress over all others, it is communication. On productions like *God of War*, which span so many disciplines and in which every team member's work affects and is affected by those around him, every mistake, each change in direction, any schedule slippage can ripple across the entire project. As valuable as a well-designed and maintained schedule is, no production is a straight line from beginning to end. To keep the entire team moving forward through the inevitable obstacles that arise, the entire team must be in a constant state of communication. The senior producer must define clear paths of communication for the production group and leads. The leads are responsible for ensuring that every team member is aware of the state of the game, changes that are anticipated, how their workload will be affected, and the necessity for them to stay on top of their tasks. Of course, communication flows in both directions on a well-functioning team, and all developers are expected to keep their leads informed of their progress, to express misgivings about a course of action, or simply to offer opinions on the next stage of development.

If communication is the key to a successful game development team, most often it is when communication breaks down that a team fails. Unclear goals being set, interdependencies being neglected, conflicts going unresolved for too long, schedules slipping without notification to leads—any number of instances in which key information is not relayed to the right person at the right time can derail a project. Team relationships cannot be designed at the outset and then ignored; rather, they must be nurtured throughout production. Team members must be constantly encouraged to speak up when they foresee problems on the horizon, when they are unsure of the immediate or long-term goals of the project, or when they think a lead or producer has made a poor decision. Mismanagement of this communication can lead to resentment and team discontent at a minimum, and can grind a production to a halt in extreme cases.

As such, when approaching a failing team, an assessment of the communication pipeline is the top priority. The communication between the producer and leads is evaluated for frequency, substance, and clarity of communication. Is information disseminated by the producer being distributed to all departments? Is the producer available to team members, engaged in problem solving, and committed to keeping the entire team involved? Identifying and correcting any breakdowns must be done before any further repair can be started. No amount of rescheduling or adjustment of game scope will get a project back on track if the team is not talking to each other.

In the hectic race toward a project's completion, it's sometimes easy to dismiss personal issues in favor of tackling the bigger problems facing the team. Those small issues can balloon quickly and should be addressed at the onset, once again by working on communication. Game development can be an arduous task, so one-on-one discussions between a manager and an employee take on added weight. We depend on our staff not to be just skilled, but inspired as well. Just as employees must show their willingness to go above and beyond the normal scope of their jobs when making an exemplary title, so must managers be willing to go the extra distance for an employee who has demonstrated consistent quality throughout production. It is also the producer's job to recognize that a developer falling behind schedule is affecting the entire team, and to take responsibility for helping reduce their workload or re-think the workflow to get them back on track.

This personal style of management can seem like a huge investment of time during the critical periods of development, but it's important to remember that a studio is being built and maintained, not just a single project. Each employee carries with them a need to grow and have their work and worth recognized and rewarded, and each deserves open and honest communication, in the form of useful and detailed reviews, promotions when warranted, and added responsibilities if so desired. The industry has experienced a boom in recent years, but you won't find many veterans who are doing this simply for the money. Making games can be a rich and rewarding experience in countless ways. It's the job of management to facilitate that by creating an environment in which talented and passionate individuals can thrive, in which good ideas can be explored and shaped into great games, and in which each team member is aware of the importance of their voice in the development of a title.

Designing and encouraging communication pathways, anticipating and resolving conflicts, and taking a personal approach to management at all levels of a team hierarchy are all sound approaches to take when managing a game development project. In practice, these simple tasks can require constant attention and energy given to tasks that do not directly relate to moving a game forward. However, production cycles mandate a team that functions well together for years, not months, and neglecting these necessities can lead to disastrous results. It may be less work to do a post-mortem on a project that has failed than to overcome the inevitable hurdles encountered during production, but we're in the business of shipping great titles, so whatever it takes to do so is more than worth the effort.

Effective team management improves productivity by creating a harmonious, problem-solving environment. Good leaders may not directly influence game design, but they empower their teams to do their best and to be objective about their work. The next chapter moves beyond the development team and looks at relationships with external groups and entities that support the game.

:::CHAPTER REVIEW:::

1. How will you incorporate the five stages of group development into your management plan for your original game project? Run a mock production meeting for your original game project, based on your production plan. How will you ensure that communication within the meeting will be as effective as possible?

2. What are some major milestones associated with your project? How will you avoid feature creep and slippage, and ensure that your team will meet these milestones?

3. Read at least three post-mortems from the Gamasutra website (http://gamasutra.com). Discuss how you can apply what you've learned from each to your own game project.

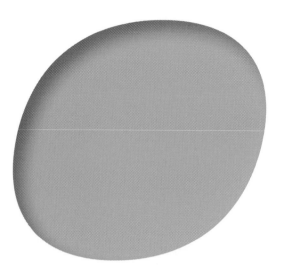

CHAPTER

8

External Relationships

managing beyond the development team

Key Chapter Questions

- What is the difference between first- and third-party publishers?

- What are the concerns of a *licensor*?

- What is the difference between *quality assurance* and *compatibility testing*?

- What are some typical assets needed by marketing for product promotion?

- What is *right of first refusal* in an agreement?

The producer needs to maintain communication with many different groups beyond the development team: publishers, licensors, press, vendors, quality assurance, legal, business affairs, and finance. Producers skilled at juggling budgets, schedules, and technical details may overlook the importance of communication. If you can't maintain consistent and responsible interaction with everyone involved, you need to get help. Projects fail when communication breaks down.

Publishers

Publishers need to know the status of the project. They are the investors backing the project and your partners in development. Some publishers are very collaborative and want input on the creative direction of the game. Other publishers adopt a laissez-faire attitude but need assurance that the project is on track.

Electronic Arts

EA has been the publisher of the *Madden* franchise (*Madden NFL 07* shown) since 1989. Over the years, many different external and internal studios have made *Madden* games for EA.

Don't make the mistake of reporting only the good news. If something isn't happening as planned or if an aspect of the game isn't hitting your goals, let them know. By the same token, don't dump all your problems on your publisher. Good producers are honest and they have multiple plans for fixing problems. Share this with your publisher and let them give input on the solution.

It's tempting to build things in a logical order for the benefit of your software engineers; however, this often doesn't provide visible progress to anyone but the engineering staff. Every milestone you submit should have a visible indication of progress. New features implemented should have final quality art—not placeholders—to best demonstrate the vision of the game. This requires extra effort, and possibly some rework down the road, but it instills confidence. You will need confidence from your publisher, the press, and your team to keep the passion and momentum going during development.

First- and Third-Party Publishing

A *first-party publisher* manufactures video game consoles and publishes games for the consoles they sell. Examples include Sony, Microsoft, and Nintendo. A *third-party publisher* produces games for multiple video consoles and is not owned by or tied to a specific console manufacturer. Developers working with first-party publishers may gain access to new technology earlier than their counterparts working with third-party publishers. In return, they usually work exclusively on a single console and optimize their software for that platform. By contrast, developers working with third-party publishers often create games for two or more platforms. Their technology needs to be adaptable for use on various consoles.

Developers

Most of this book is written from the perspective of the developer. However, some producers will find themselves working for a publisher and managing external developers. There are three categories of developers: first-party, second-party, and third-party.

First-Party Developers

A *first-party developer* is usually a combination of a hardware manufacturer, publisher, and development studio. First-party developers sometimes use the name of the company itself (Nintendo). Most first-party developers are considered part of the manufacturer, not a separate entity, and are wholly owned by the console manufacturer. Examples include Naughty Dog (which is owned by Sony Computer Entertainment of America [SCEA]) and Bungie (which is owned by Microsoft).

Second-Party Developers

A *second-party developer* is a combination of a developer and a publisher. These companies are not owned by a console manufacturer, but they might make games exclusively for one manufacturer. An example is Insomniac Games (makers of the *Ratchet & Clank* series), which is under contract with Sony to make games exclusively for Sony hardware.

First-party and second-party developers tend to have a close working relationship with their publisher. There are no other entities vying for the resources of the developer. Production pipelines tend to be tailored to closely match the procedures of the publisher. Since these developers don't work with the competition, they can be trusted to safeguard proprietary technology. Producers tend to work with these teams as they would with partners; very little information is withheld. Goals are virtually the same between producer and developer.

Third-Party Developers

Third-party developers create games for multiple platforms and various manufacturers. Most independent developers fall into this category. Liquid Entertainment and Stormfront Studios are examples of third-party developers that have created titles published by Atari. Some third-party developers publish the games they develop

Half-Life 2, developed by Valve, is the most successful and critically acclaimed of the popular third-party-developed games.

(Electronic Arts, Ubisoft), while others develop only games that are published by other companies (Treyarch, Raven Software). Third-party developers have to maintain a delicate balance between competing entities. They have to remain professional and as a result are sometimes considered distant from their publisher. Producers working with third-party developers don't have as much direct knowledge of the day-to-day activities as their first-party counterparts. They need to represent the interests of the publisher. It's important for them to develop a trusting relationship and exercise diplomacy to achieve the publisher's goals.

Licensors

Licensors want to make sure that their license will be more valuable as a result of your game. Always remember that the IP is theirs, not yours. Your team may honestly believe that their creative additions to the game are vastly superior to the ideas of the licensor, and they may be, but the licensor has the final word. You need to adopt the attitude that it's their baby and they trust you to take care of it.

Peter Jackson's King Kong was based on the movie of the same name, and it was released at around the same time as the movie.

Provide the licensor with concept sketches and get approval or direction for changes. If the direction isn't clear, it is up to you to get more information to guide your team. Don't implement final models or art until you get approval. If you must proceed without approval, set your team's expectations to allow for the inevitable change requests.

Allow sufficient time in your schedule for licensor review and approval. Ask your publisher for the licensor's contractual approval time. This is typically 10 to 15 days.

Hardware Manufacturers

Console manufacturers set standards for all games that appear on their platforms. Early in development, developers and publishers must submit their game ideas to manufacturers for approval. If they fail to obtain approval, publishers run the risk

Microsoft Corporation   Sony Computer Entertainment America   Nintendo

2006 witnessed the latest battle of the next-generation consoles: Microsoft Xbox 360 (left), Sony PS3 (middle), and Nintendo Wii (right).

that a game will not be accepted for final manufacturing and the investment in creating the game will be wasted. Producers prepare the submission documents and are sometimes invited to present the concepts to the manufacturers for their approval.

EA Exception

Electronic Arts is the only publisher that is not required to obtain approval from console manufacturers for new game concepts. They used their leverage and reputation as the top independent publisher to gain this concession.

Each gold master candidate must pass the manufacturer's technical requirements checklist (TRC), a set of guidelines that each game needs to follow. It defines elements such as how a game should interface with the hardware; displaying proper legal/copyright messages; saving and loading games; and inserting peripherals. These TRCs may vary slightly from one territory to the next.

Games are tested by manufacturers to ensure that they meet both quality standards and technical requirements. This testing is usually referred to as compliance testing or final product quality assurance (FPQA). Producers are tasked with responding to the issues reported by FPQA and resolving them with the team.

No Surprises

To avoid costly surprises at the end of production, developers check for TRC issues at least twice prior to submitting their gold master candidate.

Vendors

Vendors may be subcontractors or companies providing services or assets for your game. Be sure that your agreements with them reflect your agreement with your publisher. You will probably need to have subcontractors execute a "work-for-hire" agreement to assure that they have no additional claims to the intellectual property (IP). Try to get a fixed price for services and an agreement on pricing for change requests. Avoid deals that require substantial upfront payment. If your vendor is small, pay them promptly. If they're especially talented, treat them right; they can always find someone else to work with.

Quality Assurance

Quality assurance (QA) is the process of playing the game in order to find issues that interfere with experiencing the game as intended. Typical issues are:

- flaws that impede progress
- balance problems that make the game too difficult
- pacing inconsistencies that make the game boring or tiresome

QA starts with in-house testers. They are focused mostly on checking new additions to the game and providing immediate feedback to the development team. They look for the fun factor as well as verifying that new features are implemented. The results may be reported informally via verbal feedback or formally via written reports. Average projects will have from one to four testers on staff. Large, next-gen projects may have 10 or more for short periods of time.

The next phase of QA involves an external testing team. This team is usually managed directly by the publisher. A QA team has a manager and one or two leads overseeing a team of 20–30 testers. The testers are divided into teams that work different shifts or test specific areas of the game (e.g., multiplayer vs. solo modes). QA does not look for TRC issues. This is handled by compatibility testing.

Playability Testing

Playability testing can take place once a portion of your game is fully playable. Early testing (pre-Alpha) should be limited and focus on the game mechanics and interface. If your game requires extensive background knowledge or a vivid imagination to enjoy, you need to work on the fun factor. It's a good idea to bring in small groups of players and watch them play the game. You can do this formally using focus test rooms or informally by inviting them to play at the desks of your designers. The one rule is to keep your mouth shut and just watch; don't explain anything. If it isn't obvious, you need to make it obvious. No one ever reads the manual. This can be a very frustrating and useful learning experience for your designers. Be sure your players represent likely customers (some casual gamers, some hard-core gamers). Avoid using the same people twice.

Don't confuse this testing with *focus* testing, which is done by marketing to determine how well the game is received by the target market and what messages need to be included in the advertising campaign. Focus testing should be performed post-Alpha and it should not influence the game's design. At that point, it is what it is.

Usability Testing

With regard to usability testing, [the] answer is always going to be "the earlier the better." I know that making something universally accessible is difficult—but if you commit to one user group (e.g., the visually impaired), you need to start talking to visually impaired gamers . . . early on, get them into a usability lab, and learn what needs to be done at the very earliest stages of your testing plan. [These players] are out there; they are making their own games because they can't play yours.

— *Michelle Hinn (Vice President, Game Division, DonationCoder.com)*

Test Plan

By Alpha, your publisher assigns a QA lead who will be responsible for writing the QA test plan and coordinating the testing efforts for your game. As mentioned previously, large developers may have their own QA manager. If not, daily communication with the QA lead is the job of the producer or an experienced assistant producer (AP).

The test plan covers all aspects of the game for testing. It includes permutations, or choices, that lead to multiple pathways to be tested. It describes how bugs will be classified, reported, and assigned. It outlines who has responsibility for each aspect of a bug: reporting, fixing, closing, and waiving. The plan covers headcount, equipment, and budget estimates for the QA staff. In some cases, testers will be located on-site with the developer for quick turnaround and resolution.

Bug Report

The test plan should include a sample *bug report* and instructions for how to report and reproduce bugs. Testers try to reproduce bugs multiple times so they can list the simplest steps to recreate the bug. Testers should have a means to capture their input: VCRs connected to the video output of the console, input files from keyboard/mouse or controller, screenshots, and so forth. These should be attached to the bug report or available upon request.

Seapine Software, Inc.

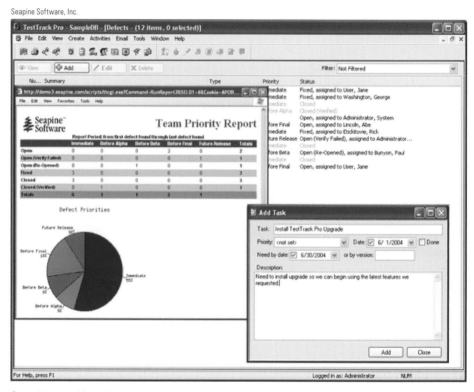

Some bug-tracking software, such as TesTrack Pro, provides detail reports and charts to help producers sort through the data.

Bug reports are entered into an online database. There are some good off-the-shelf software programs that help the team report and track bugs. These programs offer various sorting and reporting features so that producers can get a good snapshot of the game's current status.

Bug descriptions need to be clear and concise and pertain to a single issue. If you uncover a related problem, open a second bug report. Be consistent in bug classification. Opinions about gameplay should be classified as suggestions. Nothing frustrates the development team more than to see a tester's opinion listed as a high-priority bug. The best bug reports list clear, repeatable steps to replicate the bug. It may take several replays for a tester to determine the minimum action or set of actions that will reproduce a given bug.

Bug Classification

Most publishers and developers use a letter scheme to classify bugs:

Diagram by Per Olin

- A: *Highest priority.* These bugs interfere with a player's ability to complete the game. Most are crash-bugs that either crash the system or cause the game system to freeze. Some bugs involve the player getting stuck in an area, not because of difficulty, but because of geometry. Technical violations are also A bugs. These are issues that a console manufacturer requires to be fixed, such as controller warnings. Most legal issues are A bugs. These usually occur when copyright notices or credits are missing or incorrect. The game cannot ship with these bugs present.

- B: *High priority.* These bugs severely detract from the player's enjoyment of the experience. They affect the quality of the game or cause the game to be played in a manner that is not as designed. These bugs should be resolved prior to release; otherwise, the quality level is reduced and sales may be reduced.

- C: *Medium priority.* These bugs are typically aesthetic issues or game balance problems. Taken by itself a single C bug should not hold up the release of the game. A large number of C bugs is usually a sign of an incomplete product. The team should be allowed time to address as many C issues as possible.

- S: *Suggestions.* These are comments by the tester to the development team. They are usually ideas to improve game balance or appearance. They should be within the scope of the game design and not require that new features be added or new assets be created.

Often multiple testers will report the same bug in slightly different ways and with different classifications. The QA leads collate all the bugs to minimize duplicate reports and, along with the QA manager, they review classification for consistency. Most game developers strive to eliminate all A and B bugs before they ship. C bugs may affect overall quality if there are too many in a game.

Bug Fixing

Teams start testing between Alpha and Beta. If the game's assets are complete and the game play is well tuned at Alpha, testing can commence right away. At this stage, you should look for bugs that impede progress in the game and problems with game balance and pacing.

By Beta, the game should be fully playable and balanced so that most players can complete the game. If your team has been diligent about maintaining quality throughout production, there should be few A bugs at this stage. Now is the time to clear out the B bugs and as many C bugs as you can.

Diagram by Per Olin

Day	Bugs Reported	Bugs Fixed
1	30	5
2	40	10
3	35	12
4	25	15
5	20	15
6	30	17
7	20	12
8	15	15
9	10	12
10	15	11
11	10	10
12	7	12
13	5	9
14	3	10
15	7	9
Total	272	174
Rate	18	12

By Beta you should be tracking the rate at which your team is able to fix bugs; this is their *bug fix* rate. If testers are reporting more bugs on a daily basis than your team is able to fix on a daily basis, you need to focus on closing issues and, if necessary, cut any features that are incomplete or unstable. Consider the example shown in the accompanying table for a 15-day period during the QA of a game.

The rate at which new bugs are reported averages 18 per day. The rate at which bugs are being fixed is 12 bugs per day. Until the fix rate exceeds the reporting rate, this game will never be bug free.

Once your team is able to close more bugs daily than the testers report daily you are heading toward completion. You can estimate the fewest number of days required to make the game bug free by dividing the total number of bugs reported by the fix rate. For example, if the total number of bugs reported is 300, the fewest number of days required to fix them is 25, assuming the bug fix rate of 12 from the example. This doesn't take into account new bugs that crop up, so it's a good idea to add another 50% to this estimate (for a total of 450 bugs fixed in 38 days in our example). This has proven to be accurate on many projects.

Keep in mind that testers are your friends. Don't punish the messenger; be thankful that issues are being discovered before your product gets released. Every game starts out with hundreds, even thousands, of issues at Beta. With good tracking and diligence, your team should be able to address bugs quickly. It's much better to have a tester find the issues than a customer.

Archives

After the game is released, there's still more work to do. It's now time to create detailed archives of the game. Some publishers will require an archive as part of the final delivery. Even if they don't, keep one for yourself. You may miss a lucrative opportunity down the road if you neglect to keep an archive of the game's assets.

Archives should contain all software source code and assets (art, audio, designs) and the scripts required to rebuild the game. Include documentation on processes used to build intermediate assets. Be sure to retain original 3D models, concept sketches, and audio recordings. If your game becomes a big hit, these will be in demand and may be used in a sequel.

Most publishers will require that a copy of the archive be provided as the final milestone in a project. You should also keep a copy for yourself; your insurance company may even require it. Keep your archives safe, preferably off-site in a location that is fireproof, insect proof, moisture proof, and not susceptible to magnetic or electrical interference. There are many reputable firms that will store your archives for a fee.

Marketing

Marketing budgets can rival production budgets for popular games. Games that are expected to sell millions of units get television advertising, web advertising, and full print campaigns. The key to getting this sort of marketing support is that your game

must be perceived as a winner. From the very first pitch of your concept until your game hits the shelves, you need to promote the game.

It is very difficult for a new IP with no market awareness to command a substantial marketing budget, no matter how clever the game is. It is risky, perhaps foolhardy, to devote a big budget to an unproven game. That is why sequels and licensed products typically get all the attention. They already have the momentum of market awareness. Customers don't have the time to research all the games available to determine which ones are quality products. Even if a game is good, it might not suit most consumers' tastes.

More often than not, new IP catches hold by building a grassroots campaign. The Internet has helped these efforts. Developer diaries, demos, and game movies are posted at regular intervals to stimulate interest in the game. This material is a necessity, not just an option, for a successful marketing campaign; however, it isn't free, and the development team needs to generate most of the source material. Often this is not planned for ahead of time in the schedule, and producers are torn between promoting the game and building the game. The best policy is to plan on it from the beginning, whether the publisher has requested it or not.

Marketing Asset List

After the game is green-lighted for production, the product marketing manager prepares a list of assets needed for marketing support. These assets are used to promote your game and build interest among editors, retailers, and consumers.

A typical set of assets needed for marketing support include:

- *Concept drawings*: Characters, vehicles, props, and environments.
- *Hi-res 3D models*: Characters, vehicles, props, and environments. Magazines need hi-res images. If you build only one, make sure it's your lead character.
- *Rendered scenes*: Place characters in the environment. You need these for the art style guide anyway.
- *Developer notes*: Have the leads keep notes, especially the design lead. Fans love to read about how games get put together.
- *In-game screenshots*: As soon as the game starts looking good, start grabbing screens. Have your artists position the camera, lights, and characters for dramatic effect. Build versatile screenshot tools into your level editor. Don't forget particle effects, which are often implemented last; instead, have the engineering team build them early on.
- *In-game movies*: Camera movement should be in your level editor, along with character animation. Your game should be able to set up and run pre-scripted sequences for video capture. Ideally, it should store individual frames as separate files for later video editing. You want the best quality possible. If you simply capture video ouput from the back of the console and then redigitize, you'll lose quality. Don't forget to add sound effects and music.
- *Demo*: This is a controversial area. A lot of time and money goes into building and testing a demo. Some believe that demos can actually hurt sales because they satiate the consumer's interest. If your game includes an online multiplayer component, you should definitely test it with a large group (1,000–10,000 players) to get all the network and tuning issues resolved before releasing to a wider audience. Be sure that your demo doesn't contain the code or assets for the full game. Hackers might discover this and compromise your product launch. Always assume that you will need to have a playable version

of the game for shows such as the Electronic Entertainment Expo (E^3), Game Developers Conference (GDC), European Computer Trade Show (ECTS), and the Tokyo Game Show (TGS). You will also need playable versions for focus tests and editorial previews.

- *Interviews*: As the game nears completion and after it is released, you will be contacted to provide interviews. These may be e-mail questionnaires, phone interviews, publisher-sponsored events, or on-camera interviews. Select interviewees who are charismatic and passionate about the game. It enhances team morale to include more than one person in interviews. Don't always select the leads, and share the limelight. Some game industry media professionals may suggest new features for the game; politely accept their ideas but don't commit to adding them. Otherwise, you will look foolish with the team and your publisher when the feature appears in a preview article.

Try to be proactive and plan for the creation of these assets ahead of time in your production plan. Regardless of whether they have been requested, they will be used. I've never seen marketing assets go to waste.

The Critical Game Demo

The game demo plays a critical strategic role in our marketing plans. Game demos offer our target audience the opportunity to not only test drive a game, but to also generate a buzz about the game before launch. (Of course, you must have to have a great game to pull from!) This targeted sampling becomes more important than traditional advertising because you have a great tool to create evangelists on the spot.

— *Jeff Reese (Director of Marketing, Sony Computer Entertainment America)*

Marketing Plan

After the GDD is complete and the project is green-lighted for production, the product marketing manager creates a *marketing plan*. Larger publishers may assign a separate public relations (PR) manager to create a PR plan in parallel with the marketing plan. You should ask for a copy of both plans. The asset list should combine the needs of both plans as well as a schedule for PR events and marketing deadlines. Ideally, this schedule is the result of a collaborative effort between marketing and production so that the schedule can be integrated into the product plan.

The marketing plan should also describe the product, the target customer, and the competition. If this doesn't match with your own vision of the product, you need to discuss it with your marketing product manager. If the game doesn't fulfill the promise, as advertised, it will likely fail in the marketplace. You might enhance things that are considered important to customers, but you shouldn't try to change your game to fit the marketing plan. Instead, you need to make sure marketing fully understands the game and its intended audience.

Most new developers expect to see press releases the moment their game goes into production. Don't be surprised if marketing wants to keep it under wraps for a while. Seasoned marketing people know that it is important to maintain steady momentum once the game is announced. If there is nothing new to say or show about a game every week, consumers will lose interest. You want to limit exposure until you have sufficient assets to create weekly excitement until product release.

Marketing people are also a bit cautious because the track record for timely delivery among developers is terrible. Many games miss their scheduled release date by months, some miss it by years. The worst thing for a marketing product manager is to spend the entire marketing budget before the game actually ships. If you manage your game well and maintain frequent, honest communication with marketing, they'll know exactly where the game stands and can make well-informed decisions about how and when to promote it.

Resist the temptation to take matters into your own hands. Many well-meaning developers jump the gun and accept an interview with a favorite online game editor, only to find out later that it cost them coverage in a more widely circulated magazine. Editors are looking for exclusives; nobody wants news and screenshots that are already available elsewhere. All unsolicited calls should be directed to the publisher's PR manager so that PR is a coordinated, well-orchestrated campaign.

Focus Testing: Getting Immediate Feedback from Your Market

Focus testing can be a great way to gauge how well your target market will receive your game. The best experience I ever had in the game industry was a focus test with some kids who were playing a new game to provide feedback. At some point, the focus group moderator wanted to stop the kids from playing the game, but the kids refused!

— *Jesper Sorensen (Business Unit Manager & Game Director, ncom.dk)*

In-Game Advertising

Production costs rise with every successive generation of new consoles. Game budgets now rival those of feature films, but, unlike films, there is little exploitation of aftermarket revenue for games. In-game advertising is quickly gaining acceptance as a means to supplement development costs and obtain additional revenue sources postrelease. Early advertising in games followed traditional models with video commercials or advertiser-sponsored mascots.

As more homes began to connect their game PCs and consoles to the Internet, more sophisticated methods of advertising began to appear. Like product placement in a movie, in-game advertising was inside the game world. Like television, the ads could change on a regular basis.

Advertising companies such as Massive stream new ads into connected games and replace the generic billboards and signage with sponsored art. Some games even feature movies at strategically important places.

For games set in modern or future time periods these ads can actually impart a degree of authenticity to a game. What advertiser wouldn't want to have its logo in a game set a hundred years from now? Of course it does look funny years later if that company no longer exists! For example, the sci-fi movie *2001: A Space Odyssey* features spaceships with the Pan Am logo. This airline went out of business in 1991, although the name has been used by smaller regional carriers.

In-game advertising can help reduce the costs of production and potentially bring higher-quality games to consumers at lower prices. If it is not handled with care, it may also clutter the creative vision of a game with intrusive, out-of-context advertising. The decision whether to include advertising and how to include it should take into account both creative and financial interests to best serve the consumer.

Splinter Cell uses subtle in-game advertsising that changes weekly for players connected to the Internet. Advertisers pay a fee to publishers for the number of people who view their ads.

Anarchy Online: Lost Eden has a more direct advertising approach. Players encounter billboards that display video ads.

Legal and Business Affairs

Game projects start with a contract of some sort: a letter of intent, a prototype agreement, or a production agreement. Large projects involve dozens or even hundreds of contracts for content providers, licenses, talent releases and performance

Illustration by Ian Robert Vasquez

contracts, nondisclosure agreements, and so on. The contracts themselves are drafted or reviewed by attorneys, but the producer or executive producer usually negotiates the business points.

Negotiation

Development agreements are typically negotiated between a publishing executive (usually the executive producer) and the president of the development studio, but that is just the beginning. The list of negotiations continues throughout production and well after release of the game: budgets, schedules, royalties, advances, creative direction, ownership, credits, third-party licenses, technology licenses, termination conditions, transfer rights, derivative works, sequel options, warranties and indemnification, employment agreements, talent agreements, subcontractor agreements, and nondisclosure agreements (NDAs). Publishers retain a full-time staff of attorneys just to keep up with all the agreements that get created for games.

Fight Hard for What You *Really* Need

Plan on any negotiations to take twice as long as you wish they would. Be pessimistic in estimating how hard the tasks at hand will be. I try to treat the other side as my partner, not my adversary, or my mark. I am trying to make something cool, and make a profit too. The publisher as my partner is a better relationship for creating, as opposed to an adversarial relationship. Identify in advance what you really need to have from the publisher to succeed in making the game and fight hard for that. Be more flexible with the rest of the deal points.

— *Rich Adam (CEO, Mine Shaft Entertainment, Inc.)*

Think Long-Term, Not One-Off

Operate from a standpoint about what is best for the long term. Where does your business want to be down the line? Do not think about the deal as a one-off—good just to make current expenses. Agreements aren't just about financial compensation, but also are concerned with shared liabilities and goodwill.

— *Frank T. Gilson (Senior Developer of Digital Games, Wizards of the Coast)*

Negotiation Guidelines

Always tell the truth and negotiate in good faith. If you build an agreement based on lies or deception, it *will* come back to bite you in the butt. Always look at the other parties' math… if you understand their bottom line, it will help you both with negotiations. Don't expect to negotiate a deal where someone loses… while you may be able to squeeze a rookie developer because they're trying to earn their way in, at least be up front about it so everyone understands how the math works and what they are getting into. Be certain you build detailed pre-production schedules into the agreement. Honestly, when you sign a development agreement, you should be looking mostly at the prototype and pre-production. Once you have a rock-solid pre-production, the rest is easy… and if they struggle to get to that, you know that you need to re-evaluate your prior assumptions. Don't assume… anything. Always do your due diligence, and you'll be very glad you did. Question absolutely everything… not because you don't trust, but because getting those answers builds trust both ways.

— *Graeme Bayless (Director of Production, Crystal Dynamics)*

Strike a Balance

My guiding principle: Assume the game will be a hit, that you should be treated fairly, and that you'll really want the other side to work with you again under a different contract. That gives both sides a motive both to protect their own legitimate interests and to make the deal fair so they get to do the next deal and make still more money. Many times over the years I've seen supposedly clever negotiators out-maneuver people and get one-sided contracts signed. Then the game is a hit, the fact that someone was shortchanged becomes clear… and the "clever" negotiator has no chance to ever work with the successful partner again. That's not being clever, it's being short-sighted. The person brings in a few extra dollars in the short term, and loses ten times as much over the long haul.

— *Don L. Daglow (President & CEO, Stormfront Studios)*

Getting a game from concept to release requires *negotiation* skill. Here are a few basic principles of negotiation:

- Understand what the other side wants. Don't make assumptions. Take the time to really understand the other side's interests, hot points, and position. You need to create a marriage between your own interests and theirs.
- Know your best alternative to a negotiated agreement (BATNA). Ask for more but be realistic about what you would settle for.

- Don't be afraid to say no. If the deal isn't going where you want it to, be prepared to walk away. If someone is difficult to negotiate with, they'll be difficult to work with.
- Pay attention to body language. Crossing your arms creates a barrier. Arching your eyebrows means doubt. Be conscious of the other side as well as yourself.
- Practice. Have someone play devil's advocate and negotiate with you beforehand. This will prepare you and improve your confidence during the negotiation.
- Be patient. Unless you're under time constraints, don't be too eager. Let the other side do the talking and, if possible, make the first offer.
- Create a win-win scenario. Get what you want and make sure the other guy gets what he wants. If the other side feels taken advantage of they won't live up to the spirit of what's on paper.
- Stick to the agreement. Don't try to wiggle out of a commitment through crafty misinterpretation of the legalese. You know what the intent was; now honor it. Your reputation is worth far more than shaving a few points off the other guy.

After the basic deal points have been agreed to, meet with your attorney and review the deal. Let your attorney know what is important for both sides. Attorneys are very important. They can save your company from costly litigation or lost opportunities. Their job is to identify the areas of risk and minimize the risk.

No deal is perfect, and sometimes the negotiators have to move things forward. Deals can get bogged down as attorneys for both sides try to maximize future benefits for their clients. You may have to step in and make the call as to whether another round of revising the "legalese" is worth the time and trouble.

Project Termination

It is entirely possible that your project may not reach completion. Many games never see the retail shelves. It's important to understand your options and the consequences of termination.

Cause

Termination for cause represents a serious breach of contract on the part of the developer. You can be held in breach if you fail to deliver a milestone on time, but this is usually cured by delivery within a reasonable time period. You can also be held in breach if the milestones you deliver are unacceptable to your publisher (e.g., poor in quality, incomplete). You usually forfeit all rights to the game, including royalties, should the publisher decide to complete the project with someone else. In extreme cases, you may be required to pay back any advances received.

Termination for cause rarely happens. Most developers want to get their games done and most publishers realize that the best team to finish the game is the one that started it. Publishers also try to avoid the bad publicity that surrounds a cancelled project. If things have gone terribly wrong, the developer usually goes out of business shortly after termination. It's hard to find a new publisher if you have a bad track record.

Convenience

Termination for convenience occurs when the publisher decides it doesn't want to move forward with developing the game. This may happen because market conditions change and the game is no longer perceived as competitive. It may also happen when the publisher runs short on cash, although if the game is particularly good, the publisher will try to finish it by borrowing money or selling it off to another publisher. This form of termination usually happens when the game doesn't live up to expectations. It just isn't coming together and, despite multiple attempts, the team just doesn't "get it."

You may retain some rights to the game or the software used to create the game when the contract is terminated for convenience. You will likely be entitled to termination fees to compensate your company for the cost of finding another project. Some contracts allow for the developer to buy back the game and seek another publisher. Don't expect this if your game is based on a license acquired by the publisher. Licenses rarely have transfer rights.

Sequel and Porting Rights

Sequel rights grant your company the option of developing sequels to the game, assuming you successfully completed the project. These rights are not automatic; they are usually an agreement to negotiate the terms by which the sequel will be created:

1. *Right of first refusal*: The publisher agrees to come to you first and negotiate in good faith to develop the sequel. If you refuse, they are free to go to another developer.

Riven is the sequel to *Myst*, one of the most successful games of all time.

2. *Right of last negotiation or last match*: The publisher may negotiate with other developers to develop the sequel but agrees to give you the right to match the best deal they find.

3. *Right of first negotiation*: The publisher agrees to come to you first and negotiate in good faith to develop the sequel. This may be coupled with right of last match.

Porting rights are essentially the same. Porting involves moving your game from its original platform to another platform (e.g., from PlayStation 2 to PlayStation Portable).

It is usually in everyone's best interest if the original developer does the sequels and ports, assuming it has competent staff to handle the job. The original developer understands the IP and has the most vested interest in seeing the sequel or port be a commercial success.

Electronic Arts

James Bond fans can fly a jetpack in *James Bond: From Russia with Love.*

Derivative Works

Derivative works are any products based solely on your game that are not direct ports or sequels of your game. Examples include theatrical films, television shows, novels, comic books, action figures, toys, and T-shirts. If your game is based on a license, it is actually a derivative work of the original product it is based on. For example, James Bond games are derivative works of James Bond books and films.

You may be able to negotiate some royalties on derivative works if the game idea was wholly your own and you spent some resources developing the game concept before pursuing a publishing deal.

Talent Rights

If you want to use the in-game performance of an actor (voiceover or onscreen) for advertising, you'll need to secure those *talent rights* separately. If you want to film voice-over talent or musicians for a "making of" or "behind-the-scenes" video clip, you'll need to negotiate those rights as well. You can't put an actor's name prominently in your advertising or packaging unless you get that person's permission.

Some "name" talent will want approval rights before you release products or advertising containing their name, likeness, or performance.

Vin Diesel lent his voice and likeness to the *Chronicles of Riddick: Escape from Butcher Bay* game; this is no surprise, since he owns the company (Tigon) that developed it!

Errors and Omissions (E&O) Insurance

Errors and omissions (E&O) *insurance* covers a developer or production in the event that content in the game was unintentionally included without proper copyright or license. This may occur in many ways. Examples include hiring contractors without specific "work-for-hire" language in their contracts or failing to secure talent releases, even from employees, for voiceover work.

Most errors and omissions go unnoticed or without incident. Occasionally, a lawsuit is filed and damages are sought. E&O insurance protects developers and publishers from legal action, up to a limit. Typically, a developer needs to carry $3 million in E&O insurance, although with game budgets increasing and the high visibility of games, this may not be enough.

Games are a part of mainstream entertainment and they are increasingly the targets of high-profile lawsuits. Individuals and companies seek punitive damages from copyright or patent infringement. Class action groups claim damages suffered as a result of crimes committed by people influenced by videogames. Insurance and legal expenses are becoming a necessary and costly addition to the production budget.

In the early days of electronic games, a producer wore many hats: programmer, artist, designer. Now, game production involves huge teams and hundreds of complex external relationships. A single producer can't keep up with it all. Many developers delegate the various internal and external jobs to a group of producers. The modern producer is highly specialized, relying more on management and communication than technical or creative skills.

Now that you've learned what it takes to put together and manage a game project, it's time to apply your skills to an original case study. This will be the focus of the final chapter of this book, along with a discussion of the future of game project management and advice for those who want to be game producers.

:::CHAPTER REVIEW:::

1. As a developer, how will you handle external relationships with your publisher, licensor, vendors, hardware manufacturer, and funding sources? Which of these relationships will be necessary for your original game, and why? Run a mock negotiation session with one of these entities. How might you come to an agreement?

2. Using your test plan, run a QA testing series for your original game. Manage the testing process, including the creation of bug reports.

3. Create a marketing plan for your original game. How will you integrate the areas of sales, advertising, and promotion to come up with an effective marketing strategy?

CHAPTER

9

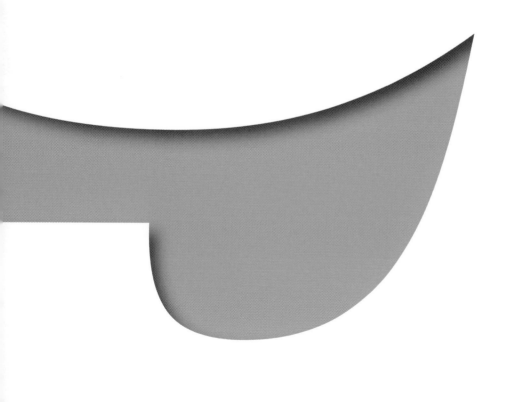

Putting It All Together

from idea to reality

Key Chapter Questions

- What are the components of a game proposal?
- What are the steps required to create a game?
- What technologies will have a major impact on games in the near future?
- How can you get started as a producer?

This chapter contains thoughts and anecdotes related to the future of game project management supplied by several leaders in the industry. It also outlines the major steps in taking a game from initial idea to final release.

Galactic Buccaneer: A Case Study

Let's walk through the steps of developing a hypothetical game project, *Galactic Buccaneer*.

Create the Concept Proposal

The first step is to create the concept proposal based on your idea. Here's a brief rundown of the concept sections for *Galactic Buccaneer*.

High Concept / Premise

Pirates in space. Fight, trade, and steal with abandon in the space colonization wave of AD 2500.

Illustration by Ian Robert Vasquez

Story Synopsis

You are the captain of a space schooner. Begin by taking mercenary jobs to earn extra money: transport a group of colonists, run a blockade with smuggled goods, or pirate a yacht. As you gain wealth and notoriety, you upgrade your ship or expand to a small fleet. The missions get more interesting: duel an alien in a game of chance, kidnap a planetary governor for ransom, or locate a secret mining facility in an asteroid belt. Play factions against each other: the Old Earth Empire, the New World Coalition, Alien species, and other privateers. Eventually gain enough wealth and power to build space stations and control entire planets.

Unique Selling Points / Game Features

Consider putting together three to five strong features for your game. These features can be related to genre, platform, market, graphics, audio, gameplay, level design, interface design, or new technologies.

- Captain a ship, govern a planet. Combines flight combat with galactic conquest.
- Build to suit your tastes. Customizable ships: hundreds of weapons and technologies, thousands of combinations.
- Explore, evade, and conquer. Open-ended gameplay in a huge world, thousands of planets.
- Be good, bad, or indifferent. Choice of missions and alliances.
- Be trustworthy, devious, or opportunistic. Diplomatic alliances in cooperative (or uncooperative) online multiplayer.

Genre and Target Platform

What will be your game's genre and target platform? Look at both single and hybrid genres, and consider various platforms before deciding on one or two primary systems.

Action-strategy game for PlayStation 3 and Xbox 360.

Sony Computer Entertainment America

Microsoft Corporation

The hypothetical game, *Galactic Buccaneer,* is designed to be played on the PlayStation 3 (left) and Xbox 360 (right).

Target Customer

The target customer (or market) demographic is primarily males ages 18–28. The game will be rated "T" (teen) for mild violence. Psychographics (such as behaviors, attitudes, values, lifestyles, and beliefs) will include fans of *Star Wars*, space flight sims, and strategy games.

Competitive Analysis

List features and benefits of your game vs. the competition, which includes all the major games in this genre that release within +/- six months of your game. Note any big-name games expected to release in the same three-month window.

Getty Images

The market for *Galactic Buccaneer* is primarily males ages 18–28.

There are two major competitors for our game: *Star Trek Legacy* and *Chromehounds*. Fortunately both games are on the Xbox 360, so we should have less competition on the PlayStation 3. Like our game, these games involve space combat and role playing.

Star Trek Legacy

Platforms: Xbox 360 and PC

Publisher: Bethesda; Developer: Mad Doc Software

USPs:

- Well-known Star Trek license
- Online multiplayer
- Over 60 ships and four playable races

Chromehounds

Platform: Xbox 360

Publisher: Sega; Developer: From Software USPs:

- Persistent online battles
- Customized ships

Financial Analysis

You need to estimate the costs of production and the expected sales (worldwide) for your game. Calculate the ROI and provide supporting arguments for your assumptions.

Let's assume that the budget for *Galactic Buccaneer* will be around $15 million and we'll sell 1 million units in the first year. It's reasonable to assume there will be at least 20 million PlayStation 3 and Xbox 360 players by the time we release. This means we have to capture 5% of the market. It's a lofty goal, but top-selling games can expect 5–10% of market share.

Team Roster

List the names and brief bios of the amazing people who will bring your game to life.

We'll want some seasoned pros for our core management staff.

- *Technical Director:* solid 3D and tech lead experience
- *Art Director:* relevant portfolio content (such as spaceships and interesting aliens); ability to show the development of a visual idea from 2D concept to 3D model; experience as an art lead
- *Design Director:* experience as a lead designer on a major console game, preferably in the action or RPG genre

All three should have at least five years of experience in the industry with two years as managers or supervisors. They, in turn, will help us interview and hire the rest of the team.

Pitch the Game

Illustration by Ian Robert Vasquez

Now you must find someone who wants to help pay for the game. This will most likely be a game publisher. (See Chapter 2 for a discussion of ways to meet and select a publisher.) Don't start with the publisher that you think would be best. Practice your presentation and refine your concept by trying it on a few other publishers (or trusted critics) first. Then get a meeting to pitch your game to your preferred publisher. Include visuals in the form of character/environmental concept art and/or animated sequences. Nothing is more boring than to sit through a lengthy speech or to read a lengthy document with no images to provoke imagination.

Seal the Deal

Illustration by Ian Robert Vasquez

Assuming you find a company that likes the idea as much as you do, the next step is to work out a deal. The company may want to just fund a prototype, or it may expect you to put in some of your own money in exchange for a bigger royalty. This process will take time; on average, a publishing deal takes three months from the initial pitch until a contract is signed. Some deals have been known to go a lot longer. Don't break off discussions with anyone else until you have a deal in place.

Staff Up Your Core Team

If you don't have everyone you need for preproduction, this is the time to hire them. Hopefully, you have kept some candidates "in the wings" and you know a few people who are willing to come on board once you have a signed deal. *Galactic Buccaneer* will need a core team that includes a producer, designer, art director, and technical director.

For *Galactic Buccaneer,* we'll contract with some concept artists to create stylish spaceships, futuristic worlds, and bizarre aliens. We'll also need some 3D modelers to create ships and worlds. A special effects person will give the combat example an edge of hyperrealism. An animator or two will make the characters and moving parts look good. The programming team will require someone to create the 3D render (or integrate a third-party solution); build the game engine; create tools and editors; program online multiplayer capabilities; develop the database management system; and program the interface. Some programmers can handle more than one area, but once production begins, they'll likely have to specialize. Finally, a few mission/level designers will be needed to script the missions and lay out the worlds.

Create the GDD, TDD, ASG, SDD, and Production Plan

The core team will build these documents over the course of a few months. Expect feedback from your publisher to refine the plans. Your team will also think of some great ideas later on that you'll want to incorporate into the design.

Proof of Concept or Prototype

Some developers have the resources to build a prototype before they pitch their game ideas. If a prototype isn't in the concept proposal, it should be part of the preproduction milestones. For this game we want to show how cool the space combat will be. We also want to show the depth of missions and strategic decisions the player gets to make. A good proof of concept would include a space combat demo with detailed ship models, a star-filled nebula as backdrop, and plenty of cool-looking enemy ships to shoot at. The strategic elements could be shown by way of a pre-rendered movie illustrating a half dozen gameplay moments.

Technical Design and Greenlight Review

Depending upon how your publisher handles it, you may be required to attend a technical design review (TDR) and/or a green light review. As you learned in Chapter 4, the TDR is where designers and programmers answer questions about the game and their approach to making it. They need to defend the ideas and architecture described in the GDD and TDD, respectively. The producers will get quizzed on budgets, schedules, risk mitigation, and competitive environment. During the green light review, you formally present the game concept. This is a very important meeting. The publisher makes the decision to move forward and fund production based on what they see at the green light review.

Into Production

You'll need a much bigger team to actually build the game. The prototype helps you work out the issues in the basic interface and establish lines of communication among the leadership. Now you and the leads need to bring in the rest of the team. You'll need to meet frequently to make sure that things are going as planned and that new staff members integrate into the group.

For *Galactic Buccaneer,* we'll have a *world* subteam assemble the galaxy: planets, ships, races, etc. In parallel, a *missions* subteam will create the various missions throughout the world. They'll also establish the network of player choices and define how these choices alter alliances and missions offered. A *combat* subteam will implement the weapons and ship designs and script the AI behaviors for solo and group combat. A *tools* subteam will support the game editor and any special needs that the designers and artists may have. For this hypothetical game, we're assuming that the designers can create whatever they need through high-level scripting with very little special case code written by the programmers. A *multiplayer* subteam will handle the user and network interfaces for hosting, joining, and playing games online. Working alongside this subteam will be a *security* subteam to make sure that at its core the game is safe from hacks and exploits; this is critical for maintaining an online community. A support group will handle maintaining everything from desktop workstations to source code archives. Big projects can't afford to be down. On the administrative side, there will be a few associate producers to track everything from task lists to localization assets.

Alpha

Assuming we've done a great job managing the team and the project, we'll hit *Alpha* right on schedule. At this point, all the features of the game should be working. All the missions have been scripted. Most of the art will be final, but some assets may be swapped out for better imagery. We'll do some gameplay testing to help us refine and do crude tuning of the game. (It's probably too difficult for most players to win the game at this stage, except for the team that built it.) We'll also start checking technical requirements. The publisher will likely submit a playable version to the console manufacturer for its approval and feedback.

Beta

At *Beta*, nothing can be altered in the game except for bug fixes and changes required by the licensor or console manufacturer. The point is to lock down the game and move on to release. The temptation to make changes is very high within the team, but the producer needs to maintain strict discipline. Failure to do so will lead to feature creep or slow down the QA process. Each change has the potential to bring in dozens of new bugs.

Release

A series of *release* candidates go through QA, compatibility testing, and finally console manufacturer certification. Once everyone agrees that the game is sufficiently bug free to ship, a gold master is sent to manufacturing. Most games have simultaneous worldwide releases, so there may be multiple masters, one for each language or territory.

Post-Release

Since *Galactic Buccaneer* has an online component, we'll have to maintain a live team for many months or possibly years if the game is successful. The live team will address bugs and security issues that are uncovered during real-world play. Marketing will have a community manager to host tournaments, research player behavior, and track customer interests for sequels and updates. We'll need to conduct a postmortem on the game with the team and incorporate their feedback into the next game. We can't forget to carefully archive the game assets for later use, since we're planning on releasing a sequel in five years.

> Two factors determine the success of a game: *quantity* (how many played sessions?), and *quality* (what does the target audience think of the game?)
>
> — *Jesper Sorensen*
> *(Business Unit Manager &*
> *Game Director, ncom.dk)*

There are hundreds of things you'll need to do to get your game from concept to completion. This case study covers only the basics. While industry veterans have the advantage of knowledge and experience, the fast pace of change makes the game industry an excellent choice for newcomers. The next section talks about some areas where the industry is likely to change in the near future.

Measuring the Success of Your Game

Interestingly, the metascore at metacritic.com is an effective way to measure potential sales. But internally, I always measure success by the quality of work accomplished within the constraints of time, budget and management. If we feel that we are able to maintain quality, the game's a success!

— *Drew Davidson (Director, Entertainment Technology Center, Carnegie Mellon University)*

I measure success on two levels. First, how did it do in the market? Sales numbers, performance in category, etc. I also like to read write-ups from real customers (not hired hacks) on the Web to get the good and the bad from the customer. Secondly, I look in the mirror and ask myself if I like the game. I guess there is also a "zero" level. If a game gets to market at all, that is the minimum metric for success.

— *Rich Adam (Chief Executive Officer, Mine Shaft Entertainment)*

A successful game is one that can somehow (even if it's not exactly how the designer idealized it) be played and be fun for as many people as possible who like to play that particular genre of game. That's not to say that you have to make sure your FPS is super fun for 57-year-old women, because now we are talking about game preferences—and that's a whole other issue. But in my mind, a game that is successful is one that can be played and enjoyed by anyone interested in that game title—especially if it's a gamer with a disability.

— *Michelle Hinn (Vice President, Game Division, DonationCoder.com)*

Everybody wants to sell lots of copies of their games, but I believe success is really measured in one's gut. Once the euphoria of gold master passes, it's not that hard for developers to look honestly at their game and say to themselves whether they are happy with it and proud of it or not. Frequently, though certainly not always, this will have a correlation in a game's sales—particularly when normalized against the popularity of the hardware platform, genre expectations, piracy tendencies (PC games get pirated a lot more for instance), and more.

— *Michael John (Lead Designer, Method Games)*

To me there are three measures, each with its own application. First would be sales, of course. Measuring your actual sales with the level of market penetration/advertising/buzz, etc., gives you a real fiscal idea on how well the game does. However, you have to remember that some games will simply always sell more than others. A Football game will almost always outsell a Submarine sim. That's why you need to know your potential market share right off the bat. Next would be critical response. Reviewers can give you an idea of how your game is received, although always take what reviewers say with a grain of salt. I remember on *Ghost Recon 2: Summit Strike*, the game came out to really good reviews. However, one review in France, the reviewer said nothing but good things about the game, and then in the "Negatives" section, said something like "Portrays the US Army in a positive light" and gave it a 7.5 (a full point lower than the average review). It was frustrating, but hey, that's just their point of view. Lastly would be fan and player response. The bigger your game is, the more naysayers there will be, so you have to be able to filter what players say. If you have an MP game, get out and play with them, and see what they are saying to each other. You will get a much better picture than the 20 guys bitching on your forum. If you have a licensed or franchise game, there will always be a certain segment of the fan base that is completely outraged by what you decided to do or change (just look at the Lord of The Rings movies for proof of this). However, if the majority of the people playing your game enjoy it, you know you are doing something right.

— *Christian Allen (Creative Director, Red Storm Entertainment)*

The bare minimum metric for success is whether we are generating enough revenue to keep the studio healthy. Beyond that "survival" measurement, we consider one of our games to be a success if people continue to play it six months to one year after they purchased it, and are recruiting others to join them. The games we build are intended to be ongoing projects that we enhance and grow over time. The initial release of the game essentially adds the game community itself to our build/test/review cycle for ongoing development. I often summarize this as: "It's a marathon, not a sprint." Another important success criteria is whether *we* enjoy and want to play our game, even after years of working on it. If the people building the game can't stand to play it, you've got a serious problem. We are all gamers, and use ourselves as filters. If we're not enjoying the game, it's a pretty good bet that the larger community won't, either.

— *Mike Booth (Chief Executive Officer, Turtle Rock Studios)*

Ned Lerner on the Future of Game Project Management Techniques :::::

Edward (Ned) Lerner works on middleware and information systems for Sony Computer Entertainment of America's (SCEA) worldwide first-party studios. Prior to SCEA, Ned was CTO of EA's Maxis studio. Ned has been making games since college when he wrote the *Arabian Nights*, a paper RPG that was ahead of its time. His first computer game was SirTech's *Deep Space* (Apple 2, C64, PC), one of the first six-degree of motion games. Next, he authored *Chuck Yeager's Advanced Flight Simulator* (PC, Apple 2, C64, Mac, Amiga)—a #1 EA seller—and its sequel. After these, he led the development of *F22 Interceptor* (the best-selling 3D Sega game), *Car & Driver* (the first game with texture mapping), and the first 3D system licensed to EA. Next, he co-founded Looking Glass Technology and ran product development—producing a few of his favorite games, including *Ultima Underworld 2, System Shock, Flight Unlimited, Madden '93* (Genesis), and Access *Links Pro* (Mac). He then produced *FireTeam*, the first team game built around a voice headset—followed by *FireTalk*, a Skype-like service. Ned has filed 19 U.S. patents.

Edward (Ned) Lerner (Director of Tools & Technology, Sony Computer Entertainment of America)

Next-generation games will cost roughly $1 million per play hour. That's more than television production, but less than movie production. It is enough that project management will be as much of a necessity as good legal or financial controls, which hasn't been true in the past. Unfortunately (or fortunately for people who like to make shiny new tools) existing project management tools, like Microsoft Project, are about as useful to helping us manage games as stone tools are for surgery. What's wrong with MS Project? Well, it can handle large lists of tasks—the infamous WBS—work breakdown structure. It can sort tasks, add up tasks, and show how task 2 can start when task 1 is finished, and display them all in tree killing Gantt charts. But it doesn't help manage your project. The best guide we have to manage your project "IFLH #7" (that's the well known game: Insert Famous License Here) is our project management statistics from "IFLH #6". If we knew, really, how much effort went into each element of the game the last time, then the next time, once we had a list of game elements we could make a reasonable estimate on what to expect in cost, time and manpower. We might even know where to allocate our resources to make certain tasks more efficient by better systems or tools. For instance I bet most games spend far more than anyone wants to admit on iterating, that is, finding and fixing bugs and performance and playability issues. If we realized we spend 75% of our budgets on rework we might become a lot more careful at planning or a lot better at iterating, and executives wouldn't be so lulled into a sense of well-being by cool E3 demos.

Project management requires knowing what percent complete each task is. This too has proved elusive. Many things that are marked done become undone because we find out later, something isn't right. Having most tasks change, seemingly randomly from 100% to 0% complete, perhaps a few times, makes game project management harder than it looks.

This problem isn't a game project management issue; it's a software project management issue. The complexity of this problem has driven the change from traditional project management (AKA the Waterfall model *http://en.wikipedia.org/wiki/Waterfall_model*) to the spiral model *http://en.wikipedia.org/wiki/Spiral_model (or basically a lot of waterfalls)* to just giving up (AKA extreme programming) and going with the flow.

There is a lot to be said for the new Agile Methods. (*http://en.wikipedia.org/wiki/Agile_software_development*). They are well named as they can make us pretty Agile, and help us spin iterations as fast as we can, but they don't give the producer control over schedules or costs.

This is a problem because, unlike software development, game development has an enormous production cost, like animated movie production. Using a method optimized for software development, and not animation development, means we save on the cheap engineering stuff to lose on the expensive animation stuff. Even worse we lose control over our schedules. Given that marketing (from TV buys to license tie-ins) is often our biggest expense—and often requires a fixed schedule —that's something most large titles just can't afford.

If we could only separate the engineering tasks from the production tasks, then we could use Agile methods for engineering, and careful movie-like planning on production. We'd need very flexibly engineered systems that could handle a wide range of production/animation needs/uses. Ideally we'd want a movie studio in a box—you'd pick your actors, sets, lights, script and just go. This is exactly what Middleware is trying to do. With the massive power of the PS3 this is a lot more believable than with the old PS2. That's not to say you can ship with your middleware, un-customized, un-optimized, out of the box. But if you can start with a stable production pipeline and a predictable set of production tasks, and use Agile methods to incrementally improve the out-of-the-box system, then someday you might be back in control.

Super Middleware will also help us adapt to the new, connected world. Once producers realize that if they can get their players to keep coming back to the game because the game keeps changing, growing and improving, then we'll kill the market for used (or pirated) software before it kills us, and, if we're really clever, we'll get the players to keep paying to keep having fun. The business will focus ever more on pumping out highly profitable, ever changing content into the same 'game.'

How does super middleware enable this? Fundamentally we'll need to learn how to make open ended game worlds, not just a game with 25 levels. All the clever special casing that makes one level work (if just barely), not only will be too expensive to build, but it will be too expensive in lost sales. Highly optimized, but limited systems, will lose to moderately optimized, but flexible systems. General purpose middleware engines will triumph over special purpose in-house engines.

The move from games to game worlds also means an acceleration of the trend concentrating most of the revenues and all the profits in a few mega-hits, which is likely to encourage even more emphasis on marketing. As we become ever more mass market, it means the flow from game back to traditional media will accelerate. Once we can make TV quality animation in real time (which the PS3 can do), what's stopping us from becoming the primary source of animated media? We are becoming the next Hollywood. Should we laugh or cry? Let's ask the focus group.

The Future of Game Project Management

Games have always been at the bleeding edge of technology. Developers continuously express their game ideas on the latest consumer electronics; some games are little more than an excuse to show off new technology. The trends of technology in the home drive what games we see and how we play them.

High-Definition Television (HDTV)

High-definition television (HDTV) is between 720 and 1080 lines and has a 16:9 aspect ratio. The effective screen resolution is from 1280×720 up to 1920×1080. By contrast, standard NTSC resolution is only 720×480. The increased screen resolution means that next-generation games need more memory and storage space for onscreen images.

Big Stock Photos

There are two formats for HD storage: Blu-ray disc (BD) and high-definition digital video disc (HD DVD). BD is the format used on the Sony PlayStation 3. A single-layer BD can store 25 GB and a dual-layer disc can store 50 GB, enough for four hours of HD-quality video. HD DVD supports 15 GB in single layer and 30 GB in dual layer. It is used for home PCs and offered as an optional peripheral for the Xbox 360.

HDTV is expected to be more widely adopted.

The impact on games is that consumers now expect more detailed scenes and characters that approach photo-realism. This takes more time to design and create. It also requires more storage and faster workstations for the artists and designers assembling these virtual worlds. Staff sizes have more than doubled on next-gen games; most of the growth is in the creative and product support areas.

Development tools will need to make it easier for artists and designers to edit and navigate these vast 3D environments. Asset management systems will need to juggle terabytes of data. Large teams and complex production pipelines make process decisions and tool choices critical to saving significant time and money.

Next-Gen Platforms: Adding More Complexity

Differentiation of platforms requires many more decisions to be made. Games are ideally not strict ports from one to another, but created to take advantage of a specific platform, and respect that platform's limitations. Should a developer hire on more staff for a separate team per platform—or outsource? Greater platform capabilities also require more content generators (artists, audio engineers, level builders, etc.) and better software. This results in larger teams and higher budgets as production values increase. Take a step back and think about whether some of the smaller platforms make better sense for your development group than the top end consoles. Finally, procedural content is definitely something to be fully investigated. Imagine if some art, sound, and game levels didn't need to be crafted piece by piece, by hand, but that a significant portion of it could be generated dynamically. What project management changes would that bring?

— *Frank T. Gilson (Senior Developer of Digital Games, Wizards of the Coast)*

Well, at least in the short term, Next-Gen means one big thing for PMs. Bigger teams or longer schedules. The amount of work that goes into the current next-gen titles is double, triple, or sometimes quadruple what was done just on the last current-gen titles. I think this will become more manageable as the technology and tools mature, but right now, you are really looking at an explosion of people-hours for the same amount of content that people are used to seeing.

— *Christian Allen (Creative Director, Red Storm Entertainment)*

The PS3-era consoles I think hold great promise, not because of their advanced compute power (which is nearing irrelevancy in actual game experiences), but because of their network connectivity and unique input methods. The Nintendo DS has already had a major impact in creating new markets with games like Nintendogs and Brain Age, both of which were heavily enabled by the stylus control input. I expect similar revolution from the Wii.

All three television-based consoles meanwhile boast robust network connectivity, which I hope will help to create a more nuanced price structure as opposed to the current very expensive model for retail packaged goods. Many game makers would prefer not to fight on the ten million dollar battlefield, and currently their avenues of distribution are limited. One or more of the three major consoles can and will change this.

— *Michael John (Lead Designer, Method Games)*

The key to developing games for Sony's next-generation platform lies in a substantial increase in the amount of up-front planning and prototyping. The next iteration of a franchise like God of War will require an exponentially larger team to develop properly. When the scale of production grows dramatically, so does the cost of false starts with level design, story elements, or any other aspect of game design that is not given the time and attention to be explored, modified, and locked down before full-fledged production begins. While the creative lead begins work on the overarching design as a whole, a core team, comprised of as few people as an implementation designer, a coder, and a producer will be relied on to develop a prototype level, determining what is possible within the constraints of the technology, as well as establishing art and design guidelines. From the initial concept, the level will be roughly built out, puzzles put in place, and rudimentary camera angles decided on. Once this prototype is completed, the art style guide is approved by the art director, pre-visualization lead, and game director. The technical director evaluates the prototype and game design for possible hurdles and suggests design changes that will satisfy the demands of current technology while maintaining the gameplay experience the core team has outlined.

The prototype level will go through multiple rounds of play testing, redesign, and refinement, until our target player is able to understand the layout and navigation of the level, is not confused by the camera, and is engaged and enjoying the gameplay from start to end. While the prototype is in the final stages of refinement, the scheduling, prioritization, and team structure for full production can begin. When the prototype is locked, the team should be well-prepared to start developing the game. Milestones are scheduled that allow the layout of each level to be properly roughed out, tested, adjusted, and locked down before the art team begins work on it.

The example provided above can work only if all parties involved invest in it completely. The publisher must be prepared to see little progress on the game as a whole while prototyping is underway. The producer must schedule properly, keeping all team members fully tasked and working efficiently while the game is being designed. The creative designer must complete the level design during the prototype phase, as the development team must be confident the levels they are handed will not change significantly once they have begun work on them. The increasing investments of both time and money needed to make games for new hardware will force the industry to become more process oriented and disciplined in its approach to development. Conversely, innovative and original titles are the result of a creative designer given the freedom to brainstorm, build, take apart, rebuild, refine, and eventually discover what the game will be. How well these two essential but conflicting ideas are balanced will dictate the success of any development studio.

— *Shannon Studstill (Director of Production, Sony Computer Entertainment of America)*

Peripherals

One of the most ubiquitous *peripheral* devices—the mouse—has revolutionized PC office software and games. Console manufacturers and some developers think that new peripherals will change the way we play games *and* the types of games we play.

Nintendo

The Nintendo Wii supports a one-handed controller that looks similar to a standard TV remote control but has sensors for motion and orientation. An expansion controller, the "nunchuk," adds an analog stick and audio. Nintendo is adapting all of its games to use these new peripherals.

The Sony PlayStation 3 is wireless and comes with sensors to detect rotational orientation and translational acceleration. PS3 games such as *War Hawk* use motion to control in-game vehicles.

The Wii's "nunchuk" and Wiimote controller (which is designed to resemble a television remote).

Sony Computer Entertainment America

War Hawk uses motion to control in-game vehicles.

Guitar Hero was released for PlayStation 2 in 2005. It included a full-size guitar and the ability for two guitars to play in a competitive mode. The success of this game has led other developers to plan more games based on performance with peripherals.

Consumers are reluctant to purchase additional peripherals, so developers have to either include them with their software or devise interfaces that work with or without the peripheral.

Guitar Hero attempts to provide an authentic guitar-playing experience with its custom peripheral.

One-Switch Games

This is such an interesting thing to think about because at GDC 2006, I saw a session on one-button mobile phone games because, think about it, it's a big pain to play a game that requires pressing a lot of tiny little buttons on your mobile. Unless, of course, big is the new small and we'll go back to having mobile phones that are the size of our heads. But one-button games have been called "one switch" games in the game accessibility community for quite some time and so this is not a "new" concept—it's just a new concept for those who now have trouble playing games on their mobile because the devices are getting smaller every day! I think that knowing about accessibility solutions—the often dramatic ways in which a gamer with a disability will access your game—will only result in solutions for the "next-generation" of game consoles and handhelds.

— *Michelle Hinn (Vice President, Game Division, DonationCoder.com)*

Size, Scope, and Skilled Management

Honestly, the biggest change is in sheer size and scope. Game teams are larger than ever, and thus have more moving parts. Focus for team leadership has become less about managing every moving part, and more about managing a set of leaders who then manage the parts. The project leader now is a leader of managers—and this requires a different set of skills and different approach. Personally, I see this trend continuing. Game teams can no longer afford to be ill-managed or recklessly run. As it stands now, sheer force of will may no longer be enough to get a project done; it requires skilled management to bring it all together.

— *Graeme Bayless (Director of Production, Crystal Dynamics)*

More Robust Art & Design Tools

The biggest problem we have to deal with is how to create increasingly more complex assets while teams and budgets stay mostly at the same sizes. A key solution is to work smarter, which involves creating better and better tools for the art and design teams, allowing them to create and iterate faster. Another challenge is how to best adapt to the paradigm shift that is happening with the new, increasingly parallel, next-gen console architectures (which are hard to program for). Again we feel that the approach of hiring only very technical programmers will benefit the creation of better tools that take advantage of the power harnessed in these new complex architectures.

— *Christer Ericson (Director of Tools & Technology, Sony Computer Entertainment of America)*

Agile Methodology Implementation

The future of game project management is Agile. [*Note: Agile is a project management methodology that emphasizes short iterations typically lasting one to four weeks. Each iteration is so thorough that it results in a mini game demo, incorporating all of the tasks necessary to release preliminary assets, coding, gameplay, and documentation.*] Next-Gen and handheld devices will have little effect on how projects are managed. Technology will change, but the game project consists of people that have to work together towards a common goal. Each game project has to be handled with methods that are open for flexibility and an explorative approach. The Agile methodology is perfect for this.

— *Jesper Sorensen (Business Unit Manager & Game Director, ncom.dk)*

RJ Mical on the New Revolution :::::

RJ Mical, at age 14, invented a tic-tac-toe game computer made of relays, flashlight bulbs, and D batteries. After that he helped create the Amiga computer, the Lynx game system, the 3DO game system, plus numerous software game engines and tools, spam blockers, bunches of video games, and more. Currently he is working on the PS3 with Sony, and hoo baby, what a job that is.

RJ Mical (Senior Software Manager, SD Tools Group, Sony Computer Entertainment of America; Co-Creator of the Amiga, Atari Lynx, and 3DO)

I believe a new revolution is coming. Consider this: In the beginning we had office PCs, which we started bringing home to "do work" but really we brought them home for entertainment. Many years ago our PCs became powerful enough to handle all our word processing and spreadsheet needs, and they could have stopped growing, but they didn't, they became more and more powerful, with ever richer graphics, theater-quality sound, burgeoning mass storage and RAM, all because we want better entertainment. It's *all* about entertainment. And then this magical thing happened to change the world. There we were with these gigantic powerhouse computing engines in our offices and homes all around the world, and out of that fantastical wealth of technology sprang the World Wide Web. Yes! The web came into existence because we created the foundation, and we created the foundation because of entertainment. Something very similar is happening now with our mobile devices. Long time ago they became powerful enough to handle our address book and messaging needs, but they don't stop, they continue to grow more powerful, with better displays, graphics hardware, GPS. And why? Because we want better entertainment! We learned from the Web and we want more! I believe that we are laying the groundwork for the next revolution in communication and entertainment. Something as important as the Web is about to come into existence, only this time it will involve us on the move, hooking up with information and entertainment and each other anywhere we are, any time we want. It's going to be huge; once again, it's going to change the way we think and act every day. The World Wide Web was radically different, yes, in its use of technology, but the underlying drives are as old as civilization itself: We want to be loved, we want to be connected. And some of us want to play games all day long.

Broadband Internet

According to the Pew Internet and American Life Project, 73% of Americans use the Internet and of these, 62% have a high-speed connection. This increased bandwidth has paved the way for multiplayer online games, voice chat, and digital distribution of games.

Digital Distribution

Digital distribution is the sale or transfer of software directly from publisher to consumer. The publisher maintains a server with front-end software for browsing a catalog of games and updates to its retail products. The consumer may purchase games directly or exchange prepurchased tokens for games.

Microsoft Corporation

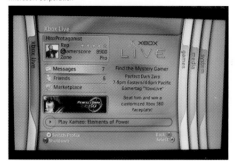

Xbox Live allows players to buy games online and download them to their consoles.

The business advantages of digital distribution include:

- Easier-to-reach international and remote markets; anyone with a broadband connection can purchase the game.
- Lower cost of sales; no distributors or sales staff required.
- No inventory to maintain; just one copy stored on a server.
- Elimination of used game sales and piracy; each game is tied to a specific console.

But the biggest gains in digital distribution may be realized in creativity. Publishers will have a direct connection to their customers. Developers will be able to try out new ideas and get quick feedback. Customers will form online communities focused on common interests, regardless of geographic location. This new form of distribution will lower the barriers of entry for new developers and open up another golden era of innovation.

Voice Integration

For many years, third-party software has been available for PC gamers to *voice chat* with each other in real-time. Recently, console games have included this capability. It enables quick communication between players during multiplayer games, and it also provides a more social environment for online communities.

There are issues that the producer must face when integrating voice chat:

- Bandwidth: Voice chat uses a portion of the Internet bandwidth that would otherwise be devoted to the game. As such, it may require sacrificing some aspects of game quality.
- Censorship: There is no effective way to censor players. Consumers, especially children, may be exposed to foul language or verbal abuse from other players. They may not have, or understand, options for squelching or blocking undesirable players.
- Translation: There are no real-time voice-recognition language translators. Players may tend to avoid playing with someone from another country simply because they don't understand the language being spoken.

Another exciting area of voice integration is *voice recognition*. Games will be able to interpret spoken words and react. *Brain Age* for the Nintendo DS takes simple voice input from players. Eventually games will be able to interpret the chat between players and, with sophisticated AI, react to what is being said.

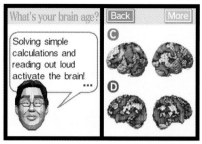

Players speak their answers in *Brain Age*.

The Third Wave of Game Production

Game project management will become not only more crucial, but also more central. As teams are comprised increasingly with freelance and/or outsourced talent, the producer will take on a role that far exceeds the current typical producer role. In particular, producers will be key in bringing non-publisher funding sources into projects, which is a trend I very much hope to see increase in the future.

The producer has gone through a number of evolutions, and is about to go through yet another. At each stage, the producer's role has become more important and central. In the early 1990s, producers were seen as an unnecessary hindrance to creativity; Boss Game Studios (now long-since defunct) famously advertised a "producer-free environment" in its job postings in 1994/95, and this had some resonance with game creators. Producers within development teams were rare, though publishers (i.e. the money) had producers as the "front man" to interface with the development team, be it internal or external. Producing was a thankless job, and unsurprisingly frequently attracted something less than the elite. [Note: My job title in 1994 was "Producer."]

We're now in the second wave of production, and producers have a much more integral role. Most development teams have a producer as part of the team, and I would define the role perhaps best as being in opposition to the lead designer: that is, whereas it is the lead designer's job to attempt to put as many ambitious ideas as possible into the game, it is the producer's job to triage those ambitions and see to it that those with the most favorable risk/reward ratio are implemented. Making that judgment requires both an intimate knowledge of the game production resources implicit in an idea, and also its value to the game. In this second wave period, producers have also taken on very formal roles in scheduling and budgeting, and often are seen as important facilitators of communication on larger teams.

The third wave of game production is coming, but is a couple years away before it becomes a major force. That is when producers are put in the position of being key visionaries on projects. They will still maintain their triage, scheduling and budgeting roles, but will add to that the crucial function of actually assembling the team for a specific project. The industry has already trended toward cost-oriented outsourcing, which puts a major added load on the producer, but will trend further toward "insourcing" of experienced creative specialists brought on board into leadership positions. In this case, the producer becomes crucially important to every stage of the project.

— *Michael John (Lead Designer, Method Games)*

Drew Davidson on the Evolution of the Producer :::::

Drew Davidson
(Director,
Entertainment
Technology Center,
Carnegie Mellon
University)

Drew Davidson is the Director of the Entertainment Technology Center at Carnegie Mellon University. He is a professor, producer and player of interactive media. His background spans academic, industry and professional worlds and he is interested in stories across texts, comics, games and other media. He chaired Game Art & Design and Interactive Media Design at the Art Institute of Pittsburgh and the Art Institute Online, and he has taught and researched at several universities. He completed his Ph.D. in Communication Studies at the University of Texas at Austin. He was a Senior Project Manager in the New Media Division of Holt, Rinehart and Winston, and he was a Project Manager in Learning Services at Sapient. Before this, he produced interactive media and games at HumanCode. He chairs the Sandbox Symposium, an ACM SIGGRAPH conference on video games, and serves on the IGDA Education SIG and the ACTlab Steering Committee.

I think producers are really going to come into their own. Currently, there is a bit of "all the responsibility, and none of the authority"—but producers will serve to help best guide the creative design and development of games in balance with the demands of management.

Next-gen is only going to increase the importance of good producers who can orchestrate huge projects. In contrast, I think handheld and casual games will enable even more creativity and innovation and producers can help their teams make some great games that don't take too long—or cost too much—to make. Again, being able to guide the team to excel will only become more important.

So You Want to Become a Game Producer . . .

Producers need to know a little bit about everything. A student of game production should understand the fundamentals of gameplay, programming, modeling, texturing, animation, audio, storytelling/character development, level design, interface design, and software testing. These are all disciplines that offer introductory courses, and the aspiring producer should take them all.

The producer's primary role is to be the project manager for the game. This requires a solid understanding of task breakdown, scheduling, tracking, team management, risk analysis, and reporting methods. These tend to be taught in business and operations management courses. They are also learned on the job. An internship with a publisher or game developer will give you access to this knowledge.

Deborah Mars on the Skills Necessary to Be a Great Game Producer :::::

Deborah Mars is currently a producer at Sony Computer Entertainment of America - Santa Monica (SCEA), where she works with external development teams on creating next-gen products. During her tenure at SCEA thus far, she has produced such titles as *Siren* and *The Con* (PSP). She has more than 15 years of experience in product development and has held positions at Scient Corporation, The Tribune Company, and Encyclopaedia Britannica. She has also provided consulting on a number of assignments for McKinsey & Company and Launch Capacity, Inc. Deborah holds a bachelor's degree from the University of Michigan in English and Creative Writing, and certification in project management from the International Institute for Learning Inc., a charter member of the Project Management Institute.

Deborah Mars
(Producer,
Sony Computer
Entertainment of
America)

Prior to my job with SCEA, I spent the better part of my career working in publishing, educational software development, web development, and management consulting. This cross-discipline experience provided me with a solid foundation for taking on the roles and responsibilities of being a game producer. It's my firm belief that all these skills acquired in those previous positions directly transferred, allowing me to apply what I've learned to my current position. Now there may be several people who disagree with me—and I suppose I'm willing to take some heat on this, or at least fight those who try to challenge it—but I'm absolutely convinced that you don't necessarily need to have tons of game-specific experience in order to be a strong game producer. To be honest, my approach to game production has not been drastically different than my approach to those other positions in product development and strategy consulting. The bottom line is this: You need to have the chops for the job, and that means:

- Excellent communication skills.

- Ability to juggle without dropping the proverbial ball. Being a producer means heavy emphasis on organization, tracking, and keeping a watchful eye on the big picture *and* the tiny details.

- Fearlessness and trust in judgment. It's important to be aggressive and know what you want, and work hard to deliver on a vision. But also, an important lesson to learn is having the ability to say "no," especially if it's the best thing for the project. A producer must make those tough decisions.

- Willingness to take risks and learn from mistakes. Not every undertaking can be successful, but each provides a learning experience and step toward growth and a future success. Understanding and accepting this is critical.

- Sharp analytical skills combined with creative and strategic problem solving. There's always a problem, a crisis, something going wrong. A good producer will assess the situation and provide solutions to resolving those issues.

- Flexibility, but know your limits. A producer takes on so much of everything, that it's important to recognize when you need support—either technical, design, or art. If there is something you don't know, be sure to ask questions or work to get the right person on board to help address those concerns.

- Typical project management skills, such as creating and maintaining schedules, budgets, status reports, development plans, useful process and workflow templates, etc.

- Desire to learn and grow with the industry. Stay abreast of developments in the industry and the competitive landscape by reading books, attending conferences, seminars, and networking.

- Of course this is not an exhaustive list. As a producer, it's also essential that you are proactive, demonstrate strong leadership, work equally well as part of a team, have exceptional presentation skills, excellent time management skills, and the ability to work effectively with all the departments involved (development team, Marketing, PR, Legal) to ultimately deliver top-notch fun products that sell.

Historically, most producers start in QA as testers and work their way up. This is changing as project managers and producers from other fields, such as film, are migrating to the game industry. Regardless of their background, producers need to have an understanding of software development methodologies. This is a key component of mastering game production. Games are essentially software programs, and they are managed in much the same way.

The best way to understand production is to try it and learn from your mistakes. There are many third-party tools that help novices create interactive games, from Flash to the Unreal 3 or Aurora toolsets. Some games have integrated level editors. Start with one of these tools, design a game, and implement it. You can use public

BioWare Corp.

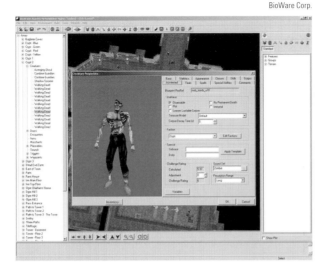

Epic Games, Inc.

Both the Aurora (top) and UnrealEd (bottom) editors ship with their respective games (*Neverwinter Nights* and *Unreal*)—allowing players to customize and extend gameplay.

domain assets or create new ones. You can also enlist the help of aspiring artists and programmers to help you. After all, project management is about collaboration.

There is no better time than now to be developing games. Technology has made it easy for creative ideas to become slick, playable games in a matter of weeks, if not days. The audience has grown from small groups of isolated enthusiasts to an entire planet of people connected to each other via the Internet. The generation of would-be producers, designers, artists, programmers, and sound designers all grew up playing video games. Hopefully, the knowledge contained in this book will provide you with some insight or motivation to realize your dreams in this exciting and ever-changing form of entertainment.

chapter 5

::: CHAPTER REVIEW :::

1. Create a proposal for one of your favorite games. Imagine going through the production process necessary to create this particular game. How does the proposal and process differ from your original game project experience?

2. How will game project management change in the next 5 to 10 years with regard to processes, tools, leadership, and team roles and responsibilities? How will technology affect game production?

3. Come up with your own personal strategic plan for becoming a game producer. How will you attain this position in terms of skill building, education, networking, research, internships, outside projects, and contributions within the game community?

Resources

There's a wealth of information on game development and related topics discussed in this book. Here is just a sample list of books, news sites, organizations, and events you should definitely explore!

News

Blues News—www.bluesnews.com

Computer Games Magazine—www.cgonline.com

Game Daily Newsletter—www.gamedaily.com

Game Developer Magazine—www.gdmag.com

Gamers Hell—www.gamershell.com

Game Music Revolution (GMR)—www.gmronline.com

Game Rankings—www.gamerankings.com

GameSlice Weekly—www.gameslice.com

GameSpot—www.gamespot.com

GameSpy—www.gamespy.com

Game Industry News—www.gameindustry.com

GIGnews.com—www.gignews.com

Internet Gaming Network (IGN)—www.ign.com

Machinima.com—www.machinima.com

Music4Games.net—www.music4games.net

1UP—www.1up.com

PC Gamer—www.pcgamer.com

Star Tech Journal [technical side of the coin-op industry]—www.startechjournal.com

UGO Networks (Underground Online)—www.ugo.com

Video Game Music Archive—www.vgmusic.com

Wired Magazine—www.wired.com

Directories & Communities

Apple Developer Connection—developer.apple.com

Betawatcher.com—www.betawatcher.com

Fat Babies.com [game industry gossip]—www.fatbabies.com

Gamasutra—www.gamasutra.com

GameDev.net—www.gamedev.net

Game Development Search Engine—www.gdse.com

Game Music.com—www.gamemusic.com

Game Rankings—www.gamerankings.com

Games Tester—www.gamestester.com

Moby Games—www.mobygames.com

Overclocked Remix—www.overclocked.org

Organizations

Academy of Interactive Arts & Sciences (AIAS)—www.interactive.org

Academy of Machinima Arts & Sciences—www.machinima.org

Association of Computing Machinery (ACM)—www.acm.org

Business Software Alliance (BSA)—www.bsa.org

Digital Games Research Association (DiGRA)—www.digra.org

Entertainment Software Association (ESA)—www.theesa.com

Entertainment Software Ratings Board (ESRB)—www.esrb.org

Game Audio Network Guild (GANG)—www.audiogang.org

International Computer Games Association (ICGA)—www.cs.unimaas.nl/icga

International Game Developers Association (IGDA)—www.igda.org

SIGGRAPH—www.siggraph.org

Events

Consumer Electronics Show (CES)
January—Las Vegas, NV
www.cesweb.org

Game Developers Conference (GDC)
March—San Jose, CA/San Francisco, CA (cities alternate)
www.gdconf.com

Serious Games Summit (SGS)
March (San Jose/San Francisco, CA; at GDC) & October (Washington, DC)
www.seriousgamessummit.com

D.I.C.E. Summit (AIAS)
March—Las Vegas, NV
www.interactive.org/dice

SIGGRAPH (ACM)
Summer—Los Angeles, CA; San Diego, CA; Boston, MA (location varies)
www.siggraph.org

Tokyo Game Show (TGS)
Fall—Japan
tgs.cesa.or.jp/english/

E3 Business & Media Summit
July—Santa Monica, CA
www.e3expo.com

Austin Game Developers Conference
September—Austin, TX
www.gameconference.com

Indie Games Con (IGC)
October—Eugene, OR
www.garagegames.com

E for All Expo
October—Los Angeles, CA
www.eforallexpo.com

Books & Articles

Adams, E. (2003). *Break into the game industry.* McGraw-Hill Osborne Media.

Ahearn, L. & Crooks II, C.E. (2002). *Awesome game creation: No programming required. (2nd ed).* Charles River Media.

Axelrod, R. (1985). *The evolution of cooperation.* Basic Books.

Bates, B. (2002). *Game design: The art & business of creating games.* Premier Press.

Bethke, E. (2003). *Game development and production.* Wordware.

Brandon, A. (2004). *Audio for games: Planning, process, and production.* New Riders.

Brin, D. (1998). *The transparent society.* Addison-Wesley.

Broderick, D. (2001). *The spike: How our lives are being transformed by rapidly advancing technologies.* Forge.

Brooks, D. (2001). *Bobos in paradise: The new upper class and how they got there.* Simon & Schuster.

Business Software Alliance. (May 2005). "Second annual BSA and IDC global software piracy study." www.bsa.org/globalstudy

Campbell, J. (1972). *The hero with a thousand faces.* Princeton University Press.

Campbell, J. & Moyers, B. (1991). *The power of myth.* Anchor.

Castells, M. (2001). *The Internet galaxy: Reflections on the Internet, business, and society.* Oxford University Press.

Chase, RB, Aquilano, NJ & Jacobs, R. (2001). *Operations management for competitive advantage (9th ed).* McGraw-Hill/Irwin

Cheeseman, HR. (2004). *Business law (5th ed).* Pearson Education, Inc.

Chiarella, T. (1998). *Writing dialogue.* Story Press.

Cooper, A., & Reimann, R. (2003). *About face 2.0: The essentials of interaction design.* Wiley.

Crawford, C. (2003). *Chris Crawford on game design.* New Riders.

Csikszentmihalyi, M. (1991). *Flow: The psychology of optimal experience.* Perennial.

DeMaria, R. & Wilson, J.L. (2003). *High score!: The illustrated history of electronic games.* McGraw-Hill.

Egri, L. (1946). *The art of dramatic writing: Its basis in the creative interpretation of human motives.* Simon and Schuster.

Evans, A. (2001). *This virtual life: Escapism and simulation in our media world.* Fusion Press.

Friedl, M. (2002). *Online game interactivity theory.* Charles River Media.

Fruin, N. & Harringan, P. (Eds.) (2004). *First person: New media as story, performance and game.* MIT Press.

Fullerton, T., Swain, C. & Hoffman, S. (2004). *Game design workshop: Designing, prototyping & playtesting games.* CMP Books.

Galitz, W.O. (2002). *The essential guide to user interface design: An introduction to GUI design principles and techniques.* (2nd ed.). Wiley.

Gardner, J. (1991). *The art of fiction: Notes on craft for young writers.* Vintage Books.

Gershenfeld, A., Loparco, M. & Barajas, C. (2003). *Game plan: The insiders guide to breaking in and succeeding in the computer and video game business.* Griffin Trade Paperback.

Gladwell, M. (2000). *The tipping point: How little things can make a big difference.* New York, NY: Little Brown & Company.

Gleick, J. (1987). *Chaos: Making a new science.* Viking.

Gleick, J. (1999). *Faster: The acceleration of just about everything.* Vintage Books.

Godin, S. (2003). *Purple cow: Transform your business by being remarkable.* Portfolio.

Goldratt, EM & Cox, J. (2004). *The goal: A process of ongoing improvement (3rd ed).* North River Press.

Hamilton, E. (1940). *Mythology: Timeless tales of gods and heroes.* Mentor.

Heim, M. (1993). *The metaphysics of virtual reality.* Oxford University Press.

Johnson, S. (1997). *Interface culture: How new technology transforms the way we create & communicate.* Basic Books.

Jung, C.G. (1969). *Man and his symbols.* Dell Publishing.

Kent, S.L. (2001). *The ultimate history of video games.* Prima.

King, S. (2000). *On writing.* Scribner.

Knoke, W. (1997). *Bold new world: The essential road map to the twenty-first century.* Kodansha International.

Koster, R. (2005). *Theory of fun for game design.* Paraglyph Press.

Krawczyk, M. & Novak, J. (2006). *Game development essentials: Game story and character development.* Thomson Delmar.

Kurzweil, R. (2000). *The age of spiritual machines: When computers exceed human intelligence.* Penguin.

Laramee, F.D. (Ed.) (2005). *Secrets of the game business. (3rd ed).* Charles River Media.

Laramee, F.D. (Ed.) (2002). *Game design perspectives.* Charles River Media.

Levy, P. (2001). *Cyberculture.* University of Minnesota Press.

Lewis, M. (2001). *Next: The future just happened.* W.W.Norton & Company.

Mackay, C. (1841). *Extraordinary popular delusions & the madness of crowds.* Three Rivers Press.

McConnell, S. (1996). *Rapid development.* Microsoft Press.

Mencher, M. (2002). *Get in the game: Careers in the game industry.* New Riders.

Michael, D. (2003). *The indie game development survival guide.* Charles River Media.

Montfort, N. (2003). *Twisty little passages: An approach to interactive fiction.* MIT Press.

Moravec, H. (2000). *Robot.* Oxford University Press.

Morris, D. & Hartas, L. (2003). *Game art: The graphic art of computer games.* Watson-Guptill Publications.

Mulligan, J. & Patrovsky, B. (2003). *Developing online games.* New Riders.

Murray, J. (2001). *Hamlet on the holodeck: The future of narrative in cyberspace.* MIT Press.

Negroponte, N. (1996). *Being digital.* Vintage Books.

Nielsen, J. (1999). *Designing web usability: The practice of simplicity.* New Riders.

Novak, J. (2005). *Game development essentials: An introduction.* Thomson Delmar.

Novak, J. (2003). "MMOGs as online distance learning applications." University of Southern California.

Oram, A. (Ed.) (2001). *Peer-to-peer.* O'Reilly & Associates.

Rheingold, H. (1991). *Virtual reality.* Touchstone.

Rheingold, H. (2000). *Tools for thought: The history and future of mind-expanding technology.* MIT Press.

Robbins, SP. (2001). *Organizational behavior (9th ed).* Prentice-Hall, Inc.

Rogers, E.M. (1995). *Diffusion of innovations.* Free Press.

Rollings, A. & Morris, D. (2003). *Game architecture & design: A new edition.* New Riders.

Rollings, A. & Adams, E. (2003). *Andrew Rollings & Ernest Adams on Game design.* New Riders.

Rouse III, R. (2001) *Game design: Theory & practice.* Wordware.

Salen, K. & Zimmerman, E. (2003). *Rules of play.* MIT Press.

Sanger, G.A. [a.k.a. "The Fat Man"]. (2003). *The Fat Man on Game Audio.* New Riders.

Saunders, K. & Novak, J. (2007). *Game development essentials: Game interface design.* Thomson Delmar.

Sellers, J. (2001). *Arcade fever.* Running Press.

Standage, T. (1999). *The Victorian Internet.* New York: Berkley Publishing Group.

Strauss, W. & Howe, N. (1992). *Generations.* Perennial.

Strauss, W. & Howe, N. (1993). *13th gen: Abort, retry, ignore, fail?* Vintage Books.

Strauss, W. & Howe, N. (1998). *The fourth turning.* Broadway Books.

Strauss, W. & Howe, N. (2000). *Millennials rising: The next great generation.* Vintage Books.

Tufte, E.R. (1983). *The visual display of quantitative information.* Graphics Press.

Tufte, E.R. (1990). *Envisioning information.* Graphics Press.

Tufte, E.R. (1997). *Visual explanations.* Graphics Press.

Turkle, S. (1997). *Life on the screen: Identity in the age of the Internet.* Touchstone.

Van Duyne, D.K. et al. (2003). *The design of sites.* Addison-Wesley.

Vogler, C. (1998). *The writer's journey: Mythic structure for writers. (2nd ed).* Michael Wiese Productions.

Williams, J.D. (1954). *The compleat strategyst: Being a primer on the theory of the games of strategy.* McGraw-Hill.

Welch, J. & Welch, S. (2005). *Winning.* HarperCollins Publishers.

Wolf, J.P. & Perron, B. (Eds.). (2003). *Video game theory reader.* Routledge.

Wysocki, RK, Beck, R, Jr. & Crane, DB. (2003). *Effective project management (3rd ed).* John Wiley & Sons.

Index